# A SLOVENIAN VILLAGE

# A
# Slovenian
# Village

## ŽEROVNICA

IRENE WINNER

BROWN UNIVERSITY PRESS

PROVIDENCE

International Standard Book Number: 0–87057–128–1
Library of Congress Catalog Card Number: 77–127367
Brown University Press, Providence, Rhode Island 02912
© 1971 by Brown University. All rights reserved
Published 1971
Printed in the United States of America
By Connecticut Printers, Inc.
On Warren's Olde Style
Bound by Stanhope Bindery
Designed by Richard Hendel

# Contents

## I. The Background

## II. The Developing Socioeconomic Structure

## III. The People and Their Institutions

# List of Illustrations

## Figures

## Plates

*Following page 50*

# List of Tables

# *Preface*

THIS STUDY of a Slovenian village was made possible, in part, by a grant from the Wenner Gren Foundation for Anthropological Research, which is gratefully acknowledged.

After exploratory trips to Žerovnica and surrounding areas in 1962 and 1963, and after consultations with ethnologists of the Slovene Academy of Sciences in Ljubljana, field work was begun in May 1964 and continued for eight months during two separate periods ending in August 1965. The results of this study were first presented as a doctoral dissertation for the Department of Anthropology of the University of North Carolina, in 1967. In a third, shorter period of field work, the village was revisited in the summer of 1969. This book is a revised and expanded version of the original study that also incorporates the later findings.

I am indebted to John J. Honigmann for his kindness, encouragement, and always helpful advice. I also take pleasure in acknowledging my debt to John Gillin and Ruth Benedict, who introduced me to their stimulating and rewarding approaches to anthropological studies. I also wish to thank Conrad Arensberg for reading, and offering valuable comments on, a part of this study concerned with the early history of the family.

I wish to thank all those friends in the village of Žerovnica, as well as in Grahovo, Cerknica, and Ljubljana, who taught me about Slovenia, who offered my husband and me their constant hospitality, and who spent many hours with us in amicable and useful discussion. A special debt of gratitude is owed to Franc Jakopin of the University of Ljubljana, who gave us his unqualified support and introduced us to the villages of the Cerknica valley where his parents were born. I also wish to thank Rado Lenček of Columbia University for his assistance concerning linguistic problems and Vladimir Rus of Case Western Reserve University for his translation of the Slovenian folk tales that we had recorded. I am grateful to Miss Ruth Sanford of the Brown University Press for her meticulous and tactful editing and to Mrs. Margaret Hayman and Mrs. Harriet Mayerson for the great care with which they typed the various versions of this study.

Our daughters, Lucy and Ellen, who accompanied us to Žerovnica and took part in village life, contributed to the enjoyment and scope of our work. Lucy's friendship with village children provided us with insights concerning the children's world. Ellen furnished the drawings in this study. My greatest debt is to my husband, who helped me conduct this study in all its phases and whose knowledge of Slavistics enriched my work.

# A SLOVENIAN VILLAGE

# Introduction

IN THE mountains and valleys surrounding the broad and flat plain of the Cerknica lake in southwestern Slovenia, one can see many small villages in which what appears to be traditional peasant life is still carried on. Men, women, and children cultivate fields, either by hand in the steep mountainous areas or with the aid of ox- or horse-drawn implements where the land is flatter. The remains of feudal castles and ancient churches crown the distant hills, and wayside shrines mark the dusty mountain crossroads. In many villages the church occupies the highest land, and the common well is located in a central square. Village men wear high boots, old work clothes, and felt or straw hats; women wear dark, full skirts, aprons, kerchiefs, heavy stockings, and boots or felt slippers. Everywhere there is a general quiet and the slow but steady pace of unmechanized labor. Yet, not far out of reach are asphalt roads leading to urban centers like Cerknica, headquarters for the *občina*—the basic administrative unit in Yugoslavia—in which the village of Žerovnica is located.[1] Buses travel to the paved highway that stretches from Ljubljana, the industrialized and cosmopolitan capital of Slovenia, to Rijeka and Trieste on the Adriatic. Interspersed among the villages of the district are sawmills, and furniture and plastics factories located in rural areas in order to utilize local labor. Young men wearing black leather jackets, goggles, and city shoes, and young women wearing tailored suits, nylon stockings, high heels, and modern hair styles, commute to factories by bicycle, motorized bicycle (*moped*), or motorcycle.

In this broad valley of the Cerknica lake lies a large, modern, working co-operative farm (*kmetijska obdelovalna zadruga*—KOZ). Its extensive holdings, worked primarily by agricultural migrants from Yugoslavia's poorer southern republics, stretch to historical village lands. Today some mountain villagers have abandoned their land, which, rejected as too rugged and stony by the state and the private peasant, lies uncultivated. Furthermore, some peasant proprietors in villages or towns located close to factories in the Cerknica plain have leased their fertile fields to the encroaching co-operative farm and have joined the ranks of commuting wage laborers. Villages that surrender a large part of their land and labor force to socialized enterprises of farm and factory are most directly affected by modern trends. But the inhabitants of Žerovnica and the immediately neighboring villages surrounding the basin of the Cerknica lake, and many other peasants in Slovenia, still continue to cultivate their inherited strips in the traditional way.

Žerovnica was chosen for this study for a number of reasons. Since earliest times the flat terrain and fertile soil of the Cerknica basin have provided favorable ecological conditions for agriculture compared to the more mountainous neighboring areas. Although the village is relatively isolated (the nearest paved highway lies several kilometers away), it has not been unaffected by new developments. It is serviced by a main bus line and is within commuting, but not easy, distance (about five kilometers) of the factory and the co-operative farm. Its size and plan were suitable. A population of about 250 inhabit fifty-nine houses, compactly arranged along a central road. It is general knowledge that Žerovnica has had a long and relatively stable history. Although its people have suffered war and revolution (in the last war the village, a partisan center, was set afire twice by enemy forces), nevertheless its population can be traced back to the 1600s. Earlier records are lost, but the village is much older. A model of Žerovnica and its landholdings, displayed at the Geographical Institute of the University of Ljubljana, is described as representing an unusually well-preserved example of a typical Slovenian village, with its ancient land divisions. Yet, Žerovnica has never been the object of anthropological study.

In May 1964 my husband and I and our two daughters accepted a lodging in the house of a relative of our friend Professor Franc Jakopin, in the village of Grahovo, about one kilometer from Žerovnica. Grahovo is the center on which Žerovnica and other small villages are dependent for school, stores, and other services. I had previously studied Serbo-Croatian and Slovenian in the United States, and was aided in the field work by my husband, who is a Slavist. A young friend, Primož Jakopin, acted as interpreter in the initial period until we felt we could handle the village dialect.

Soon after our arrival we presented ourselves to the *občina* officials in Cerknica. We explained that we hoped to write a description and history of what might be in some respects a representative Slovenian village and showed the officials other village studies by American anthropologists, undertaken in various areas of the world. We generally met co-operation and interest, and few difficulties were placed in our way. The villagers themselves were accustomed to being visited by American relatives, although tourists were rare. After explaining our project to the school director and the priest, both of whom lived in Grahovo, and receiving their suggestions for initial informants, we began our work in the village itself. Several weeks were spent in casual visiting and establishing contact. We were gradually accepted as friends of villagers' relatives and as visiting Americans, and with few exceptions, we were offered friendship and help.

The methods we used changed as the study progressed. It was clear that a primary task was the reconstruction of the history of Žerovnica. Although it could hardly be complete, such a history would contribute not only to an understanding of the present culture but also, I hoped, to an understanding of some of the processes of culture change particular to Žerovnica as well as to peasant villages of similar types.

In order to gain historical perspective we used the following sources: church records going back to 1618; the school records, initiated with the founding of a one-class, one-room school in 1888; village records, the first entry of which was for 1861; records of the village firemen's association formed in 1907; library sources, one of the most important of which was J. W. Valvasor, *Die Ehre des Erzherzogthums Crain* (1686–89), in which Žerovnica is described and which includes early maps; statistical data collected by the Slovene Academy of Sciences, the Ljubljana University Geographical Institute, and governmental agencies; and, finally, the accounts of older informants who remembered conditions in the kingdom of Yugoslavia as well as those of the Austro-Hungarian days. These data illuminated problems of population trends, traditional family forms, marriage and inheritance practices, land divisions, traditional occupations, and the status of local crafts and markets, as well as the history of the changing social, economic, and political structure of the village and past relations of the village to the institutions of the world outside.

Our field methods were those of participant observation and interviews, supplemented by tape recordings of traditional tales and songs. In the first period of our work we considered each family as a basic unit of study. We documented the history, inheritance practices, and size of each family, and the number and kind of possessions. We reached every family in Žerovnica except one. From those informants with whom we established good rapport we secured more subjective information, in particular, life histories. Extensive consultations with the school director, the priest, and officials of the *občina* and the cooperative farm provided additional valuable information. In September 1964 we completed the first period of research, devoted to gaining an understanding of the village's past and its present composition. The problems that I wished to investigate further required a new approach.

On our return to Žerovnica in May 1965 we were warmly greeted as old friends. In the second period of study, although we continued unstructured interviews, they were less important than guided discussions based on specific topics relating to the present political, social, and economic structure of the village, to the role of religion, to child rearing, and to the education of the young. It was also important to define the villagers' attitudes toward the past, present, and future in the light of changing official policies that were directly affecting peasant life. Among the subjects discussed that bore on the latter concerns were projected reforms in agriculture and land tenure, state regulation and control of peasant-owned agricultural and forest land, plans for economic improvement of the lake land, the taxation program, aspirations of the young, and the general question of the current status of the peasant.

During the second period we reinterviewed each *gospodar* (male head of a household) and also devoted more individual interviews to women and the young, as we began to isolate various groups that, as well as individual families, became units of study. Material gathered by our elder daughter during her attendance at the village school contributed to our understanding of the attitudes of the young. Finally, even so small a village was divided into economic and social strata and implicit factions. There could be distinguished a small group of richer peasants; a core, farming group, the members of which frequently were forced to combine factory and cultivation; a poorer, almost landless group, whose livelihood did not depend on cultivation; and also a developing, small, crosscutting group, which I call a "new elite." These strata needed to be understood both in relation to the prewar social and economic structure, and in relation to new pressures and changes affecting the peasants—processes that have been called "modernization."

While the basic data of the study are from the period through 1965, we conducted a limited and further study in 1969. When we returned for a month's study we talked again to leading *gospodars* representing the main village strata, while our two daughters and a Slovenian student from the University of Ljubljana discussed problems with young villagers. I wished to know how village life was affected by national reforms adopted between 1965 and 1969. After the adoption of the new Yugoslav constitution in April 1963 administrative decentralization became the stated goal of new legislation. While new measures were not directed immediately toward the private peasants, who still composed the basis of the Yugoslav rural economy, this sector could not remain unaffected. I found, as I had expected, that the village itself was not fundamentally altered. It is true that villagers did enjoy somewhat more of the benefits of modern technology, and they believed that the relation of the village to nearby socialist farming enterprises was improved. No longer did they fear that their land might be absorbed by the socialist sector of the economy. However, joint ventures of the village and the working co-operative remained undeveloped.

My objective in this study is to understand Žerovnica from several points of view. The first places the village, as far as possible, within the perspective of its history. The second encompasses the internal structure of the village as it is today. What are its social, economic, and political institutions, and its internal strata; and how are they interrelated? What attitudes and activities define its individuals and groups? In what sense do villagers share a common life-style and world view, and in what sense do the various strata diverge? The third view focuses on the nature of the structural relation of this commu-

nity to the larger society of which it is a part, and the way this relationship has changed. It asks how Žerovnica survived; what changes
in the culture made this survival possible; how profound these
changes are; and what kind of a future there is for a peasant village
like Žerovnica in the modern state of Yugoslavia.

I hope that the findings of this study may have implications relevant
to other peasant societies. In a country as diverse as Yugoslavia, and
even as Slovenia, where sharp dialectal differences divide neighboring
valleys, it cannot be assumed that one village is the typical representative. I suggest, however, that Žerovnica embodies some representative
Slovenian patterns, that it has demonstrated considerable vitality, and
that it still represents a Slovenian way of life.

# I

# THE BACKGROUND

# I

## The Village and Its Setting

THE VILLAGE of Žerovnica lies in the republic of Slovenia, about seventy kilometers from the Slovene capital, Ljubljana. The highway from Ljubljana is connected to the village by a hilly, partially asphalted road twenty-five kilometers long. The *občina*, or administrative district, of Cerknica, in which Žerovnica is located, encompasses the plain of the Cerknica lake and the mountain ranges to the northeast and southwest.

## Slovenia

Slovenia, the northwesternmost republic of Yugoslavia, occupies a frontier region where Slavic, Germanic, and Mediterranean influences meet. Its green Julian Alps descend from the Austrian border, while its southern karstic ranges reach Italy and Dalmatia to the west and south. To the south and east lies the republic of Croatia. The area of Slovenia is 20,000 square kilometers, and the 1961 census gave its population as 1,584,368, only a small percentage of the 18,549,000 inhabitants of Yugoslavia.[1] Its population density, however, according to a study of 1958, was 78 inhabitants per square kilometer, ranking it with the two other major republics, Serbia, with 87, and Croatia, with 74.[2]

Slovenes are linguistically homogeneous, with the exception of a small Hungarian minority at the extreme northeast and an Italian minority on the Istrian Peninsula. The Slovene language, one of the South Slavic group of the Slavic family, is one of the most archaic of the Slavic languages. It includes thirty-six dialects and twenty-nine subdialects,[3] many of which are distinct enough to be unintelligible to Slovene speakers of different areas.

On the north and northwest Slovenia is rimmed by the Julian Alps

FIG. I. *Yugoslavia*

and their eastern extensions, the highest point of which is the Triglav, 2,864 meters. The Alpine ridges meet the Dinaric fold, which extends along the western side of Yugoslavia. The largest part of Slovenia is mountainous. Only a small eastern section lies within the Pannonian Plain, which reaches into Hungary. Summers are short, often cool, and sometimes rainy. July temperatures in the Ljubljana area reach only 64° to 66° F.[4] Average temperatures, listed twenty kilometers from Žerovnica, are 30° F. in January, 46° in April, 67° in July, and 50° in October.[5] The average for Slovenia is 48°, and there is a range between January and July of thirty-nine degrees. The precipitation for the Ljubljana area averages 1,546 millimeters and is lower in winter than in other seasons.[6]

Rugged mountains, stony valleys, and karstic soil limit agricultural areas in Slovenia, and consequently expansion of agriculture must rely primarily on increased productivity.[7] With the exception of the Pannonian Plain, soils in all of Yugoslavia tend to be starved out by crop rotation that exhausts the soil and by the lack of sufficient fertilizer, either natural or commercial. Only at the high altitudes in Slovenia are Alpine black soils found.[8]

Slovenia does not produce enough grain for its own needs and must therefore rely on supplementary imports.[9] Today wheat cultivation, which requires flat areas, occupies 20 per cent of Slovenian fields, while rye, barley, and oats are grown in higher areas. Maize is cultivated primarily in Prekomurje (northeastern Slovenia) and Primorje (southwestern Slovenia) but also in other areas. In addition, clover is general, and potatoes are everywhere, especially in central Slovenia and the Drava valley. Turnips, carrots, beets, and cabbage are cultivated for animal as well as for human consumption. The animal economy includes milk cows, beef cattle, pigs, sheep (in the mountains), and poultry. Horses and oxen are the primary sources of power in the peasant village. The Slovenian agriculture is thus a mixed economy with a small surplus for the market.[10]

Forest exploitation is basic to the economy of the Slovene peasants, who owned 80 per cent of all woodland in the period between the two world wars.[11] In many parts of Slovenia (the Cerknica area is one example) sale of timber and employment in sawmills and furniture factories are the chief sources of cash for the peasants.

In 1960 Slovene land was divided into the categories shown in table 1. Almost half the land was forested, and 29.01 per cent was pasture land or meadows, while fields and gardens occupied only 14.5 per cent. In other parts of Yugoslavia, as well as Slovenia, population pressure on limited land resources is an old problem. In 1931 the average farm size in Slovenia was 8.27 hectares; 11.8 per cent of the farms measured 0.5 hectares or less; 64.3 per cent were from 0.5 to 10 hec-

TABLE I

*Land Categories in Slovenia, 1960*

| Category | % of Total Area |
|---|---|
| Forest land | 47.33 |
| Meadows | 10.71 |
| Hay land | 7.04 |
| Grazing land, including mountain pastures | 11.26 |
| Fields and gardens | 14.51 |
| Fruit orchards | 1.44 |
| Vineyards | 1.14 |
| Marshes and fish ponds | 0.15 |
| Unproductive land | 6.37 |

SOURCE: Melik, *Slovenija*, p. 373.

tares; 22.8 per cent were from 10 to 50 hectares (15.8 per cent were from 10 to 20 hectares); and only 1.1 per cent were over 50 hectares.[12] In all of Yugoslavia in 1931 small farms under 10 hectares represented 55 per cent of farm holdings, medium sized farms (10 to 50 hectares) represented 35 per cent, and large farms of 50 hectares or over represented 10 per cent.[13] Thus Slovenia was a land of small peasant holders even before the first land reforms of the 1930s, and it remains so today. In 1961, 73.3 per cent of the land was in private hands, and it is assumed there were no longer any farms of over 10 hectares. Of the total land area of 2,025,000 hectares, 1,486,000 hectares were private, and 540,000 were socialized, of which a disproportionate amount was forest land (342,000 hectares).[14]

While Slovenia has more limited agricultural resources than Croatia and Serbia, it is the richest industrial region of Yugoslavia, since its resources include natural gas and oil, and its mountains contain deposits of coal, lead, silver, and zinc. Furthermore, Slovene production of electrical energy provided, up to 1958, over one-fourth of the needs of the entire country.[15] There are developing paper, textile, metal, wood, and chemical industries.[16] The shift toward industrialization is evidenced by the following statistics: in 1900, 75 per cent of the total Slovene population was engaged in agriculture, in 1931 the figure was 61 per cent, and by 1960 farming was limited to 32.3 per cent of the population, as is shown in table 2.

TABLE 2
*Occupational Categories in Slovenia, 1960*

| Category | % of Population |
|---|---|
| Farming | 32.3 |
| Industry | 24.6 |
| Crafts[a] | 6.1 |
| Transportation | 4.1 |
| Trade | 4.7 |
| Administration | 2.9 |
| Education | 2.3 |
| Building | 4.2 |
| Unemployed | 13.3 |
| Various | 6.0 |

SOURCE: Melik, *Slovenija*, pp. 269–70.
[a] This group includes village specialists such as carpenters, smiths, and cobblers.

These figures, however, obscure the fact that many peasants in Yugoslavia combine factory and agricultural labor. In 1960, 822,000 individuals in Slovenia lived on agricultural holdings (see table 3). This means that while only 32.3 per cent are listed in table 2 as farmers, over 52 per cent of the population of Slovenia in 1960 lived on the land and were either full- or part-time peasants, as table 3 shows.

TABLE 3

*Members of Agricultural Households in Slovenia by Occupational Group, 1960*

| Occupational Group | Number (× 1,000) |
|---|---|
| Peasants: | |
| Men | 140 |
| Women working primarily on land | 106 |
| Women working part-time on land | 117 |
| Total peasants | 363 |
| Others: | |
| Peasant-Workers | 139 |
| Housewives | 22 |
| Children, students, elderly, infirm | 298 |
| Total others | 459 |
| Total living on land | 822 |

SOURCE: *Statistički Godišnjak SFRJ, 1964,* vol. 11, Federal Office for Statistics, Belgrade, 1964, quoted in Halpern, "Farming as a Way of Life."

## The Cerknica Basin

The karstic formations covering most of western Slovenia are composed of limestone of varied ages. In the area known as Notranjsko, in the southwest of Slovenia, where Žerovnica is located, the karstic terrain is characterized by large enclosed basins—poljes (*polja*) or valleys (*doline*)—the floors of which are generally level, while the walls rise sharply around them.[17] Two of the most important are the Lož valley (*Loška dolina*) and the Cerknica polje (*Cerkniško polje*), about fifty kilometers southwest of Ljubljana. The two basins, separated only by a small series of low hills, stretch from northwest to southeast, paralleling the Dinaric range. They are bordered on the southwest by the Javornik mountain range, rising to a height of 1,268 meters, which formed the Yugoslav-Italian border in the period be-

FIG. 2. *The Cerknica* občina

-called
occa-
ooded,
nunal
rned

ake
u-
he

a h
on a
ooked
wer. It i
lds, with t
of the area. I
ere the *občina*
s down on a bro
water, the depress
opes. High on the Kr
oke range there is visib
xcept on a few Catholic h
rossed by fields utilizing all
as well as that laid bare when
the northeast and east of the lake
d worked by tractors and combin
south and northwest. Here peasants
Grahovo, Žerovnica, Lipsenj, Goriči
two villages at the lake's northern e
Jezero) work their traditional fields v
and by hand. If one follows the ne
through the mountains, the plain is soon
would see more isolated, poorer mounta
cattle grazing on high slopes, their precipi
The karstic Cerknica lake is described
(*presihajoče jezero*). Its flat bottom is cov
The lake is filled by water from undergrou
mountain streams, as well as by small surface
slowly emptied by drainage holes (*požiraln*
structure. By summer, only marsh grass and a
marks the lake, but in early fall, rain water fro
replenishes the underground and surface waters
rapidly than the drainage holes can empty it.
At its lowest period the lake water covers half
while at its highest it floods twenty-five to twen
meters, approximately half of the Cerknica polje

tween the two w

ranges of Menisij

Slivnica. To the so

peak being the Snež

tip of the Lož valley

In the Cerknica po

meters. To reach Že

Ljubljana at the town

passing through karstic

ants), the administrativ

cal government, of the

prise Brest. Here also ar

They are a department

and refrigerators to pap

service grocery store that

are also a small movie hous

there remain the ruins of ar

The large Catholic church

From Cerknica the road

Cerknica basin, which is par

and spring, but which, excep

is dry in summer. To the left

on the right, on the flat land

co-operative farm. After passing

operative farm, with its large b

ters for workers, the road enters

is now the home of an importan

prise that produces furniture for

the road reaches the village of G

small villages with a post office, th

the local parish house. Grahovo's cl

destroyed during a battle between

groups. Barely in evidence are an ii

and a butcher shop, the dark exterior

From Grahovo a straight, dusty road

ing past the Co-operative House (za

munity center with a small store, now

end. The land uncovered in summer is mowed in August. Its so

sour grass (*kisla trava*) is used for cattle bedding and, on rare

sions, for fodder. The northeastern parts of the polje, never flo

provide excellent, fertile land. Once cattle also grazed on comm

pastures at the edge of the lake lands, but most villages have tu

this desirable level land to cultivation.

In the seventeenth century a Slovene nobleman described the l

in his now classical study of Slovenia. Marveling at the lake's mira

lous disappearances and its riches in fish and crabs, he wrote: "T

Cerknica lake . . . can be entitled in all honor a rarity of all lakes, ar

a true wonder of Nature. For this reason it has been classed as one o

the most noble curiosities of waters by older and newer scribes

through whose pens it has flowed."[18]

Legends about the origin of the lake are known throughout the

area (see chapter 4). Until ten years ago, when a road was con-

structed around the lake, villagers transported wood across it on rafts.

Timber was cut from the hilly forest lands around the lake. Many

nostalgically recall fishing expeditions and fantastic catches made pos-

sible when the lake dried out in late summer, exposing crabs and fish.

Ambitious plans by the *občina* to reduce the area covered by the lake

at its height, by a system of dams, and to drain and improve the un-

covered area, are met by mixed reactions on the part of the villagers,

many of whom believe the lake is unconquerable and all of whom

fear the loss of their hay lands.

## Žerovnica

Most of Žerovnica's fifty-nine houses are lined up close together, half

on one side of a dusty road and half on the other. The houses are rec-

tangular, with a narrow end of the rectangle facing the road. The

single entrance to the house is reached by a side path at right angles

to the road. At either end of the village the pattern breaks, and a few

poorer houses straggle out of line. Then, taking off from the central

road, along the Žerovnišča River, are the widely spaced and larger

houses of the five millers, whose sawmills once worked long hours,

representing the industry of the village.

The Slovene historian Grafenauer has classified Slovene villages into two main types.[19] He believes that the earliest form, in which houses were clustered irregularly, surrounded by unsystematically arranged plots of many different shapes, was associated with cultivation by the wheelless plow (*ralo*) or even by hoeing. During the main period of the settling of Slovenia, from the ninth to the twelfth century, when the wheeled plow (*plug*) was employed, the planned village, or long village (*dolga vas*), with a rationalized land arrangement, superseded the earlier type, according to Grafenauer. The long village took three main forms. The road village (*obcestna vas*) was composed of houses lined up close together on either side of the road, with a narrow end of the house facing the road, a type which is illustrated in Grafenauer's study by the plan of Žerovnica. In a second subtype, the line village (*vas v vrsti* or *gozdna vas*), houses were built only on one side of the road. Finally, in the centrally planned village (*središcna vas*) houses faced a central square with a church. Land associated with the planned villages, and particularly with the road and central types, was divided into complexes or sections (*delce*), also referred to as open fields.[20] Sections were, in turn, subdivided into long parallel fields or strips without visible borders between them. Traditionally each peasant possessed one or more strips in each section of the village land, and all villagers co-operated in a village-wide system of crop rotation (*kolobarjenje*), a system that is still partly followed in Žerovnica. After the harvest the fields were opened for pasturing the cattle of the entire village.[21]

The present land division of Žerovnica is assumed to be ancient. Old families believe that their ancestors have held the same strips for hundreds of years. The village map of 1887, a copy of a somewhat earlier document, depicts a land distribution very much like the present. Furthermore, the earliest complete church records, which begin with the late eighteenth century, list fifty-nine homesteads, the same number as today. According to the map of 1887, the village then owned 518 hectares, 16 ares, 69 meters, as it still does today. (See fig. 3, which is similar to, but later than, the 1887 map.)

A relief map of Žerovnica in the Ljubljana Geographic Institute includes the following explanatory remarks: "Žerovnica is a typical road village on the southeast side of the polje. The village houses are situated on both sides of the road." Concerning the arrangement of

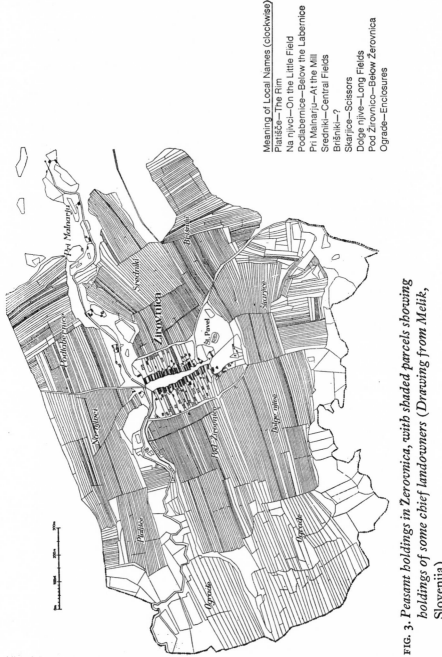

Meaning of Local Names (clockwise)
Platišče—The Rim
Na njivci—On the Little Field
Podlabernice—Below the Labernice
Pri Malnarju—At the Mill
Sredniki—Central Fields
Brišniki—?
Skarjice—Scissors
Dolge njive—Long Fields
Pod Žirovnico—Below Žerovnica
Ograde—Enclosures

FIG. 3. *Peasant holdings in Žerovnica, with shaded parcels showing holdings of some chief landowners (Drawing from Melik, Slovenija)*

land in relation to the village, the inscription explains that Žerovnica is located in one of the most typical Slovenian areas, in which land is divided into strips. This is a large triangular area, in the center of which lies the Cerknica basin. There are "narrow, impossibly divided strips that compose clearly defined land complexes. . . . On each complex the most significant families each have one piece."

The road from Grahovo leads to the northern entrance to Žerovnica, marked by a bridge over the Žerovnišča River, which here borders a small village green, the only common gathering place today.[22] The green is shaded by the wide boughs of a linden (*lipa*) tree, beneath which there are a few benches and a table.[23] Alongside the linden tree rises a partisan monument, a roughhewn stone obelisk with a polished side on which are engraved the names of war heroes. Its heavy state style is lightened by the linden tree and by the flowers at its base. Next to the monument is the *balina* field, where a few men and boys meet on evenings and Sundays to play the *balina* game, a form of lawn bowls. It is found everywhere in this area and is a recent introduction from Italy.

The central road leading from the green is faced by houses of plastered stone, many of which need paint. To each house is affixed a shiny red plaque bearing a number. Villagers, however, have never learned the numbers so convenient for the tax collector; their dwellings are still identified by traditional house names, registered in the earliest church records. Houses are fronted by wooden benches and some by small, fenced-in flower and vegetable gardens. Behind each house are attached sheds for fowl, pigs, cattle, and horses, next to which are storehouses (see fig. 4). The manure pile, used for fertilizer, is close by. Generally there is another shed that houses a special stove on which to cook feed for pigs, and, with few exceptions, there is an outhouse. Then come the fruit trees—apple, plum, and pear—and finally the detached storage barn (*skedenj*) where hay and cattle bedding is stored (see figs. 5, 6). Behind the homesteads are paths leading to the fields, where wheat, maize, fodder crops, potatoes, beans, and other vegetables are grown.

On a spring afternoon a few elders sit on benches in front of their houses. Small children play along the road, in the stream, and under the linden tree on the green. A villager with his ox-drawn cart, carrying his wife and children and perhaps one or two grandparents with

FIG. 4. *House and attached sheds*

FIG. 5. *Detached barns*

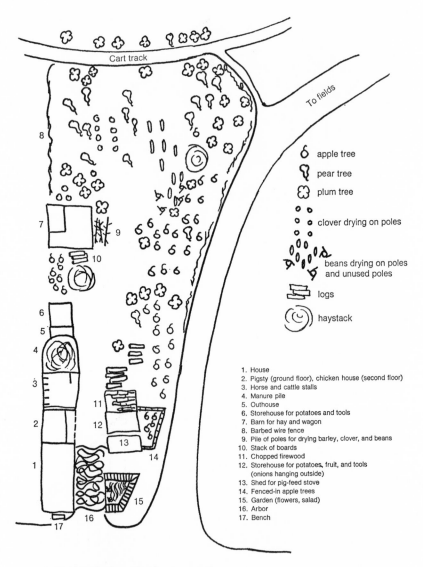

Cart track

To fields

δ apple tree

φ pear tree

❀ plum tree

∘ ∘ clover drying on poles

beans drying on poles and unused poles

logs

haystack

1. House
2. Pigsty (ground floor), chicken house (second floor)
3. Horse and cattle stalls
4. Manure pile
5. Outhouse
6. Storehouse for potatoes and tools
7. Barn for hay and wagon
8. Barbed wire fence
9. Pile of poles for drying barley, clover, and beans
10. Stack of boards
11. Chopped firewood
12. Storehouse for potatoes, fruit, and tools (onions hanging outside)
13. Shed for pig-feed stove
14. Fenced-in apple trees
15. Garden (flowers, salad)
16. Arbor
17. Bench

FIG. 6. *Ground plan of a homestead*

their hoes and rakes, leaves for the fields. All but the very old and very young are at work, and the village is quiet and empty. The road leads through the village to the hill on which the church stands and near which is the oldest structure in the village (fig. 7). Anyone

FIG. 7. *The oldest structure in the village, a former storehouse, no longer in use*

climbing the hill is rewarded with another excellent view of the area. In the churchyard, enclosed by an old stone wall, are the family graves of the villagers as well as a collective grave of seven partisans. The bell in the baroque, red-painted steeple no longer rings, but the church itself is freshly whitewashed. Until the autumn of 1964 Sunday masses were celebrated in Žerovnica. Now they are celebrated only in Grahovo.

Extremes of climate are familiar in this area. Heavy spring rains may cause severe damage to crops and forests. Cool, wet summers may be interrupted by periods of steppelike heat when dust and sun are oppressive.

Drinking water is now piped to the village from Grahovo. According to villagers this project was under discussion for fifty years. A few years ago, when the water from the Žerovnišča River was found to be polluted by an army camp upstream, villagers agreed to finance the pipeline by individual contributions. Electricity has been available since shortly before World War II.

Žerovnica is serviced by a post office in Grahovo, which is reached by a daily mail truck. The post office has one telephone. Because of Žerovnica's strategic location between various large centers, numerous busses (we counted thirteen) speed daily through the village to Ljubljana, Rakek, Stari Trg, and other centers, causing villagers to caution children frequently. Before the last war no bus reached Žerovnica.

The road from Cerknica to Grahovo was asphalted after the war. The Žerovnica road is still unpaved. Since 1910 Žerovnica has been linked to the smaller village of Lipsenj by a dirt road, replacing the earlier footpath. (This sister village, located only a half a kilometer away, has been tied to Žerovnica by intermarriage for many centuries.) Today bicycles, motor scooters, some motorcycles, and busses complement the horses and ox carts on the village road, but automobiles are rare. Until 1965 only one villager, the richest miller, owned an automobile. In the last few years one more has appeared.

The population of Žerovnica numbered 264 in 1961, according to the data of the Geographical Institute in Ljubljana, and 248 according to church records of 1962. A review of the figures since 1868 shows a rise of population until 1890, then a decline through the first decade of the twentieth century. A second increase continued until some time in the twenties, but there has been a decline ever since. This pattern in the twentieth century is shared by the two other small villages in the church district, but not by Grahovo, the population of which increased in the early forties, reflecting urban trends (see table 4). During this entire period, when the population of Žerovnica declined from 323 to 248 persons, the number of occupied houses varied from 57 to 59.

Several factors explain the decline of the rural population from the 1890s until the period just before World War I. In the nineteenth century the typical Slovene family was large. With the growing shortage of land and a depression at the end of the nineteenth century, emigration rose sharply, attaining its greatest height in the period between 1890 and 1914. Most Slovene emigrants went to the United States, where they worked in mines or factories or at railroad building. Others found employment in Germany and Austria. After 1918 emigration was slowed by American restrictive quotas. The gradual increase of industrialization in Yugoslavia provided a new outlet for

TABLE 4

*Population Trends in Žerovnica and Neighboring Villages*

| Year | Žerovnica | Lipsenj | Bločice | Grahovo |
|------|-----------|---------|---------|---------|
| 1868 | 323 | | | |
| 1880 | 344 | | | |
| 1890 | 361 | | | |
| 1900 | 332 | | | |
| 1910 | 327 | | | |
| 1911 | 326* | 269* | 136* | 498* |
| 1921 | 366* | 271* | 294* | 470* |
| 1931 | 354 | 223* | 176* | 466* |
| 1941 | 343* | 215* | 162* | 500* |
| 1948 | 289 | | | |
| 1953 | 275 | | | |
| 1961 | 264 | | | |
| 1962 | 248* | 153* | 117* | 445* |

SOURCES: The starred figures are based on church records. The others are from unpublished data of the Geographical Institute of the University of Ljubljana.

rural overpopulation. However, some Slovenes continued to emigrate to South America and to central and western Europe.[24] An increase in population after World War I was halted by the depression. After World War II the general use of birth control and the movement to cities caused over-all declines in the rural population in spite of gains from better medical care and the reduction of infant mortality.

The trend in Slovenia as a whole since 1931, in contrast to the rural trend, has been one of population increase. However, for a long period Slovenian population growth has not paralleled that of other areas in what is now Yugoslavia. For example, from 1878 to 1910 the total population increase in Serbia was 71.3 per cent, while the Slovenian increase was only 9.4 per cent.[25] The low population increase in Slovenia is explained by a lower birth rate and heavy emigration caused by the early exhaustion of free land.[26] Between 1921 and 1941 the population in Slovenia increased by 14.5 per cent, while in Yugoslavia as a whole the increase was much greater, 33.3 per cent.[27]

Slovene population grew from an estimated 1,266,604 in 1931 to 1,439,800 in 1948, 1,504,427 in 1953, and 1,584,368 in 1961.[28]

Table 5 indicates that the sexes were approximately evenly divided in Žerovnica from the later nineteenth century until the first part of the twentieth.[29] However, since 1890 the male population has de-

TABLE 5

*Distribution of the Population of*
*Žerovnica by Sex, 1866–1961*

| Year | Male | Female | Total | Houses |
|------|------|--------|-------|--------|
| 1866 | 158  | 165    | 323   | 57     |
| 1880 | 170  | 174    | 344   | 58     |
| 1890 | 180  | 181    | 361   | 58     |
| 1900 | 169  | 163    | 332   | 59     |
| 1910 | 162  | 165    | 327   | 59     |
| 1931 | 172  | 182    | 354   | 58     |
| 1948 | 136  | 153    | 289   | 58     |
| 1953 | 125  | 150    | 275   | 56     |
| 1961 | 124  | 140    | 264   | 57     |

SOURCE: Geographical Institute of the University of Ljubljana, unpublished data.

clined. While the female population also has declined, it has become significantly larger than the male population. The change in proportion of male to female reflects the loss of men to industry as well as the losses caused by the two wars. In recent years, however, more young women have been leaving the village for training beyond grade school, and therefore it is not clear whether the disproportion of the sexes will persist.

Birth rates in Žerovnica remained fairly stable from 1900 until the depression years, after which they dropped. In the nineteenth and early twentieth centuries birth rates were high. Generally there were nine to fourteen persons in a house, members of three generations, and frequently these included unmarried brothers and sisters of the *gospodar*. Since World War II, two or three children have been considered enough by most families. Death rates have also declined in the last decades, reflecting improved medical care.

TABLE 6

*Births, Deaths, and Marriages in Žerovnica, 1900–1965*

| Year | Births[a] | Deaths | Marriages | Year | Births[a] | Deaths | Marriages |
|------|-----------|--------|-----------|------|-----------|--------|-----------|
| 1900 | 5 | 4 | 1 | 1930 | 10 | 3 | 2 |
| 1901 | 11 | 8 | 1 | 1931 | 8 | 3 | 4 |
| 1902 | 10 | 9 | 2 | 1932 | 6 | 5 | 2 |
| 1903 | 7 | 7 | 3 | 1933 | 6 | 9 | 0 |
| 1904 | 17 | 4 | 3 | 1934 | 7 | 6 | 6 |
| 1905 | 10 | 10 | 2 | 1935 | 5 | 3 | 0 |
| 1906 | 14 | 10 | 2 | 1936 | 0 | 5 | 6 |
| 1907 | 7 | 7 | 1 | 1937 | 7 | 3 | 1 |
| 1908 | 11 | 11 | 2 | 1938 | 2 | 5 | 2 |
| 1909 | 12 | 8 | 2 | 1939 | 8 | 5 | 6 |
| | | | | | | | |
| 1910 | 14 | 3 | 2 | 1940 | 5 | 3 | 5 |
| 1911 | 16 | 9 | 1 | 1941 | 4 | 4 | 6 |
| 1912 | 12 | 4 | 3 | 1942 | 3 | 4 | 2 |
| 1913 | 12 | 4 | 3 | 1943 | 2 | 3 | 0 |
| 1914 | 12 | 8 | 3 | 1944 | 3 | 4 | 0 |
| 1915 | 13 | 9 | 0 | 1945 | 4 | 11 | 3 |
| 1916 | 9 | 5 | 0 | 1946 | 4 | 5 | —[b] |
| 1917 | 10 | 7 | 2 | 1947 | 4 | 1 | 5 |
| 1918 | 9 | 5 | 2 | 1948 | 2 | 2 | 6 |
| 1919 | 13 | 8 | 6 | 1949 | 4 | 3 | 1 |
| | | | | | | | |
| 1920 | 15 | 7 | 5 | 1950 | 10 | 2 | 1 |
| 1921 | 9 | 10 | 3 | 1951 | 3 | 2 | 1 |
| 1922 | 14 | 8 | 3 | 1952 | 5 | 2 | 3 |
| 1923 | 14 | 3 | 2 | 1953 | 3 | 3 | 1 |
| 1924 | 11 | 4 | 2 | 1954 | 3 | 4 | 3 |
| 1925 | 13 | 6 | 3 | 1955 | 4 | 3 | 7 |
| 1926 | 10 | 6 | 0 | 1956 | 7 | 3 | 0 |
| 1927 | 12 | 16 | 2 | 1957 | 3 | 3 | 4 |
| 1928 | 9 | 8 | 3 | 1958 | 3 | 3 | 0 |
| 1929 | 8 | 6 | 3 | 1959 | 4 | 3 | 1 |

(*Cont.*)

TABLE 6—*Continued*

| Year | Births[a] | Deaths | Marriages |
|------|-----------|--------|-----------|
| 1960 | 6 | 2 | 8 |
| 1961 | 9 | 2 | 3 |
| 1962 | 1 | 4 | 3 |
| 1963 | 4 | 3 | 4 |
| 1964 | 0 | 2 | 2 |
| 1965[c] | 1 | 0 | 1 |

SOURCE: The Bureau of Vital Statistics (*Matični urad*) of the Cerknica *občina*, unpublished data.
[a] The figures until 1950 show only births in Žerovnica. After 1945 some infants were delivered in the hospital in Postojna. These births are included from 1950 on.
[b] Not recorded in Cerknica.
[c] Through August.

There were more marriages in the years 1933–65 (at least ninety-one) than in the years 1900–1932 (seventy-five in all), in spite of the decrease in population, reflecting improved economic circumstances allowing people to marry younger (see table 6). Earlier, lack of economic opportunity forced some individuals to remain in the category of unmarried relatives and unpaid helpers of the *gospodar* for indefinite periods.

The dialect spoken in the area of Žerovnica and the Cerknica basin is classified by Ramovš as a western subdialect of Lower Carinthian (*dolenjski dialekt*).[30] It is bordered by the Inner Carinthian dialect (*notranjski dialekt*) spoken on the western side of the Javornik Mountains along the prewar Italo-Yugoslav border. To the north is the so-called *rovtarski* dialect. Morphologically and syntactically, the Žerovnica dialect does not deviate significantly from standard literary Slovene. The reduction of vowels, however, does differentiate its phonemic system. Thus, for example, *tukihle* ("here") is pronounced "tle," and *Martinjak* (the name of the nearby village) is pronounced "Martnjak." Lexically, the Žerovnica dialect is also distinguished from standard literary Slovene by its inclusion of a large number of Germanisms.[31]

All village children begin school at the age of seven or eight. English is introduced in the fifth grade and Serbo-Croatian in the sixth. Literacy has been general for at least the last two generations. Many villagers subscribe to a local monthly paper, *Glas Notranjske*, the organ of the Socialist Union of the Working People of the Cerknica *občina*. Some read the partisan monthly *TV 15*. About fifteen families subscribe to the weekly *TT*, a Slovene movie magazine. Only a few receive the national Slovene daily, *Delo*, published by the Union of

Communists of Slovenia. Many villagers said they liked to read newspapers, but few thought they had time to read books, which were hardly available. The nearest source of books is a small selection of paperbacks and a few textbooks in the general store in Cerknica, eight kilometers away.

A small cinema in Cerknica offers old American, Soviet, and Yugoslav films twice weekly. Other cultural events are lacking, and local officials expressed no interest in encouraging community cultural activities that might replace the traditional market gatherings, religious holidays, and social events that are a fading part of village life.

# 2

## *The Village in History*

### From Prehistoric Times to 1848

MUCH REMAINS to be known of the long Paleolithic period in central and eastern Europe. It has been suggested that at the close of the Paleolithic, groups in southeastern Europe, who were relatively close to the cradle of agriculture in the Near East, participated in the formation of the farmer tribes that penetrated to the north, gradually assimilating hunting, fishing, and collecting groups.[1]

In the area that is today Slovenia, the culture indicated by late Paleolithic finds was followed by a Neolithic culture lasting until approximately 1900 B.C. Copper Age dwellings on swamps in the Ljubljana area and on lake shores are dated from 1900–1800 B.C.[2] More numerous finds, signifying denser settlement in the early Iron Age (Hallstatt, 1000–400 B.C.), are attributed to the Illyrians, an Indo-European cattle-herding people who lived along the Adriatic coast between the Julian Alps and present-day Bosnia.[3] During the late Iron Age another Indo-European group of cattle herders, identified with the La Tène culture, arrived and freely intermingled with the Illyrians. The Roman influx began in the third century B.C., and by 14 B.C. all of Illyria to the Danube River was under Roman control.[4] In the fifth century A.D. other groups, including the Visigoths, Huns, and Ostrogoths, caused new disruptions, which were followed by the devastations brought by the Avars (called *Obri* by the Slavs).

For a considerable period Slavic tribes from the east also moved into the Balkan area, and by 650 A.D. they were in full possession of Illyria.[5] Among the Slavic groups that turned west and southwest after crossing the Carpathians, the northernmost were the Slovenes, who replaced the Germanic Langobards in the territory of present-day Slovenia.[6] In the middle of the seventh century Slovenes were included in the Slavic union led by King Samo (627–58), whose rule extended from the area of present-day Slovenia to what is now central Germany.[7] The union fell apart after Samo's death, and the Slovenes subsequently came under the domination of the Franks, and became the object of intensive Christian proselytizing, especially during the reign of Charlemagne (768–814). During the Middle Ages Slovene lands became a part of the duchy of Carantania, created by the Holy Roman Emperor Otto I in 952. In the thirteenth century the Slovenes were again included in a Slavic union, led by King Otokar II Přemysl of Bohemia, who was, however, defeated in 1278 by a new Holy Roman Emperor, Rudolf of Hapsburg. By the middle of the fourteenth century Hapsburg domination over the duchies of Carinthia (German: Kärnten; Slovene: Koroško) and Carniola (German: Krain or Crain; Slovene: Kranj) was firmly established.

The Slavic ruling group having been eliminated from early Slovene society before the tenth century, the chief representatives of the feudal order in Slovene lands became the German lords and the Catholic church.[8] Between the tenth and twelfth centuries, Grafenauer states, there were two basic social classes, the nobility (*plemstvo*) and the peasants (*kmeti*). The latter were not a homogeneous group but included three strata. The manorial serfs (*pridvorni hlapci*) lived in bondage in or near the castle. A second group of serfs (*hlapci*) had been awarded separate homesteads but were heavily obligated for corvée (*tlaka*), or, if they lived at a distance, they paid taxes in kind or in money. They could be sold with the land or lose their land to the lord. The third and best-situated group, the half-free (*polsvobodni*), colonized hitherto uncultivated lands, a significant process under the early Hapsburgs. While they paid heavy taxes to the lord, they had been freed from corvée, hence they were also called *prazniki* (from *prazen*, "free").[9] During the period from the twelfth to the beginning of the fifteenth century the majority of the Slovene rural population obtained their own homesteads, but were obligated for taxes and often for corvée.[10]

The later feudal period was marked by unrest and the ferment of new ideas. In the sixteenth century the Reformation encouraged the rise of a Slovene national consciousness. Thus the Slovene language was adopted in church services, and in 1584 the first Slovene grammar appeared. But Protestantism was vigorously opposed, and the Counter Reformation was nowhere more successful than in Slovenia,[11] where it led to persecution of heretic believers and sects, and even to witch-hunts and burnings.[12]

Between the fifteenth and seventeenth centuries Slovenian life was disrupted by peasant revolts. The earliest, protesting heavy taxation, occurred in 1474–76.[13] In the most important uprising, in 1573, Slovenes joined their Croat neighbors in a revolt led by a Croatian peasant leader.[14] A significant response to peasant protest was the enlightened policy of agrarian reform during the reigns of Maria Theresa (1740–80) and her son Joseph II (1780–90). While the power of the central government to tax was strengthened, the feudal lord's control over the peasant was limited by a series of decrees that drastically reduced the corvée,[15] abolished personal servitude, and gave peasants the right to move away or marry without the lord's permission.[16] Furthermore, various economic reforms were undertaken to rationalize agriculture, including the introduction of new crops and fertilization.[17]

The Hapsburg rule was briefly interrupted from 1809 to 1813 when, under Napoleon, Carniola became part of the French Illyrian provinces, of which Ljubljana was the capital. French influence furthered the rise of nationalism and the development of the Slovene language. The first newspapers in Slovenian were published. Broad but short-lived reforms were adopted declaring all men equal before the law and serfs full owners of the land.[18] After the Austrian restoration Slovene national consciousness continued to grow. In the revolutionary year 1848 the society named Slovenija called for the creation of a Slovenian kingdom under Austrian rule.

The accomplishments of the period of reform initiated by Maria Theresa were significant. Legal bondage to the land was abolished, and the rights and obligations of serfs were defined, protecting them from extreme exactions of labor and produce. Peasants were serfs only in the sense that they paid tithes or levies and performed compulsory labor for land occupied. By fixing the total area of peasant land, legislation protected peasant holdings from absorption by the landowner. Thus a proportion of the land was in peasant occupation when serf obligations were finally fully abolished in 1848.[19]

The oldest fragments of church records for Žerovnica refer to the year 1618. Earlier documents were lost or destroyed. Complete church records have been preserved only since 1780, by which time there were fifty-eight homesteads, essentially the same number as today, each with its housename (referred to in the church records as *nomen vulgaris*), which generally was derived from the name of the first founder, although sometimes it was altered later. Villagers believe that Žerovnica was settled many centuries ago. According to legend the first inhabitants were twelve free Slovene families who cultivated their lands until they were forced into serfdom by the count, or feudal lord (*graščak*). Village tales of the feudal period describe Turkish raids and life under the reign of the count of Šteberk, whose domain included Žerovnica. A central story explains the origin of the lake, which is ascribed to the era of the count of Šteberk.

Turkish incursions in the Cerknica area, though brief, were significant. Remains of fortifications against the Turks in Cerknica are still visible, and details of the largest Turkish conflict, during which Cerknica was burned in 1472, are recorded on a tablet in an old church in Cerknica that is said to have been erected in 1482.[20] According to folk tradition, while other villages were destroyed, a clever woman saved Žerovnica. This event was recounted by an elder villager, a former itinerant musician and singer at weddings: "It is said that in the old days the Turks came to Žerovnica. Everyone fled and took their cattle with them. But in one house an old woman was left. She heated a pot and put everything evil-smelling into it, bones, manure, and so forth. The people said they could smell it for a half an hour's walk away. So the Turks did not enter the village. They came to another forest and another village and they burnt it down. This is why Žerovnica was saved."[21]

The count of Šteberk is an important dramatis persona in a series of tales. The castle from which he ruled his domain stood on a hilltop overlooking Žerovnica and must have been an imposing sight until it was destroyed by a neighboring ruler in 1492. Today a narrow path climbs a steep, wooded slope to a clearing, where extensive ruins of the once mighty castle remain. In a folktale, the origin of the lake is attributed to the miraculous action of a young prince of Šteberk who lived in the ancient castle. At that time, it is said, a bog, studded with oaks and other trees, covered the area that is today under water. In the most frequent version told today in the village, a narrator recounts a story that was related to him by a friend as they went boating on the lake.

When I was young, I used to go boating on the lake. Well, almost our entire village went there once. And we were sitting in the boat talking about all sorts of things—our men. Then one spoke, and said, "That is nothing, I heard how this lake came to be."

"Well, then, tell us," I said. And he began to tell us. He was a carpenter, a small little man, and a hunchback.

"Well," he said, "there, where the Karlovica [one of the main drainage holes of the lake] is, there was a castle—there is still a small section of the wall there—but at Šteberk much of the wall is still left." [Šteberk and Karlovica are on the opposite sides of the present-day lake.]

We own a small wood, right by that castle there, below and above it. And there is also a cellar there, a big one—I do not know what they used it for. During the war, the second one, the partisans hid in that cellar—they had benches and a stove in there so they could warm themselves.

"When the young prince of Šteberk was the master," he said, "there was a girl at the Karlovica, the poor girl. That prince wooed her, but the count at Karlovica, her father, refused to give up his daughter. He told the young prince, 'Only if you come for her in a boat can you have her.'

"And the young prince felt a premonition of something terrible. He went [riding]—he had a beautiful white horse. And a man appeared from a valley and said, 'Why are you so deep in thought and sad?'

" 'How can I help it,' said he. 'There is a girl I would like to marry, but her father will not allow it at all. If I come for her in a boat I may have her. How can I do this? What should I do?'

"And that man said, 'I shall tell you. Cover a drainage hole with a grid, make strong iron grids, and put a lot of dirt over them, and when it rains a lake will form.'

"And he did so. It began to rain, and the lake appeared. Then he made a boat, a large boat, and sailed across. And truly, the father was not happy at all—but he had given his word and he had to keep it. The boy and the girl agreed that she would set a light for him in the evening. And he used that light as a guide and came to see her every evening. But suddenly others came from elsewhere asking for the girl's hand. And her father was glad—but the girl was not. She said, 'I have my man—he comes to me every evening—I just set the light on the window for him and he comes up on the boat.'

"But the father plotted with one of her suitors, or he bribed one of the maids, to carry the light over to the Karlovica. The young man from Šteberk followed the light and came to the Karlovica. The water swallowed him—the boat was so big and listing so heavily that its name was visible on its side.

"The girl was looking for the young man, wondering why he had not come. She looked at the window—there was no light. She walked around the castle and glanced at the Karlovica—the light was still burning there in the daylight. And she saw the boat —its name was there as before. She said, 'Someone set the light there on purpose,' and she also threw herself into the water.

"And so then there was the lake. No one could reopen the hole —and so the lake came to be."

Other tales describe the autocratic rule of the count. It is said that the people were prohibited from fishing in the lake except when a bell rang in Cerknica. But no sooner had the villagers caught their fish than the count would rule that all the fish were for the castle. The people would then have to throw the fish back into the lake as the count cursed them, saying, "Death to all."

Another tale ridicules the countess: "Once the peasants were mowing on all sides. There was the corvée then, and the peasants went up there to mow. Well, the countess came to take a little walk, to cool off a little. She had a parasol and watched the peasants mowing. When they stopped to sharpen their blades, she said, 'Do not scritch-scratch, finish the job [Nix figl-fajgl, durch mahaj].'[22] The mowing went so slowly with dull blades that finally the countess said, 'First scritch-scratch, then finish!' "

Witches also appear in the early tales. One story describes the burning of a village to rid it of a witch (*copernica*). In a map drawn by Valvasor around 1686, the top of the Slivnica is labeled as a gathering place for witches (*Hexenzusammenkunft*). Under Count Šteberk, it is said, witches were tortured, the gallows were filled, and peasants were beaten, as excerpts from early tales recounted by an old village woman demonstrate:

> Šteberk Castle controlled all these villages. They were all raising cattle for him up there, all these villagers. And they say there also were large prison cells in the castle. If someone would not obey and was not submissive, they would throw him into that prison. In those earlier times, when people believed strongly in witches, if a woman was accused of being a witch, they would chain her and chase her from the castle through Žerovnica to Grahovo—and to Martinjak. Then the hangman would take her and close the gates where the big gallows were.
>
> While they chased a witch, all the church bells would toll for her last hour. Saint Pavel, here in our village, and Mary of the Immaculate Conception in Grahovo, it is called so, and in Martinjak there is another church, it was called Saint Leo; Saint Leo would toll till the end, until she was hung. And if she should cry out on her way—they would cut off her tongue.
>
> There, where they were catching fish down the lake and along those shores, there was a guard, or a policeman, with a whip. If someone did not want to catch fish, he would beat him on the naked back—he would let him have it with a real whip, they say.
>
> Each peasant also had to work for the count for fourteen days. Then the local count—that old one—died, and they brought one of his relatives from Germany, but again it did not work out— that one also left. Then all fell into decay.
>
> Now, at Saint Ann, up there on the top, they have found the cemetery of these counts. And they found a skeleton there; it is now some two or three years since—and there were golden chains and golden rings still on the skeleton, which was still intact. And it is perhaps two, three, or four hundred years old, or even older. Well, the castle came to be. And then, after it fell apart, it was no more.

At some time after the legendary era of the counts of Šteberk, and until 1848, the peasants of Žerovnica served the more distant count of Planina, called by villagers the *grašcak* Hasberk, who was a member of the Windischgrätz family. The remains of the castle, set afire in the last war, are visible from the main highway that leads from Ljubljana to Trieste and Rijeka, but are far out of sight of the village. In folktales Šteberk Castle retained the dominant role.

# From the End of Serfdom through World War I: 1848–1918

Austrian decrees of 1848 and 1849 ended tithes and the corvée. By that period most of the agricultural land in Slovenia was already in peasant hands, and peasant-landowner disputes centered primarily over the important question of forest rights, and the use of Alpine pasture lands by the nobility as game preserves.[23] There were efforts on the part of the government and agricultural societies to improve farming practices; to expand maize, dairy, and livestock farming; and to help home industries such as spinning flax and wool, weaving, and basket-making.[24] However, grain imports continued to be necessary.[25] Aid also came from co-operative organizations, which, as a result of efforts by the Catholic clergy, reached a high level by the end of the nineteenth century. Credit societies were well developed, and marketing societies handled dairy produce, cattle, eggs, fruit, and vegetables.[26] Machine co-operatives existed also. The increase of industry, mining, and railways in the later nineteenth century offered some peasants new occupations. Finally, the avenue of emigration was open to all.

Throughout this period, however, there was a general increase in taxes, an increase in subdivision of the land, and the mortgaging of farm property, which eventually led to foreclosures and the agrarian crisis of the 1890s. Consequently the years 1890–1910 saw large-scale emigration of Slovenes to the United States.[27]

In the later nineteenth century Žerovnica gained forest land, which remains a basic village economic asset. Before 1880 the peasants did not own forest land, although they had been awarded certain rights to use the forest and to buy wood. One family still guards land documents that record a sale of forest land by Count Windischgrätz in 1802. Whether this was a common practice is not known, but this family is still one of the richer ones in Žerovnica. In 1880 approximately two hundred hectares of the count's forest land was divided among the peasants of Žerovnica. Each family received three parcels, one in the valley, and two high in the mountains across the lake. The five millers, who by this time all had sawmills, obtained more forest land than the others. However, everyone in the village knows that the count was supposed to give 1800 *joch* (1,026 hectares) but instead cheated the village and gave only 300–400 *joch*.

Life under Austrian rule has both positive and negative associations for village elders. Villagers recall the inconvenience of communicating with officials in German; that language was never really learned, and no one in the village remembers more than a few words. Many recall poverty, poor housing, a lack of farm machinery, and families too large to support. At the same time this era is associated in the minds of the peasants with a limited feeling of respect for some of the paternalistic measures and the order and efficiency ascribed to the old regime, as well as the ease of emigration.

## The Interwar Years: 1918–41

Austrian rule in the area that is now Yugoslavia finally came to an end in 1918. The new South Slav state was at first called the Kingdom of the Serbs, Croats, and Slovenes. The province of Slovenia included the former Austrian territories inhabited by the Slovenes, the former duchy of Carniola (Krain), a considerable section of Styria, and a small section of Carinthia.[28] According to the census of 1921, Slovenia then had a population of 1.05 million inhabitants.[29] Slovene nationalism had yet to receive full expression, however, since the provisions of the new Yugoslav constitution of 1921 supported Serbian centralism. Democratic forms ended with the establishment of a royal dictatorship in 1929. After the assassination of King Alexander I in 1934, however, a milder autocratic government continued its rule until World War II.

During the interwar period limited land reforms in Yugoslavia attempted to break up large land concentrations. The Interim Decree of 1919 announced the government's intention of expropriating large estates, with indemnity. (For the most part this meant estates of over

100 cadastral yokes, but in some areas 500 cadastral yokes were allowed.)[30] Estates owned by foreigners were excepted. Large forests were declared state property, and owners were to be compensated. Peasants were also given the right to use these lands for grazing, woodcutting, and household needs.[31] Provisions for implementation of these reforms, however, were lacking, and necessary legislation was delayed for fourteen confusing years. With the Law of Agrarian Reform of Large Estates of 19 June 1931 the maximum areas that could be retained were finally defined, and in 1932 the terms of compensation were fixed. By the end of 1935 from ten to twelve thousand landowners had surrendered some land. The interwar reform transferred an area of approximately two million hectares (about one-fourth of all cultivated land in 1938) to the ownership of 637,000 families. More than one out of every four peasant families benefited. In addition, another half million hectares of forest land came under state ownership.[32] However, the northern estates, including those in Slovenia, were only partially expropriated, and Žerovnica and many other villages were not affected at all.

Over the whole interwar period the crop yield rose slowly by about one million tons every five years,[33] doubling by 1939. During this period Yugoslavia was a net exporter of its two most important crops, wheat and maize, as well as of pigs.[34] In spite of agricultural reforms, however, Tomasevich estimates that in 1921, 3,892,000 persons, or 41 per cent of Yugoslavia's agricultural population, were surplus, while in 1938 this figure was 5,011,000, or 43 per cent. This is based on a norm of one and one-quarter hectares of cultivated land per person.[35] In 1938, for Slovenia alone (or the Drava *banovina*, the administrative unit that replaced the province of Slovenia in the latter part of the interwar period), 58.5 per cent of the agricultural population was considered surplus.[36]

Slovenia, as distinguished from the rest of Yugoslavia, maintained an agricultural credit system that had been initiated during the last decades of the Austrian rule. Nevertheless, peasant indebtedness increased during the interwar years, and mortgaging land was common. With the financial crisis of 1932 came a moratorium on peasant debts. In spite of the better-developed agricultural credit system, 48.3 per cent of all agricultural debts in Slovenia in 1932 were owed to private moneylenders and storekeepers; 45.9 per cent of all rural

households were in debt, and this affected 59.9 per cent of all cultivated land.[37]

Villagers expressed less positive feelings concerning life in the interwar period. The strongest memories were of the depression—with
its severe poverty, hunger, unemployment, and limited possibilities of
emigrating—and the requirements of army service.

Žerovnica was affected by one delayed land reform during this
period. Among the early nineteenth-century reforms that Austrian
rulers had encouraged was the conversion of the common pasture
lands (*gmajna*) into fields and haylands in order to increase barn-
cattle economy and the cultivation of feed crops. Some of the landless
villagers thereby obtained pasture land that they ultimately used for
cultivation.[38] However, this reform was carried out only slowly, and
the common pasture remained intact in most of Slovenia through the
middle of the nineteenth century.[39] In some areas, including that of
Žerovnica, this land was not divided until even later. Villagers first
divided part of it in 1915, and a further and final division took place
in 1925. These steps brought disagreements between neighboring villages over land rights, which were finally settled by the Commission
for Agrarian Operations (Komisija za agrarske operacije). Some villages maintained the communal pasture, but Žerovnica and nearby
Lipsenj decided to divide. Each villager received three parcels and
could decide how to use the land; since few had the time to pasture
their cattle, most turned the land into fields or forest.

# World War II: 1941–45

On 24 March 1941 Yugoslavia signed the Tripartite Pact, and two
days later the pro-German Yugoslav government fell. On 2 April the
Germans invaded Yugoslavia; after twelve days the Yugoslav army
formally capitulated. This period also saw the beginning of the resistance, which grew to such strength that the greater part of the
Yugoslav countryside remained under partisan control throughout
the war. The Germans occupied Slovenia except for the southwest,
which was controlled by the Italians, and a small portion of Preko-

murje, which fell to the Hungarians. But in the mountains and small villages the partisans were active. The peculiar ability of the peasant to survive wartime disasters and disruption of services was demonstrated in the partisan war. Even if a villager is forced to retreat to the mountains, he can return to cultivate his land and live off his crops, while urban groups have no such recourse. The inhabitants of Žerovnica provide one example of the character of the resistance of the rural population, and of the will of the people to return to their villages in the postwar years, to reunite dispersed families, and to repair the destruction of the war years, as the following chronicle of events will illustrate.

On the partisan monument that marks the entrance to Žerovnica are engraved the names of victims of the last war; at the far end of the village in the cemetery on the church hill is a collective partisan grave; and in the main room (*hiša*) of many houses hang the framed photographs of young men who did not survive the war. During the four war years Žerovnica was a center of partisan resistance. Peasant fighters took refuge in the mountains while their village was shelled and burned, their crops and animals stolen, and some members of their families, left behind to cultivate the crops, were transported to prison camps.

It is a truism that the chaos of war brings with it many uncalculated changes. This observation is all the more relevant when conflict brings about the rise of a relatively autonomous and unstructured resistance movement that relies on individual initiative and guerrilla warfare, and that opens new channels of leadership to all strata of society. The Domobranci (Home Defenders), also called Bela Garda (White Guard), the antipartisan movement in Slovenia that paralleled the Ustaši and other groups elsewhere in Yugoslavia, claimed some adherents in Žerovnica, but the village was known as a partisan center. In the war years the traditional village structure received severe shocks, laying the basis for profound changes in the postwar years.

The school records for the six villages of the school district faithfully chronicle the bare events of the years 1941 to 1945. The following outline is based on the chronicle, with supplementary details gathered from villagers of Žerovnica.

1941:            The Italians occupied the Cerknica area;
                 Yugoslav defense ended; the mobilized
                 soldiers returned; and the underground de-
                 fense began with the formation of the
                 Slovene National Liberation Front (NOF).

2 April 1942:    The first partisans left the area to fight. In
                 this same month the partisans executed one
                 villager in Žerovnica, accusing him of
                 treason.

11 May 1942:     Thirty partisans attacked an Italian motor-
                 ized column in Grahovo, and a six-hour
                 battle ensued. The partisans were forced to
                 retreat when the Italians brought reinforce-
                 ments.

16 May 1942:     The Italians shelled Grahovo and Žerovnica.
                 Ten houses in Žerovnica were set afire.

27 July 1942:    Italian revenge on the population of the
                 region culminated in deportations to the
                 prison camp on the island of Rab. Villagers
                 estimate that forty to fifty inhabitants of
                 Žerovnica, aged sixteen to sixty, were trans-
                 ported. Prisoners recall severe treatment on
                 the island and near starvation. (When the
                 camp was opened after Italian capitulation in
                 September 1944, it was learned that many
                 Slovenes had died; they were left buried on
                 the island. Large numbers of the liberated
                 prisoners joined partisan units.)

Fall 1942:       Strife between Italians, Domobranci, and the
                 partisans continued. The Italians executed
                 a number of villagers including women. A
                 priest, held guilty of organizing the Domo-
                 branci in Žerovnica, fell victim to partisan
                 justice. In December 1942 the Italians occu-
                 pied the school building in Grahovo. They
                 never established garrisons in the surround-
                 ing, small villages but operated through
                 the co-operation of local Domobranci.

June 1943: Over half the houses in Žerovnica were set afire in a second shelling by Italian artillery.

3 September 1943: The Italians capitulated. They burned their barracks in Grahovo, and their munitions exploded. The partisans occupied the area up to Rakek—12.5 kilometers from Žerovnica—but were prevented from going further by the Germans in Rakek.

26 October 1943: Following the withdrawal of the Italians, new occupiers, the Germans, arrived. In an intervillage meeting they threatened the population of Grahovo and Žerovnica with mass executions should a single German officer be shot. Aided by the Germans, the Domobranci were strengthened, and on 3 November this force established a garrison in Grahovo.

23 November 1943: In a battle between the partisans and the Domobranci the latter were forced to retreat to the Grahovo church. The partisans then burned the church to the ground.

Spring 1944: Two allied bombers (one American and one British) crashed nearby, and partisans rescued the surviving crew members. An American flier was buried in the Žerovnica cemetery. His body has since been returned to the United States.

June 1944: The Domobranci arrested fourteen people in Žerovnica and sent them to prison in Ljubljana, where some villagers spent months in crowded cells. Some were freed, but most were sent on to German prisons.

4 May 1945: The Domobranci withdrew and the National Liberation Army (NOV) occupied the area.

The following losses are listed in the school records for the school district with its six small villages: 39 persons were killed in battle; 26 were killed by bombing; 30 were executed; 1 died from torture; and

12 died during internment. In addition to these deaths, totaling 108, 31 persons were wounded and 214 imprisoned. The population of the four major villages totaled 1,220 in 1941, and the total for the district is a few hundred more.

The economic losses resulting from the destruction of villages and disruption of trade and cultivation cannot be calculated. Nor can we know the extent of the psychological effect of a conflict that united many, but also severely divided some villagers from each other. Villagers assert that only three Domobranci were active in Žerovnica.[40] One remains in the village today, but his position approaches that of a social outcast. A mother whose son was executed by the partisans for treason has withdrawn from village life. Of approximately eighty men between the ages of sixteen and sixty, it is said that seventy-five co-operated with, or were members of, the partisan group. Sixteen partisans from Žerovnica were killed, many villagers were imprisoned, and several were shot by the Italians.

Each village family relates its own war story, but certain themes recur. The men were away—in prison, doing forced labor for the Germans, or fighting as partisans. The women, children, and old men stayed home, farmed, and supported the partisans in the hills. "Everyone came through the village and took" is a frequent comment. Peasants hid their calves in storage rooms to escape the nightly forays of the Italians and later the Germans. The partisans and Domobranci also came at night for food. The following are some typical recollections.

An old woman remembered that Italians, Germans, and partisans were all quartered in her house; three of her sons were partisans, and two were killed. "Many fine boys were killed and for what? What do they have now?" was her lament.

Another mother lost her son:

> The partisans mobilized my two sons, they were seventeen and eighteen. The younger one was wounded by the Domobranci. He begged for his life, but they shot him in the head. Before he left that day he had asked me to bake him some bread and leave it on the table. Then my other son came home and cried and told me he had seen his brother killed. The partisans brought his body to the house. He was a beautiful boy in his finest years. . . . Our

house was burned down. . . . We lived in terror. The Domobranci came in the evening—the partisans were in the fields. We had to give to everyone and everyone frightened us.

A widow, whose three sons had joined the partisans, carried messages for the partisans with the aid of her eight-year-old daughter. One day, she said, a young partisan confided that he longed for salad. "I made it for him, with oil and vinegar, and put it in a wooden bowl. I heard later from the Domobranci that a partisan nearby had been killed, and he had a salad bowl in his knapsack."

Others told of starvation on the island of Rab, imprisonment in Ljubljana, forced labor in Germany, and the violence and killings of the Italians, who lived in fear of peasant retaliation. The vicissitudes of one villager exemplify the fate of the weak at the mercy of the strong. Matija, who was working in the forests in France at the outbreak of the war, was shipped to Germany as a forced laborer. In 1943 he was granted permission to visit his village in Yugoslavia. He arrived in Žerovnica in July 1944, where he encountered the Domobranci, who were dispensing justice. All the village men were divided into two groups: twenty-five were ranged on the right of the road, and twenty-five on the left. Matija's group was sent to Ljubljana to prison, while the others remained free. For six months Matija was held in a small, crowded cell. Then the prisoners were divided again. Some went to concentration camps, but the lucky ones, among them Matija, became slave laborers in Germany. In 1945 Matija escaped and walked back to his village.

In 1945 the surviving villagers returned to Žerovnica and set about the task of reconstruction. One individual recalled, "Everything was burned and destroyed. There were no cattle, no clothes, not the smallest thing to eat. It was as though we had fallen from the sky onto the land."

# The Early Postwar Period
## 1945–48

On 29 November 1945 the Federal People's Republic of Yugoslavia (FNRJ) was officially formed.[41] The republic of Slovenia gained a part of the Istrian Peninsula inhabited by Slovenes[42] and the territory surrounding Trieste, as well as certain regions west of the Italian city of Goricia. Yugoslavia entered the postwar period under Communist leadership, but a militant past contributed again to Yugoslavia's independent stance, this time within the Communist entente.

The government of the newly formed Federal People's Republic of Yugoslavia embarked on a series of revolutionary reforms that attacked anew the old problem of land distribution. On 29 August 1945 a new land reform became law according to provisions of the constitution of the republic. Individual holdings were limited to from twenty-five to thirty-five hectares of arable land, with the total holdings no more than forty-five hectares; those who did not cultivate the land were allowed only three hectares; large estates of private landholders, land corporations, and banks were liquidated without compensation; churches and monasteries could retain from ten to thirty hectares of arable land and up to thirty hectares of forest; the remaining German settlers were expelled. Nevertheless, only 1,566,000 hectares were expropriated in Yugoslavia, far less than after World War I. Some 797,000 hectares were distributed to 316,000 poor and landless peasants and new settlers, and 49 per cent of the newly gained land eventually went to the state, for state farms, state forests, and other uses.[43] In Slovenia 266,000 hectares were obtained from 2,355 owners, including banks, corporations, large estate owners (mostly Austrian), and rich peasants. However, since land in this area had long been subdivided, only 167 peasants held more land than the allowed maximum, providing merely 4,000 of the total hectares acquired. This may be compared with Serbia, where of 732,000 hectares expropriated, 93,000 came from 6,865 peasant owners, and to Croatia, where of 345,000 hectares, 9,000 were taken from 630 peasant owners.[44] Yugoslav leaders recognized that the amount of land available for confiscation and redistribution was small and that Yugoslavia would remain a nation of small holders.[45] While industrialization proceeded under state planning, agriculture went along its traditional ways in spite of these reforms. Yet, by 1948 grain production had reached 90 per cent of the prewar level.[46]

As villagers entered the postwar reconstruction period, the spirit that had unified many in a war of survival contributed to a mood of guarded optimism concerning the future. Peasants returned to culti-

*The southeastern side of the Cerknica basin.*
*Grahovo is at the center and Žerovnica beyond it, to the right.*

*Žerovnica before World War I (Foto Znidarsic)*

*Žerovnica in summer 1964*

*Washing clothes in the river, beside the partisan monument*

*View from the churchyard*

*The Cerknica lake (Foto Znidarsic)*

*Haying on the lake bed*

*Fodder crops drying on poles*

*Harvesting potatoes*

*Harvesting wheat*

*The threshing machine owned by Marof*

*The school yard in Grahovo*

*Factory worker–peasant*

*The new buffet and store*

*Inside the new buffet*

vation of their traditional strips of land and complied with emergency measures requiring that each household supply to authorities a designated quantity of potatoes, milk, calves, pigs, and wood, or face confiscation. These unpopular policies were at least partially accepted as necessary steps to recover from wartime devastation.

The village was unaffected by the land reform of 1945. Two neighboring large estates, however, came under the 1945 provision confiscating holdings exceeding three hectares from those who did not cultivate the land. The estate of one landowner that lay between Martinjak and Cerknica became the basis of the co-operative farm Marof. A second estate near Martinjak, owned by an entrepreneur whose name was Premrov, included woods, fields, and a small factory. The latter has been replaced by the large state furniture factory at Martinjak. The common pasture lands that villages had not divided by 1941 were appropriated by the *občina* and, if wooded, are used as lumber reserves for construction of schools and public buildings. Because Žerovnica had divided its communal pasture earlier, it was not affected by this law either.

THE PROGRAM for collectivization of agriculture, which has taken many forms in Yugoslavia, was first introduced in 1948. Although the private peasant remains the basis of the Yugoslav rural economy, since 1948 peasant villages have been fundamentally affected by national restrictions, new controls, and new institutions that have directly impinged upon, and altered, peasant society. Thus the year 1948 marks the beginning of the contemporary era in the village of Žerovnica.

# II

## THE DEVELOPING
## SOCIOECONOMIC STRUCTURE

# 3

## The Early Society

### Inheritance Practices

THROUGHOUT THE history of Žerovnica its inhabitants have been obliged to cope with foreign rulers, wars, and revolution, as well as with the ordinary hazards of agriculture. Despite a favorable physical environment and periods of agricultural and land reforms, possibilities for expansion of the land base were almost entirely exhausted long ago. With the exception of a grant of forest land in 1880, villagers have exploited the same limited resources with much the same methods for centuries. Historical and environmental contingencies have presented a sufficiently severe challenge to raise the question of how this community survived and adapted to changing circumstances. The following three chapters are an attempt to provide part of the answer to this question through an analysis of the social and economic structure of the village and its relation to the world outside within a historical perspective. Particular attention will be given to the change and development of two closely related and focal structural principles: family form and inheritance rules. These principles bear a close relation to the gradual increase in heterogeneity and socioeconomic stratification and to the character of the involvement of this community with the outside.

Traditional ideals of the village are well represented by the opening lines of a passage written by an elderly peasant woman, "We are an old and friendly village. There are sixty houses. [One house has since been destroyed.] We are all peasants [kmeti]." Villagers commonly remark that gospodars own one-quarter zemlja. The Slovene terms zemlja and kmetija designate a land unit that traditionally, during feudal times, supported one peasant family.[1] In Žerovnica, one-quarter zemlja approximates fifteen hectares, which includes hayfields, woodland, and perhaps two and a half hectares of plowland.

Villagers also agree that the homestead and its land have traditionally descended from *gospodar* to the eldest son, according to the rule of primogeniture, while other sons have gone elsewhere to earn a living. Younger sons, as well as daughters, may be awarded grants in money or movables, but not land, which should not be divided.

There are, however, deviations from the ideal of a homogeneous, equalitarian, and friendly peasant community ruled by the tenets of primogeniture. The spatial structure of the village itself indicates differentiations in status and occupation. Indeed, inequalities in landholding can be traced back for several hundred years. Furthermore, inheritance practices suggest conflicts that the rules obscure. By 1840 church records showed the size of the landholding, or estate (*stan*), of each homestead or the notation "cottager" (*hišar*)[2] or the occupation—for example, carpenter, cobbler, or smith. These records establish the existence of three or even four economic strata in the village, which, other documents and oral history suggest, reflect a considerably older pattern. Thus by 1840 the village was composed of a group of landless or nearly landless villagers, a few of whom became village specialists, thereby forming a stratum intermediate between the landless cottagers and the landed peasants; a larger, core group of peasants owning approximately a quarter *zemlja;* and a small group of larger holders owning up to a half *zemlja.*

Furthermore, although records establish that since 1780 land has not been divided to any significant extent and primogeniture has been the dominant rule followed, and although villagers believe that this rule is three hundred or more years old, nevertheless, records show and villagers report that occasionally some land was granted to a younger son or a daughter; and in certain cases a younger son, or even a daughter, was designated as the main inheritor of the homestead. When an inheriting daughter married, the new son-in-law was identified as one who "came to the land from the outside" (*pristupil je v kmetijo*). Again, in spite of the rule that disinherited brothers should depart for other occupations, in fact they often did not. Some remained as adult but dependent unmarried helpers of the *gospodar.* Or an individual with greater resources might build or buy a hut in the village and join the cottager class or, more advantageously, marry an inheriting village daughter. It appears that the normative rule of primogeniture, which enjoins all but the eldest son to depart from the village, may be counterposed to ancient and traditional ties to the village. Indeed, a village legend describes an earlier social order based on differing family forms and on rules of inheritance that recognized the principle of equality of brothers.

# A Village-Origin Legend

A village legend tells us that the patriarchal peasant family ruled by primogeniture has not always dominated the world view of the inhabitants of Žerovnica. There is said to have been an earlier family organization that was eventually modified by the villagers in response to special conditions and economic necessity. Leading *gospodars* relate a story of four legendary epochs in the village past. The dim early epoch of the free Slovenes was, it is said, followed by the second epoch, when the twelve founding families of Žerovnica, or their descendants, became subject to the rule of a feudal overlord. The twelve original homesteads were said to have stood in the center of the village. Each, according to legend, was occupied by a large family that co-operatively worked one full *zemlja*, or four times the present-day normative village holding. These landholdings had been established, it is said, when each of the seven large complexes of apparently communal, cultivable village land was divided into twelve equal parts, thus facilitating a village-wide system of crop rotation. Each of the twelve families then held one *zemlja* composed of seven separate fields, one in each complex.

In the third epoch, it is said, family lands began to be divided equally among brothers, and all the sons except the eldest, who inherited the father's house, built their new houses close by on the family land. Villagers believe this practice accounts for the crowded appearance of the village today. The eldest son was then surrounded by his brothers, which suggests a form of neighborhood family. Finally, legend refers to a fourth period, which extends to this day. Approximately three or four hundred years ago, when each *gospodar* owned only a quarter *zemlja*, equal division was halted, since land scarcity required the adoption of impartible and single inheritance. After primogeniture was accepted, younger sons were expected to seek their livelihood elsewhere.

Legend is reinforced by specific beliefs held by leading families as well as by particular funds of village data. Thus certain peasants whose ancestors have long held the same land claim descent from the twelve original settlers. Other information was offered by the former village head (*podžupan*), who had reconstructed the history of several full-*zemlja* holdings by determining boundaries from ancient maps. He pointed to several groups of four contiguous but now independently owned strips of land in the different complexes, each group of four, he asserted, having once been a single unit, owned by a single *gospodar*. He showed that they were once owned by the forebears of certain leading village families, and that today some of the small contiguous strips are still in one family, being owned by relatives bearing the same surname. Seven such units (one group of four strips in each of the seven complexes) together composed, he believes, the traditional full *zemlja* once worked by the ancient enlarged family. Legendary history is further validated, he believes, by the fact that some peasants own small irregular additional fields; these are said to have accrued to the original twelve settlers at the beginning of the second epoch, being what was left after the division of the seven large complexes into twelve equal parts.

The view supported by legend that prototypical families worked a full *zemlja*, or approximately sixty hectares, raises some interesting questions. Today, although village agriculture is essentially unmechanized, some technological improvements have considerably lessened the number of working hours required for cultivation. Nevertheless, today the cultivation of a quarter *zemlja* demands at least three full-time field workers. This would suggest that at a lower level of technology the working of one full *zemlja* would have demanded far more than twelve fulltime field workers. We know that the nineteenth-century patriarchal family was large and included three generations, many children, and unmarried siblings. However, villagers recall that with nineteenth-century equipment the family was fully employed in the cultivation of the average quarter *zemlja*. Thus a family labor force adequate for the cultivation of one full *zemlja* implies some form of an enlarged or joint family.

# The Question of the Zadruga in Slovenia

The legendary reconstruction of the early social organization and inheritance customs of Žerovnica raises a controversial issue. What is the position in early Slovene society of the traditional South Slavic zadruga, or joint family, a basic rural institution that persisted in all South Slavic countries, with the exception of Slovenia, until the nineteenth century?

The minimal characteristics of the zadruga are given in Mosely's definition: "A household composed of two or more biological or small-families, closely related by blood or adoption, owning its means of production communally, producing and consuming the means of its livelihood jointly, and regulating the control of its property, labor, and livelihood communally."[3] Collective property is generally held to be the hallmark of the zadruga. As Tomasevich has stated, "The property belonged to the family as a collective, and the head of the family, who was the first among equals, was able to dispose of it only with the consent of the majority of the adult zadruga members."[4] Furthermore, if a son wished to leave the zadruga and claim his share of the property, he received either his property or an indemnity, according to majority decision. If he worked outside but remained in the zadruga, his earnings went to the zadruga.[5] However, according to some Yugoslav scholars, the ethos ascribed to the zadruga is as important as its economic basis. Thus the zadruga is praised as a "peasant family order with special family law, incorporating in the zadruga not only its property and labor, but also family love and mutual assistance. . . ."[6] Tomasic has carried this conception further in his description of a specific South Slavic ethos based on what he calls the humanistic zadruga culture of northern Yugoslavia, which is contrasted with the power-seeking Dinaric culture to the south.[7]

According to most western scholars, Slovenia is the sole South Slavic area for which there is no evidence of an earlier zadruga. Thus Mosely writes,

Slovene society shows no trace of a *zadruga* system. Under serfdom, and after its abolition, Slovene peasant families followed a pattern of hereditary holdings, maintained more or less intact

as family and productive units through transmission to a single son,
the eldest or the youngest, more often the latter. Other male heirs
were assisted by the family to learn a trade or to become petty
officials; or, at worst they became urban laborers or migrated.
Once established in new occupations and usually in new locations,
they had no right to share in the family capital.[8]

The Croatian ethnographer Vera St. Erlich, in a study based on her
prewar researches in Yugoslavia, also states that the zadruga was to be
found in all Yugoslav regions except Slovenia.[9] Slovene scholars,
however, generally posit the ancestral Slovene zadruga associated
with early systems of joint cultivation, which is said to have characterized the indigenous culture before intensive feudal colonization by
German lords was initiated in the ninth century. Furthermore, some
Slovene scholars also discern evidence of the zadruga in later Slovene
society. Gruden, writing in the early twentieth century, asserted that
he had found linguistic traces of the early Slovene zadruga. In the
past a joint family, living together in one hut and cultivating together,
shared their communal property composed of land, buildings, animals, farming tools, and the house. When the hut became too small,
members built a new one alongside the old, a process that sometimes
continued until the zadruga grew to a village of one hundred to three
hundred relatives who cultivated communally. All members of the
zadruga were designated by the name of their first leader. For example, if the leader was Marko, the zadruga members were Markoviči
(the nominative plural of the patronymic *Markovič*, meaning "the
descendants of Marko"). Thus in the Bela Kraina, in eastern Slovenia,
many villagers are identified by patronymics reflecting, Gruden asserts, an earlier zadruga organization. (*Ablesiči* and *Pribinči* are examples.) In the same region Gruden found instances of joint property
administered by one of the brothers in the name of all.[10]

According to Grafenauer, the Slovene zadruga may be inferred
from medieval land-grant documents. As he describes early social organization, "To the end of the eighth century, the majority of the
inhabitants in the Slovene regions represented a distinct layer of free
members of village communities, in which according to all appear-
ances, the form of the large family, the zadruga, was still quite powerful."[11] Villagers communally exploited common pastures, forest and

water resources, and, eventually, cultivable lands. Within the community, Grafenauer asserts, the zadrugas jointly cultivated the lands temporarily assigned to them and jointly utilized the crops. A gift document (*darovnica*) of the year 888 is cited as testimony for the existence of the zadruga, since it records King Arnulf's bestowal on a grantee of a family of serfs including a *gospodar* and his wife, their sons and their wives, and all their jointly held land and property.[12]

Melik describes an early period of village-wide collective cultivation generally associated with the joint family. Fixed complexes of regular shape (*delež* or *oddelek;* German, *Gewann*) were "collectively cultivated according to the rules of the crop rotation [*kolobarjenje*] with fallow. In work as well as in produce all villagers were equal partners, just as they also jointly pastured their cattle on the large pastures near the village or in the mountains."[13]

In contrast is the position of Vilfan, who rejects as too ambiguous both linguistic and documentary evidence of the Slovene zadruga, but who nevertheless advances the hypothesis of its early presence: "For the period before planned colonization, direct proofs are hard to claim. . . . However, we do not need to prove at all costs that . . . the Slovenians had the family type known as the zadruga. During the period before . . . the beginning of the one-family feudal *kmetija*s, the zadruga is also an evolutionary necessity among the Slovenes. Therefore, we can presuppose a zadruga for that period, and it would be necessary to demand proofs for . . . an opposing view."[14]

Whereas Slovene scholars generally posit the zadruga as an institution in the earliest, poorly documented period of Slovene society, there is less agreement concerning the status of the zadruga after the ninth century. The varying practices and land tenure systems of the developing manorial economies in different Slovene areas increasingly obscured or altered the indigenous social order. During the era of intensive Germanic colonization of Slovenia, from the ninth to the twelfth century, Slovene villages became permanent settlements[15] when land was measured and divided into *kmetija*s.[16] After this period the peasant living on the *kmetija* and fulfilling feudal obligations was granted the right to bequeath land to his offspring, but the lord retained the prerogative to withdraw the land at will.[17]

In the characteristic land tenure pattern in medieval Slovenia a complex was divided into long narrow parallel fields without visible borders between them, that were used as open fields for pasturage of cattle after harvest. This system is exemplified in Grafenauer's study by Žerovnica, which he describes as typical.

Melik's hypothetical and generalized description of the process of division of communal land into such dispersed *kmetija*s in Slovenia recalls the particular historical myth of Žerovnica.

> Later—in the course of the new era—the collective system of cultivation began to be abandoned, and the joint land was divided so that each villager had one field or one part in each of the formerly joint fields. If there were twelve peasant families, each joint field was divided into twelve parallel fields which were naturally narrow, and therefore were usually called strips [*jermen*]. If there were twelve joint fields, each peasant had twelve small fields distributed all over the village land which was itself divided into not less than 144 fields. Pasture land was not divided. This system of land partition has been maintained until today.[18]

Vilfan believes the zadruga was incompatible with the one-family *kmetija* of the later medieval period and had disappeared by then.[19] Others, however, see a more gradual disintegration of the zadruga in the medieval period when peasants frequently turned to subdivision of the *kmetija* among several heirs, and finally adopted single and impartible inheritance. As Kos describes this process,

> The house and property community or the joint living . . . of families and close relatives on one piece of land, began to fall apart in the thirteenth and fourteenth centuries. At that time there remained only a remnant of the old Slovene house and property community which recalls the zadruga. . . . The zadruga could not withstand the influence of the economically stronger neighboring German farms which were not organized in the zadruga manner. . . . The whole legal concept of the Germanic state and individualistic legal views which spread as a result of the acceptance of Roman law could not favor the further existence of the house and property community. The *kmetija* was often divided in such a manner that externally in the urbarial records it was listed as one. In fact, however, it was divided into several possessions. The final step was the actual division of the *kmetija* into one-half, one-

quarter and even smaller units. . . . This process was basically completed in the fifteenth century. The divided *kmetija* could nourish more of the growing population than the undivided ones.[20]

From the fourteenth century on, Kos believes, the norm was expressed by the German legal maxim "a peasant has only one son"— that is, only one son could remain on the land, and the others, it was said, must seek their bread elsewhere. Thus there developed a Slovene landless peasantry, and during the fifteenth century members of this group appeared in growing numbers at the edge of the village.[21] Vilfan has stressed the role of the feudal lord in attempting to contain the drift toward fragmentation of land units that disturbed the stability of the peasant village:

> In most Slovene lands it [the principle of indivisibility] maintained itself to the twentieth century. As long as questions of inheritance were in large measure decided by the lords, the principle of indivisibility remained in the realm of customary law. . . . Divisions were permitted only where the two new halves would be economically sufficiently powerful. . . . A new building was constructed and fields and other land belonging to the *kmetija* were usually divided in such a way that every parcel was divided into two halves along the long side. Pastures were not divided.[22]

THE FOREGOING résumé of village folklore and some aspects of the development of Slovene society suggests conflicting trends. The full *kmetija* of the early Middle Ages may have been worked for the feudal lord by the joint family, or zadruga, if this social form persisted from the pre-German era, when it is presumed to have been dominant. However, the pressures of land shortage and rural poverty frequently impelled cultivators toward subdividing their property in spite of counterpressure from the landlords, who favored undivided inheritance. Whether or not it was the zadruga, and later the feudal lord, that mitigated the trend toward subdivision, the tendency in the feudal period seems to have been to encourage maintenance of land and homestead whenever it was economically possible. The adoption of primogeniture, presumably at some time during the medieval period, contributed to the maintenance of the village economic and social order by preventing further fragmentation of land, by establishing inheritance priorities, and by providing the *gospodar* with a pool of labor composed of dependent, unmarried siblings. It also contributed, however, to the growth of a landless peasantry within the village and thus to the development of internal economic differentiation.

# 4

## *The Stem Family and Traditional Elites*

THE PREVIOUS CHAPTER discussed evidence of an early Slovene joint family, or zadruga, which at some time during the medieval period evolved into a patriarchal, extended family ruled by single inheritance, preferably primogeniture. Such a patriarchal family is of the type called by LePlay the *famille-souche,* or stem family, which Arensberg and Kimball see as typical for large parts of Europe and some Asian peasant lands.[1] With the medieval transition from tribal landholdings and feudal tenancy to peasant proprietorship there developed, according to Arensberg and Kimball, "an intermediate size of family and household, living for generation after generation on a family holding. . . . In each generation the household has included: the peasant holder, his wife, his minor children, his unmarried brothers or sisters (living as unpaid farm laborers and helping him until they should move away or marry), and his father and mother, who perhaps had retired from active work but were still influential and assisting."[2]

As Arensberg and Kimball explain, in order to avoid endless subdivisions, "in each generation the family homestead and plot had to be kept intact and undivided. . . . Through matchmaking and other mechanisms such restrictions of inheritance to a single heir in each generation often became standard, acceptable, even ideal. The household and lands remained a stem or source of new heirs and new emigrants in each successive generation; a long line of holders kept the homestead in the line or stem: usually it even carried the name of the farm as a family name."[3]

In such a household, they point out, the position of the son is subordinate: ". . . a grown man is still a boy under a family council headed by his mother and his father who pool the family's resources and arrange a match and dowry for him and his sister; thus the family continues to the end of the old people's lives."[4]

The typical nineteenth-century Žerovnica family exemplified this ideal form in many respects, displaying associated patterns: continuous occupation of the homestead by the family line or stem that carried the name of the farm as a family name, marriage arrangements made by the parents, single inheritance, and emigration of many of the disinherited. As Arensberg and Kimball have stressed, the land had to be kept undivided. The inhabitants of Žerovnica resisted subdivision of property throughout the nineteenth century as did peasants in other areas of Slovenia, although legal provisions relating to inheritance became increasingly confused during this period. During the brief French occupation of Slovene lands, from 1809 to 1813, the Napoleonic code enforced equal division of property among heirs.[5] With the return of the Austrians, former limitations upon subdivisions were not totally renewed, and after 1848 peasants were legally free to dispose of their land as they wished. Relieved of feudal obligations, peasants found these burdens replaced by those of augmented taxation, and consequently in some areas subdivision of farm property increased. In 1868 new legislation permitted children to receive equal parts of the father's property, which caused peasant owners in some areas of Slovenia to fall into even greater debt. By 1888 the state adopted new measures to prevent the disintegration of the peasant village. The principle that the peasant household must not be subdivided was again accepted.[6] However, provisions were interpreted variously in the different areas and could not themselves offset the basic problem of the land shortage. Consequently, as economic opportunities shrank during the general agricultural depressions of the years 1890 and 1910, many Slovenes, including many inhabitants of Žerovnica, resorted to emigration to the United States.

Despite various legal changes and economic pressures throughout the nineteenth century, in Žerovnica the basic socioeconomic structure was maintained. The village benefited from relatively favorable ecological circumstances, and family forms and rules of inheritance helped to preserve the economic resources in land. Village patterns are well represented in Arensberg and Kimball's description of the alternatives open to the noninheriting sons: "Each generation knew new waves of brothers and sisters, noninheriting children who had to go out into the world to 'make their fortunes' elsewhere—on new farms, in marriages outside, in apprenticeships leading to artisan or other work in the cities."[7]

Yet, in spite of the village saying that others go elsewhere to earn their bread, some disinherited sons who left their natal households did not depart from the village, but established independent households there. And some daughters who did not marry inheriting sons also remained in the village, since they married noninheriting sons who did not leave. The effect of these processes on the internal village structure and on the relation of the village to the world outside has been significant, as later discussions will show.

## Family Size and Composition

The typical nineteenth-century family in Žerovnica was large and composed of three generations: the *gospodar* and his wife, one son (preferably the eldest) who as inheritor of land and homestead remained in the house with his wife, and their children. In addition, the household included various other relatives of the *gospodar*. Ten children in one household was not uncommon. Characteristically, some unmarried siblings of the *gospodar* remained as helpers. Illegitimate children of unmarried men and women were not uncommon and were included in the household of the mother. Eventually individuals deprived of land might be granted a field or two, allowing them to marry and move into a cottager house and perhaps practice a trade. Often, however, these individuals did not succeed in marrying at all. In 1965 twenty houses still included three generations, but the birth rate had dropped, and only rarely were collateral relatives of the *gospodar* members of the household.

Of seventy-one village marriages recorded from 1869 to 1914, twenty-seven families had eight or more children. The largest number recorded was eighteen children. There were thirteen families with seven children, and fourteen families had either five or six children. The remaining seventeen had two to four children, with the exception of one family with a single child. On the other hand, of the twenty-eight marriages recorded from 1915 to 1941, only three families had as many as seven children. Seven families had five or six children, and the rest (eighteen families) had one to four children. Of the thirty marriages recorded since 1941, all but five took place before 1960. One family has five children, and the rest have one to four.

Therefore one can conclude that the trend toward large families was broken in the interwar period, and since that time the tendency has been toward fewer children.

In the church records from 1850 to 1965, thirty-three households are listed as including collateral relatives. These relatives were unmarried brothers, sisters, uncles, or aunts of the *gospodar*, and, in some cases, their illegitimate children. Altogether this group was composed of forty-six individuals, only five of whom were born in the postwar period. Most were born from 1850 to 1899, and seven were born from 1900 to 1940. Undoubtedly, many households included collateral relatives whose names did not find their way into the church records, since their residences often changed. Thus the enlarged household, which included collateral relatives of the *gospodar*, was typical for the nineteenth century, but not for the twentieth. Today in only a few exceptional cases are collateral relatives members of the household.

## Traditional Marriage Patterns

After 1890 most men did not marry until they were in their thirties or older. Before that, earlier marriages were more common, but it seems that with the depression of 1890 marriages began to be postponed until the man could make a living. Marriages were traditionally arranged by parents and required considerable bargaining over inheritance and dowry. A *gospodar* with little land had to provide his son with money, animals, or at least a few fields. A *gospodar* who was in debt might try to find a daughter-in-law with income-producing forest land in her dowry.

In the eighty-eight marriages that occurred in the 1869–1940 period for which birth and marriage dates were listed, seventeen men were over forty, thirty-two from thirty to forty, and only one was below twenty. Of the thirty-eight men who married in their twenties, only eight married after 1890. Most women in this group married in their twenties, although there were fourteen marriages in which the woman was thirty or over. These figures do not reflect the large number of men and women who were forced to remain in the village but who could not marry at all.

In the period from 1941 to 1965 marriages continued to be delayed, partly because of the interruption of the war years. In thirty marriages listed in the church records, eight men were over forty and eighteen were in their early thirties. At least six women were in their early thirties. Most villagers believe that young people now will marry at an earlier age, although marriage before one has the means of support is hardly considered.

Traditionally villagers looked for spouses mainly in Žerovnica, while the nearby villages of Lipsenj and Grahovo were favored over more distant ones. The place of birth of the incoming spouse was not regularly included in the church records until around 1840, and even afterward there were omissions. Nevertheless, it is possible to consider 170 marriages in which place of residence was recorded from 1840 to 1965. Seventy-one of these marriages were endogamous. Except in the cases of postwar marriages, this figure does not include those couples who did not become heads of households but who lived with others or eventually left the village. Of these seventy-one cases, all but five were patrilocal. In the five matrilocal instances, village men married into families in which a daughter inherited the land. The great majority of the remaining marriages were to individuals in the villages closest to Žerovnica. Except in the few cases in which a woman inherited, these were also patrilocal, as were most of the thirty postwar marriages. Fourteen of the postwar marriages were endogamous. Eleven of these were patrilocal, one was matrilocal, and the remaining two couples left the village. Twenty of the men involved in these postwar marriages were born from 1905 to 1925. Of the ten born after 1925, five married Žerovnica women. The figures do not indicate the modern generation's attitude toward village or local endogamy. The greater mobility today and the new attitudes of youth suggest that marriage patterns will alter greatly.

While most villagers easily deny that there has been a traditional preference for marriage within the village, some recall certain customs and beliefs that express this preference. Thus some older people believe that individuals from one's own village are more reliable. Marriage within the village used to be more common, they explain, because those who grew up in the village wanted to stay there, since Žerovnica was the best place in which to live. Some recall a common conflict created by a poor father's wish to marry his son to a rich girl from another village. Such a marriage is warned against in an old proverb, "The money is gone, but the bottle [i.e., the unloved girl] remains in the home [Denar je otšel, flaša ostala doma]."

Another factor that suggests early marriage within the village is the large number of surnames common to several households. Thus twelve surnames account for thirty-nine of Žerovnica's fifty-nine houses. The confusion one would expect is avoided, however, since houses have been known by housenames for as long as villagers can remember, and they are so listed in the earliest church records. Most villagers say they cannot explain the phenomenon of common surnames, but upon reflection some suggest that it may mean relationship in the distant past.

Preference for residence within the village is directly implied by kinship relations. Records show that eleven *gospodar*s who married between 1853 and 1960 had, or have, brothers who were, or still are, also *gospodar*s in the village. Since place of birth was sometimes omitted in early records, this figure should probably be higher. Today five pairs of brothers in the village are *gospodar*s of separate village households. The number of wives with sisters in the village has always been far greater. In fact, at present the majority of wives have sisters in the village, and there is no family that believes it has no relatives within the village.

Villagers do not recognize a conflict between the implicit emotional preference for residence and marriage within the village and the ideal of primogeniture with its often stated corollary that all but the eldest brother must go elsewhere to earn his bread. An examination of nineteenth-century society leads to the conclusion that these two principles, in spite of the tensions between them, had certain complementary functions. On the one hand, the practice of primogeniture, in the qualified form that has been noted, insured that the land did not become dangerously subdivided. On the other hand, the preference for residence in the village encouraged younger brothers to remain. They were then available to take the place of an elder brother who might decide to leave or who died unmarried. At least three elder villagers stated that they had replaced a brother, and church records show other cases. This is not fully reported, however, since conflicts between brothers over inheritance are not freely admitted. Other younger brothers built new houses and served as village specialists. Noninheriting daughters who remained in the village married either inheriting sons or members of the specialist class. On the other hand, if daughters inherited the land themselves, they provided an opportunity for noninheriting younger sons to marry them and remain in the village. Furthermore, unmarried siblings who remained in the enlarged household contributed to the working force. Although landholdings were small, the reliance on hand labor required many helpers. Thus one of the principal hardships in the smaller family of today is the shortage of workers for the still unmechanized cultivation of crops. The ideal of primogeniture, then, did not itself explain the structure, for it was qualified by strong traditional ties to the village and to family.

## Emigration and Family Ties

While the low level of mechanization in agriculture necessitated many helpers on the land, it is easy to see that this requirement was overfulfilled in the nineteenth and prewar twentieth century. This problem became particularly acute in the depression years of the 1890s and the 1930s, when temporary emigration of the *gospodar* or of the son who was to become the heir was resorted to, as one solution to poverty and overpopulation, in addition to the more common solution of permanent emigration of some of the disinherited sons and their families. The earliest emigration was to nearby Croatia, where individuals worked in the forest, generally for short periods, although some remained there. By the 1870s villagers began to turn to the United States, and in the last decade of the century stays of several years in America became part of the pattern of life. A *gospodar* might travel to the United States two, three, or even four times to work in the mines and forests. To many villagers the life of those who remained in America as farmers represents a millennium in which plentiful resources have eliminated the need to struggle for existence. Cleveland, Ohio, which became the cultural center for Slovene immigrants, is known to all villagers. The main room of most village houses is typically adorned with calendars, photos, and other mementos and bric-a-brac, gifts from American relatives.

Yet no emigrating *gospodar* permanently deserted the homestead he inherited, nor did any villager ever state that he considered such a course of action. Moreover, ties with migrant kin were characteristically maintained. Departed brothers and sisters were neither forgotten nor absolved of kinship obligations. Nor has it been uncommon for migrant families to return for visits. In contrast is the ethnically German village of St. Felix in the South Tyrol, studied by Wolf, whose traditions also stress impartibility of inheritance, lineality of descent and patriarchal authority. In that community, however, "migration . . . breaks the tie between family of origin and the migrant, and the migrant becomes socially irrelevant to the remaining members. . . . the uncles who have gone to America are never heard of again."[8]

Emigration to the United States continued until the 1930s, when restrictive quotas were imposed by that country; then France became the greatest outlet for temporary work trips. Today some villagers go to West Germany for temporary work, but emigration as a way of life is past, and overpopulation has been replaced by an anachronistic form of underpopulation, for there are too few field hands for a land area that is largely worked by nineteenth-century unmechanized techniques. Greatly lowered birth rates and increasing employment of the modern generation in the new economy has caused this alteration. Should mechanized farming ever become possible for the private peasant, rural underpopulation would quickly be transformed into technological unemployment of the peasant. The American example, so intimately known to every Slovene peasant, is constantly referred to. Many point to a brother or cousin in the United States who is believed to own land equal in size to all or most of Žerovnica. Yet, villagers believe, the American relatives work the land alone or with a few helpers.

## Family Histories and Village Structure

It has been argued in the last two chapters that the earliest form of the family in Žerovnica was probably a joint family, or zadruga. Such families, it appears, lived in the central part of the village and evolved into neighborhood families. With the adoption of partible inheritance

in the later medieval period, however, the stem family began to pre-
dominate, and socioeconomic complexity increased. Finally, the nuclear family is now replacing the stem family, although a significant
number of families still include three generations, and a few include
affinal relatives. Various forms of evidence support this view—the
village legend and Slovene historical reconstructions for the early
period, and statistical data relating to the village family of the nineteenth and twentieth centuries. It is also supported by other data
gathered within the village on patterns of surnames and housenames,
the spatial structure of the village, and the history of a focal village
family from 1730 to today.

Although villagers do not consider that families bearing common
surnames are necessarily related, blood relationship of over half the
families with common surnames is easily demonstrated by an examination of the church records, which after 1840 list village of birth
and, if the birthplace is Žerovnica, house number as well. This suggests that if earlier records specified place of birth, a greater number
of families with common surnames would be shown to be related. Of
particular historical interest are those surnames that identify more
than one landowning *gospodar* whose ancestors have held their land
since 1780, the date of the earliest surviving complete church records.
Four surnames meet these qualifications, accounting for seventeen
village houses today. However, only earlier data than the records
provide would reveal whether these surnames were once borne by
some of the legendary founding families, reputedly owners of full
*zemlja*s that were later sacrificed to partible inheritance.

Casting light on processes prior to 1780 are housenames, which
villagers believe were generally taken from the surnames of first
founders, as well as the spatial structure of the village. In only eight
cases do records indicate that housenames have shifted since they
were listed in 1780. Yet, in 1780 only eleven housenames were corre-
lated with the surname of the listed *gospodar* of that date, suggesting
that housenames are considerably more ancient than the later eighteenth century.

Examination of housenames leads to two conclusions. The first is
that when related *gospodar*s with the same surnames founded independent homesteads in the village, at least one family, possibly the
earliest, retained the original housename. Apparently to avoid dupli-

cation, the housename of the second *gospodar* was frequently composed of a descriptive adjective added to his surname, or a descriptive term might stand alone. For example, a second Petrič house is called Upper Petrič ("Petrič zgornji"), and one of the Janež houses is called Upper Fieldman ("njivec zgornji"). The second conclusion is that, once established, the original housename was generally retained, even when a homestead changed ownership several times, although in a few cases the housename did shift.

These conclusions imply the antiquity of the common surnames that also served as housenames according to first records. Do certain housenames and their variants, paired with the surnames to which they show affinity, identify ancient family lines? An investigation of this question points to three of the four surnames (for which pseudonyms are substituted) borne by ancient landowning families. *Janež, Gornik,* and *Petrič* are the only village names that today are simultaneously surnames and (with their variants) housenames distinguishing at least two families owning land since the first records, and their associated homesteads. The two homesteads of the Gornik group are called Gornik. The Petrič group has Petrič dolnji ("Lower Petrič") and Petrič zgornji ("Upper Petrič"). The housenames related to the Janež group are listed in table 7 (p. 78). Together these three surnames identified ten *gospodar*s of the later eighteenth century whose homesteads bore related housenames and whose families had controlled, except in one case (no. 7, table 7), at least a quarter *zemlja* since the earliest records. In 1969 seven of these homesteads were occupied by the same family line as in 1780, and—further indication of the strength of these three groups—the three surnames accounted for fifteen village families.

If the ten early homesteads with names related to these surnames were indeed established by descendants of founding families of Žerovnica, their physical location might serve to validate legend. Earliest families were said to have settled in the central part of the village, and after partibility was adopted inheriting sons were said to have built their houses close to that of the *gospodar*, thus accounting for the present nucleated village pattern. Later settlers were said to have occupied the hilly fringe at the south end of the village. As figure 8 shows, most of the ten homesteads in question are located centrally, toward the more desirable, northern part of the village and on the

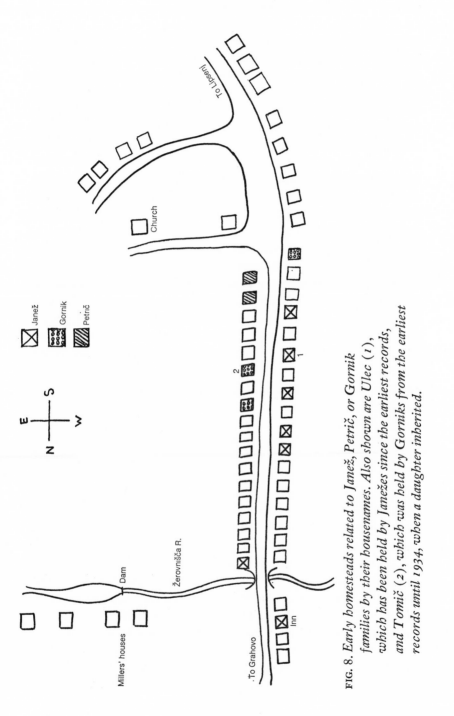

FIG. 8. *Early homesteads related to Janež, Petrič, or Gornik families by their housenames. Also shown are Ulec (1), which has been held by Janežes since the earliest records, and Tomič (2), which was held by Gorniks from the earliest records until 1934, when a daughter inherited.*

main village road, and, with a few exceptions, the related housenames belong to neighboring groups of homesteads. In addition, two other centrally located homesteads have long been occupied by Gorniks and Janežes respectively, although their housenames apparently are not related to the surnames.

Thus the legend of an ancestral peasantry composed of full-*zemlja*, patrilocal families who later adopted partible inheritance is not contradicted by these internal data. The spatial structure of the village and the patterns of housenames and surnames together suggest that the three groups of homesteads under examination grew from three ancient families who settled in the central village and later divided and redivided their land among brothers.

According to village tradition the joint surname and housename *Janež* designated one of the legendary twelve founding families. Some villagers concede that almost all village families may be related in one way or another to this family line. The surname *Janež*, the most common in the village, today designates six *gospodars*, or one-tenth of the families of the village. Furthermore, some *gospodars* admit that some of the Janež families are the most powerful in the village. Of the six Janež *gospodars*, two belong to the cottager class, one is a quarter *zemljak*, and three represent the small stratum of rich peasants who own well over one-quarter *zemlja*.

The reconstruction of the history of the Janež families in table 7 provides one model of the kinds of processes that have shaped the social and economic structure of the village from the early undocumented period, when partibility is said to have been the rule, through the more recent past, when impartibility and primogeniture brought about the growth of disinherited groups and an increase in economic stratification and differentiation of occupation within the village. The surname *Janež* is first mentioned in fragmentary documents that do not show a housename. It is recorded that on 13 March 1730 Josef Janež, the legitimate son of Mathia Janež, was baptized in Žerovnica. Evidence of the earlier history of the family was lost when the church documents were destroyed. The first complete village registry indicates that in 1791 there were five Janež *gospodars* and one other homestead identified by a Janež housename (no. 6, table 7), and each of the six controlled a quarter *zemlja* or more. Another Janež, born in 1803, is listed as an innkeeper (*gostilničar*). Subsequently, five Janež *gospodars*, born from 1804 to 1873, appear in the cottager class; four of these were disinherited brothers of landowning Janež *gospodars*, and one was reduced to this class from a landowning status (see no. 12, table 7).

In only one case was *Janež* alone the name of a homestead. In this single example (no. 3, table 7) a shift to another name was recorded when the *gospodar* sold his house and land. The housenames of other Janež dwellings included a descriptive term modifying *Janež*—as in Janež dolnji ("Lower Janež")—or were variations of the housenames *Njivec* ("Fielder") or *Brinar* ("Juniper"). *Brinar* can be a Slovenian surname, but since all *Brinar* terms in the village are associated with homesteads in which the first listed *gospodar* is a Janež, in Žerovnica *Brinar* apparently served purely as a descriptive term attached to some of the Janež housenames. Similarly, within the village, *Njivec* and its variations are associated only with the surname *Janež*.

Janež *gospodars* assert that all Janež households stem from one house called Ulec (no. 5, table 7), located in the center of a group of Janež homesteads. Its present *gospodar* believes his direct ancestors were among the twelve first settlers, who later divided their land. The significance of the name *Ulec*, which occurs only once in Žerovnica, is not clear. It might indicate beekeeping, an early village activity still important today. (*Ulj* means "beehive.") The earliest listed *gospodar* of this household was a Janež, a half-*zemljak* born in 1789. Perhaps at some early period a forebear of this early Janež *gospodar* divided his larger holding among sons who built their houses close to the original homestead (and then identified them by descriptive housenames), and this may explain the presence of four landed Janež *gospodars* today. But village records also show that some Janež homesteads were landless in the nineteenth century, as four disinherited sons and one *gospodar* who lost his land moved to landless houses. We know that two of these houses were constructed before a Janež became the *gospodar*. It seems that Janežes built the remaining three, two at the hilly southern edge of the village and one at the northern entrance. The following examples show variants in the fate of the disinherited.

1. Johan Janež (no. 8, table 7), born in 1804 at Brinar, although the eldest son, lost his inheritance to his youngest brother, and built a hut called Gričar ("Hill Dweller"), at the southern edge

TABLE 7
*The Janež Group of Households*

| House | First Listed Janež Gospodar | Date of Birth | Place of Birth (House) |
|-------|-----------------------------|---------------|------------------------|
| 1 | Caspar | 1771 | 1 |
| 2 | Michell | 1779 | 2 |
| 3 | Mathaeus | 1785 | 3 |
| 4 | Andreas | 1786 | 4 |
| 5[b] | Andreas | 1789 | 5 |
| 6 | None[e] | 1791 | 6 |
| 7 | Martin | 1803 | 7 |
| 8 | Johan | 1804 | 4 |
| 9 | Josef[d] | 1833 | 5 |
| 10 | Lovre | 1859 | 4 |
| 11 | Antonius[d] | 1861 | 1 |
| 12 | Franc | 1873 | 3 |

SOURCE: Church records supplemented by interviews.
[a] Landholdings in 1969 are indicated in parentheses.
[b] The founding Janež homestead, according to tradition.
[e] Housename indicates that prior to records homestead was owned by a Janež. The birth date is that of the first listed *gospodar*.
[d] The second *gospodar* listed.
[e] Franc sold no. 3 and built no. 12, which was subsequently destroyed.

| Landholding or Status[a] | *Gospodar* 1969 | Housename 1969 |
|---|---|---|
| ⅜ *zemlja* (½ *zemlja*) | Janež | Njivec ("Fieldman") |
| ¼ *zemlja* (½ *zemlja*) | Janež | Njivec zgornji ("Upper Fieldman") |
| ¼ *zemlja* (3 ha.) | Other | Toninec Formerly Janež |
| ¼ *zemlja* | Janež | Brinar ("Juniper") |
| ½ *zemlja* | Janež | Ulec |
| ¼ *zemlja* | Other | Janež dolnji ("Lower Janež") |
| Innkeeper (¼ *zemlja*) | Other | Pri Petru ("At Peter's") Formerly Brinar |
| Cottager | Other | Gričar ("Hill Dweller") |
| Cottager | Other | Lovre |
| Cottager | Janež | Brinarjev Lovre ("Juniper's Lawrence") |
| Cottager | Janež | Pri Njivčem Antonu ("At Anton the Fieldman's"). Formerly other |
| Cottager | None[e] | Formerly Pri Janežovih ("At the Janežes' ") |

of the village. Apparently he did not succeed in earning a living in Žerovnica for long, because after a short period another family is listed as occupying his homestead.

2. Lovre Janež (no. 10, table 7), born in 1859 at Brinar, was also a disinherited son. He became a cobbler and built the cottager house Brinarjev Lovre ("Juniper's Lawrence") at the northern edge of the village. He was forced to supplement his income by trips to Brazil and the United States, which began in the 1890s. His eldest son, also a cobbler, returned from America to help his aging father. Although the son went back to the United States for a few years after his father's death in 1904 and sent his earnings to his family in Žerovnica, nevertheless he and his family remained among the village poor. In the third generation, however, the eldest son, born in 1926, has converted disability to assets. Unencumbered by land, he has worked for twenty years in the nearby factory and has been awarded special economic benefits unavailable to peasants, such as social security and low-interest loans.

3. Josef Janež (no. 9, table 7), a disinherited younger son, was born in 1833 at Ulec and married the inheriting daughter of a cottager. However, poverty apparently forced this family to sell the house, and the six children left Žerovnica.

4. Antonius Janež (no. 11, table 7), born in 1861 at Njivec, where his elder brother became the heir, bought a neighboring cottager house, where his descendants still live. Unlike the family of Lovre Janež, this family has not been able to rescue itself from poverty, even recently.

5. Franc Janež (no. 12, table 7), born in 1873 at Janež, was the sole son and heir. While his father was one of eight children, an adequate family in nineteenth-century Žerovnica, Franc had only a sister. Since his own marriage was barren for many years, a shortage of helpers forced him to sell his quarter *zemlja* and house. The buyer was a disinherited younger brother of another family, Andrej Petrič, a tailor. His inheriting son, Anton, gave the homestead its new housename, *Toninec*, a diminutive of *Anton*. While this homestead is still owned by a Petrič, the *gospodar*'s wife is a Janež from Njivec. After selling his house, Franc Janež and his wife, born in a nearby town, built a hut

called Pri Janežovih ("At the Janežes' ") at the hilly edge of the village. The house was later destroyed, and Franc, his wife, and one daughter left Žerovnica.

Janež women have been well represented in the village, since they were considered desirable wives, as were women of other dominant families. In addition to the six homesteads headed by Janež *gospodars,* twelve more houses are related to the Janež family through marriages that took place between 1811 and 1955. In at least five of these houses two members, of different generations, had married Janež women. Thus the Janež network encompasses about twenty houses, or a third of the village. If the children of Janež women who married into the village are included, the network reaches most village houses.

Parallels could be established in other family histories. Because the name *Janež* has legendary significance, because housenames suggest the early presence of this family in Žerovnica, and because economic facts establish the traditional dominance of the Janež line in village society, this family was chosen for close study. Its history exemplifies certain principles that help to explain the village social and economic structure as it both changed and endured throughout village history.

Thus the normative portrait of Žerovnica—as composed of an equalitarian group of peasant families, each owning a quarter *zemlja* that descends undivided to the eldest son, who remains in his house of origin while other sons go elsewhere—must be placed in broader context. Only then can one account for the complexities and developments of the village socioeconomic structure and for earlier but still remembered traditions of village and fraternal solidarity that may once have held all brothers and many sisters in the village. Both the earlier tradition, of equal inheritance, and the later traditions, of primogeniture, single inheritance, and strengthened patriarchal control, contributed to the preservation of the land and community of Žerovnica. However, the later traditions were also associated with socioeconomic differentiation and the growth of a traditional elite, and brought conflicts that have become more and more difficult to resolve within the contemporary village structure. The disinherited who remained in rural life could not be absorbed into the traditional village structure without disruption and change. The disinherited, more than other villagers, were forced to look to the larger society to supplement their income. They could take little comfort in nostalgic recollections of the past, when, village tradition relates, all brothers shared equally in family property. Today this group looks outward and to the promised new opportunities in the expanding economy of the greater Slovene society, a trend that threatens the stability of the traditional social order of the peasant village.

# 5

## The Village Socioeconomic Structure and the Outside World

WHILE THE economy of Žerovnica has always been geared to subsistence needs, it has never been self-sufficient; it has always been related to the larger society of which it has been a part, and more recently to the world economy as well. Wolf has pointed out that peasants are "rural cultivators whose surpluses are transferred to a dominant group of rulers that uses the surpluses both to underwrite its own standard of living and to distribute the remainder to groups in society that do not farm but must be fed for their specific goods and services in turn."[1] Peasants have not entered into these relations voluntarily. Rather, the subordinate position of the peasant has subjected him to "asymmetrical power relations which made a permanent charge on his production. Such a charge, paid out as the result of some superior claim to his labor on the land, we call rent, regardless of whether that rent is paid in labor, in produce, or in money."[2]

The peasant's dilemma is to have to balance the demands of the external world against the needs of his own household. To meet this problem, a peasant may either increase production or curtail consumption.[3] The inhabitants of Žerovnica have tried both methods. When economic opportunities have presented themselves, most villagers have tried to increase their cash income by increasing production and by engaging in varied activities in addition to farming. If funds remained after his obligations were met, the peasant could buy new equipment, seed, and fertilizer, and sometimes, but rarely, more land. On the other hand, on the many occasions when the peasant could not find the means to increase his income, he reduced consumption, bought less, and resisted experimentation. The alternative chosen depends not only on opportunities offered by the larger social order, but also on the relative strength or weakness of the various strata and individual families making the choice.

## Poverty and Its Solutions
### 1848–1941

In 1848, when the last feudal obligations were abolished, the village entered the modern era. The mid-nineteenth-century village achieved a certain degree of economic autonomy, but at the same time peasants were obliged to meet new demands of the postfeudal society. Taxes replaced feudal dues, and the vicissitudes of the world market could be more threatening than the rule of a feudal overlord. A report of the Chamber of Commerce and Industry for the Crownland of Carniola (Kranj) describes the state of the peasant economy in 1852:

> Land is more fragmented in Carniola than in any other province of the Austrian Monarchy, with the exception of the coastal region. For example, 229,847 joch [one joch equals approximately one acre] of arable land are divided into 609,600 parcels of land; 1,382 joch of meadows into 3,250 parcels; 2,876 joch of pasture into 2,700 parcels; 2,649 joch of vineyards into 9,108 parcels, while the whole area of land in holdings is divided between 73,469 owners. As the farmers wish to produce as many varieties of crops as possible, they raise many different crops on one small area, and there are therefore many different rotations, in which buckwheat, the main crop in this region, is usually planted as a second crop in the stubble of winter wheat and barley. Necessity drives the smallholder to grow on one and the same field the greatest possible quantity of a variety of crops, and to use methods which could not be approved in more advanced larger-scale farming.[4]

It is clear that for a long time peasants in this area have not had enough land to subsist by farming alone. The inhabitants of Žerovnica have shown considerable ingenuity and perseverance in their efforts to supplement their income. The most common ways of securing cash, in addition to farming, were the sale of special services and labor, and various forms of trade. In critical periods villagers resorted to mortgaging property and to emigration.

Until the postwar period those with little land could become specialists, but not all could succeed, since the demand for their services was limited. Five grain mills were operated in the village for many years, beginning in feudal days. Peasants from Žerovnica and from five or six neighboring villages brought their grain to the Žerovnica millers and paid one-sixteenth in kind for the service. Several cobblers also served the village. The village tailor, along with an apprentice and an assistant, served several villages. Žerovnica also supported several smiths, and there were three carpenters, who were paid, in the interwar years, at the rate of four dinars an hour. Other specialties were weaving and charcoal making.

Landless peasants who did not succeed as specialists were often obliged to resort to wage labor, working as shepherds or as agricultural laborers, or splitting rocks for road building. There was no factory in reach of the village until 1939, when a small woodworking factory (Premrov) was formed in Martinjak; it employed about thirty workers at the rate of 1.5 dinars an hour for unskilled labor and 2 dinars for skilled labor.

The forest has always been Slovenia's greatest source of natural wealth. Peasants look upon the forest as a gold reserve, permanently available when a family is threatened with such unpredictable occurrences as crop failure, illness, or heavy taxes. Villagers consider the sale of lumber an essential activity, although today forest exploitation for private profit is severely limited. Even before 1880, when the peasants were granted forest land, they bought lumber from the count, paid the village sawmillers to saw their logs, and then sold the lumber for profit. The millers also bought logs from the local count before they obtained their own forest land, and then sold the lumber at market. Selling lumber required considerable effort, since the count's forests were located on the mountains across the lake. After the trees were felled, logs had to be carried down the mountainside to the lake. They were tied together to form rafts (*splav*). The most desired woods were fir (*jelka*), pine (*smreka*), maple (*javor*), beech (*bukev*), and elm (*brest*). Since beech could not be floated, it was carried by boat. Once across the deepest part of the lake, logs were left until winter, when the water level fell. They were then dragged by oxen over the snow to the village mills. Finally, with ox- or horse-drawn carts, the villagers took their wood as far as Trieste, or to nearby Rakek, about ten miles northwest of Žerovnica, where there were weekly markets frequented by merchants.

Villagers recall the fact that in 1857 a railway line was opened from

Ljubljana to Trieste, making the town of Rakek a major station for wood loading. While the new line destroyed the carrying trade for lumber carters along this route, impoverishing many Slovene peasants,[5] it brought a new source of income for others. Villagers began to cart lumber for local landowners from the Lož valley, about five miles from Žerovnica, to Rakek—an occupation that became the main source of outside income until after World War II, when carts were replaced by trucks. All those who had carts participated. The competition for carting jobs was always keen, and villagers recall that in the Austrian days magnates favored those who could show that they voted for the Liberal party. In the depression years of the thirties villagers would leave Žerovnica at four in the morning in the hope of reaching the Lož valley before their competitors. Many times the trip was in vain. Those who succeeded in securing a haul would return to Žerovnica in the afternoon and depart the next day for Rakek. Sometimes fifty or sixty carts would line the road. The two-day trip brought about one hundred to three hundred dinars in the interwar years. During this period the village sawmill owners prospered greatly, sawing for themselves and other villagers as well as for local landowners.

Throughout the interwar period horse smuggling was a popular source of income for peasants from the Lož valley to Cerknica. Until after World War II the forest to the west of Žerovnica reached to the Italian border at the Javornik mountain range. Thus villagers could buy horses in Croatia and move them through the forest to Italy, where they sold for twice their cost. Some smugglers were caught by Yugoslav and Italian border guards, and four, none of whom were from Žerovnica, are said to have been killed. This now romanticized activity is the subject of a popular novel entitled *The Smugglers* (*Tihotapci*, by M. Hace, a former partisan). While men traded horses and sometimes oxen, women smuggled meat, butter, and eggs in exchange for Italian rice and saccharine, which brought a good price. A butcher in a nearby village remarked, "Now we are a little bored without smuggling."

Cattle trading was a central activity in the earlier village. Markets (*sejem*) were held six times a year on the Žerovnica church hill, on 12 January, 14 February, 27 May, 20 June, 7 September, and 15 December. At other times inhabitants of Žerovnica attended markets in other villages. In the Austrian days purchasers were said to have come from as far as Moravská Ostrava (now in Czechoslovakia) to buy young cattle. There were also buyers from Abbazzia (now Opatija) on the Adriatic Sea. Other products were also offered: textiles, tools, ropes, sweets, and whatever else was available. An individual could buy a license entitling him to operate the market and retain the profits. Otherwise the market was a village-wide activity. Markets provided opportunities for day-long fairs and general celebrations, gambling, and feasting.

The threat of poverty was always a part of village life from the Austrian period through the 1930s. The richer peasants were better equipped to survive agricultural and world depressions than the small landowners, the specialists, and the cottagers, who were frequently without adequate resources to meet the growing burden of taxes. Many were forced into debt and even into selling land. Consequently, economic differences were intensified.

Peasants remember that during the nineteenth century failure to pay annual taxes could bring confiscation of land or resources, but that the proceeds of four days of wood carting or the sale of a calf could pay for this levy. With the depression of the 1890s villagers sought refuge in emigration, and yet indebtedness grew. In the 1920s and 30s the problem for medium-sized landowners and poor peasants became severe; many families were faced with hunger, and the poorer peasants with unemployment as well. Many resorted to the usurer (*oderuh*) in Grahovo. Any rich man with land, it is said, could become a moneylender. One landowner who traded in wood is said to have loaned money to the peasants in return for wood at a low price. If the peasant did not fulfill his obligation, the landowner went to the woods and took what he wanted.

In the years just preceding World War II, prices were inflated far beyond the means of the peasant. For example, while factory wages, for the few who found employment, averaged only 1.5 to 2 dinars an hour, and agricultural laborers received only 25 dinars a day, a pair of work trousers cost 45 dinars. Other prices that villagers recall paying in this period for various commodities are: wood, 120 dinars a cubic meter; white flour, 2 dinars a kilo; beef, 8–10 dinars a kilo; veal or pork, 10–12 dinars a kilo; bread and a flask of wine (at the inn), 4 dinars.

The widow of a peasant who owned a quarter *zemlja* told of her family's experience:

> My husband went to America at seventeen [in 1906] and stayed until the First World War. He worked with a relative in the mines of Minnesota. He went because his father's farm was terribly in debt. There were six children, and my husband's father had to send his son to America. My husband said to his mother before he left, "If I earn 1,000 forints can I come home?" She said, "You earn that much and you will be master in this house."
>
> If it had not been for earning in America this farm would have disappeared. My husband came home and fixed up the house with the money he made from America.

The son of a village specialist also resorted to emigration:

> My father was a shoemaker and had five children. He had only one field of potatoes. In the 1880s he went to Pennsylvania. Then he went to Brazil. I went to America also, but my father got sick in Brazil and returned to the village, so I came back to help him. Then my father died, so I went back to America and sent money to my mother and brothers and sisters. I worked in the mines in Minnesota. In 1914 I came back to the village, but the rest of my brothers remained in America. Then I was able to buy a little more land. But I should have stayed in Minnesota for another ten years. I came back because my mother needed me, and then I had to go to war.

The son of an impoverished quarter-*zemljak* who had lost some land in the late nineteenth century emigrated to France:

> My father called me home in 1931. The house was deeply in debt. I said, "What will be, will be [Kai bo, bo]. Either it will be sold or it will stay." When I came back, it was very bad here. It was a lucky house that had one hundred dinars in cash. I sold wood for seventy-five dinars a cubic meter. There was no trade, nothing. No one could pay taxes. The government just waited for years and years, but did not take anything.

Villagers recall that children went to school barefoot, that there was only dark bread or nothing at all to eat, and that some individuals were forced to beg for food from house to house. One villager remarked, "Bread was what cake is now, and children prayed to God for bread, but no one would eat the bread today that we used to eat."

Many women complained that their life had been filled with suffering and work. One elderly widow recalled that her father died when she was seven years old, leaving her mother with the task of cultivating their quarter *zemlja*. She remembers that she spent her childhood herding cows and that she frequently had nothing to eat. She arose at four in the morning to dig the holes to plant potatoes: "We used to have to feed the horses before ourselves, because the horses carried wood for which we got money."

During a conversation a former blacksmith, pointing to our Slovene dictionary, remarked that before the war he had had as thick a book of unpaid bills, and had spent Sundays walking around trying to collect.

Although such stories of deprivation and suffering are often repeated in the village, another view stresses individual pride and initiative, and the protective role of the traditional social fabric. A well-to-do peasant, who owns a half *zemlja*, reported that no villager was ever allowed to starve and that the village council always provided for those in want; those without enough were fed by various houses in turn. He recalled that when a poor woman who was married to a charcoal maker and lived in a lean-to in the Žerovnica woods turned to drink and moved away, leaving her child, the village had cared for the child, since it had been born in Žerovnica. The former village head expressed a common attitude when he observed with pride that Žerovnica peasants are tough, that they have always managed to find a way to survive, and that they generally have avoided getting into debt.

## Social and Economic Strata
## 1848–1941

Although villagers frequently emphasize the ideal qualities of homogeneity and equalitarianism when describing their society, this does not mean that they are unaware of social and economic differentiation within their community. It seems clear that economic strata have existed in the village for a long time. The growth of a landless class may be ascribed to land shortages and to the adoption of primogeniture, which created a disinherited group. In the nineteenth century, as chapter 4 has shown, a traditional elite, dominated by one family line, controlled more land than other comparable groups and occupied a focal and prestigious position within the village and within the kinship network. Thus by the nineteenth century, if not earlier, the community of Žerovnica exhibited patterns of stratification in the three areas distinguished by Weber—economic, social, and political.[6] Recognizable strata of the village may be differentiated by economic wealth, by life styles and associated prestige, and, to a lesser extent, by political power. While traditional descriptions of peasant societies have tended to overlook factors pointing toward stratification, there is growing evidence from many peasant communities of significant relationships between real wealth, prestige, and authority.[7]

A related problem is that of the degree of rigidity of stratification within peasant communities.[8] For even the most traditional peasant society is not unchanging. Evidence indicates that in peasant communities, economic differences and differences in social ranking are associated with a limited degree of status-striving and competition for scarce goods.[9] While in some periods peasants retrench and restrict consumption, in other times they try to raise their standard of living and are willing to experiment with new methods and to risk change. Here it is useful to consider Stirling's analysis of social ranking as related to two scales, that of power and that of prestige.[10] While these scales tend to coalesce in periods of relative stability, they may diverge in periods of upheaval. Thus in Žerovnica, from the mid-nineteenth century to the mid-twentieth, economic differentiation was intensified, but only gradually, and social ranking did not change dramatically. While the millers are to some degree an exception, since their power increased more rapidly than their prestige, in general during this interval the most powerful group was also the most prestigious. But in the period of severe social change following World War II, channels to power and prestige began to diverge sharply and even to take opposite directions, causing social ranking to become far more complex.

In the traditional village the larger landholders enjoyed the greatest prestige, followed by the core group of average holders. The specialists, some of whom owned a little land, held a relatively low position, while the cottagers, who had neither land nor recognized occupation, were barely accepted. Although the cottagers attempted to compete in offering specialized services to the village, they were often forced to resort to unskilled wage labor. Thus, in a general sense, the larger the landholding the higher the rank of the individual. However, landholders could also achieve prestige by participation in the political administration of the village and by leadership in voluntary societies.

The five grain millers who became sawmillers before the end of the nineteenth century occupied a somewhat separate position. Physically isolated from the village, they were always somewhat apart from the village community. Furthermore, although they might be classified occupationally as village specialists, the millers owned assets, so that their economic position was always superior to that of the village craft specialists. Some owned land in addition to mills, and even before they constructed sawmills, all could sell their services to a wider group than could craft specialists. In the 1850 church records two millers are listed as landless and three as owning a quarter *zemlja*. But by 1941, the end of the period under consideration, the two landless millers had each obtained a quarter *zemlja*, and the three who had originally each owned a quarter *zemlja* had increased their holdings considerably, two becoming half-*zemljaks*. According to one miller, his family had occupied his homestead for four generations. At first his forebears had owned a grain mill but no land; later each generation added land, and in the nineteenth century his grandfather added a sawmill, which his father modernized in 1900. Today the miller owns at least a quarter *zemlja*. Thus millers, as a group, had greatly increased their power during this ninety-year period. While their prestige also grew, their new power evoked some envy and resentment. Hence the larger landholding peasants, living in the central village, retained the highest unqualified positions of prestige and leadership.

The increase in social and economic differentiation within the village from 1850 to 1941, and some of the changes within the internal village structure, may be elucidated by an examination of data regarding the four traditional strata—cottagers, village specialists, average holders (mostly quarter-*zemljaks*), and larger holders (half-*zemljaks*) —distinguished by size of landholding and by occupation listed in the church records of 1850. Four criteria are used here in assessing the degree of internal stability and economic strength, and the power and prestige of each stratum over this period of approximately ninety years:

1. The frequency with which the homesteads of each group changed family lines because an owner was forced to sell
2. The number of families having a significant net loss of land over this period
3. The number of families adding land or other important assets (primarily the sawmills of the five early millers)
4. The number of *gospodars* in 1941 (about half of whom were born before 1919) who had inherited by primogeniture, had inherited as a younger brother, or had married an inheriting woman

In the following discussion stable strata are considered to be composed primarily of family lines that have retained ownership of their homesteads within the male line throughout the ninety-year period, and that have maintained (or enlarged) their landholdings. Unstable strata are composed primarily of more fluctuating family lines that were not able to maintain ownership of their homesteads over generations and that lost land or were even forced to abandon their homesteads and leave the village. Power and prestige are related both to stability and, in a general way, to size and increase of landholdings, as well as to the way of life associated with the larger, more stable landholding group.

## Cottagers
### Eleven Families in 1850

Six of the homesteads owned by cottagers changed ownership between 1850 and 1941. One of the most stable family units in this group was a line of cobblers, although the homestead did not achieve this listing in the church records. Two houses were destroyed and not rebuilt. While all members of this group received small amounts of land from the division of the common pasture and forest land, none was able to improve his position significantly, although the cobbler and one other family bought a few small fields.

The criterion of inheritance can be applied to only seven of the eleven households of this group. Two family lines died out, and their houses remained vacant for a time; one house was destroyed early in this period; and for one family the record is incomplete. In the seven households considered, only three of the *gospodars* in 1941, all of whom were eldest sons, had inherited their houses. A fourth had married an inheriting woman, and the other three had bought their houses. One of these three was a younger son (a tailor from another village), one a younger son from another house in Žerovnica, and one an elder son from one of the poorest houses in the village.

Thus the cottager group remained impoverished and unstable, representing the shifting element in the village. During this ninety-year period over half the cottager families were forced to sell their houses, and several houses were abandoned or destroyed. Two of the poorer quarter-*zemljaks* were reduced to joining the cottager class.

## Specialists
### Eight Families in 1850

No members of this group were listed as landowners in 1850. They included one inn owner, two shoemakers, one church sexton, two millers, one blacksmith, and one carpenter. The specialists showed greater stability than the cottagers as well as more upward mobility. None of the houses of the specialists changed family lines before 1941, but one, that of the sexton, was abandoned when the family moved to a cottager house. Three of these families had obtained close to a quarter *zemlja* by 1941. (Two of these were families of grain millers who had obtained sawmills around 1850; the other secured land shortly before 1941 as a result of an inheritance conflict.) One other family bought a little land, and only two remained without significant holdings. All the *gospodars* of these families inherited their houses; three were eldest sons and five were younger sons.

## Average Holders
### Thirty-Seven Families in 1850

This group was composed of thirty-five quarter-*zemljaks*, one owner of a sixth of a *zemlja*, and one owner of a third of a *zemlja*. Thirty-six of these families are considered here.[11] While in some cases the records are not clear, it does not appear that any house changed family line during the period under consideration. Moreover the large majority of the *gospodars* of 1941, thirty-two in all, inherited house and land. Twenty-one of these were eldest sons and eleven were younger sons. In the four remaining cases the *gospodar* married a woman who inherited the house and land. Two of these *gospodars* came from outside the village. Of the two born in Žerovnica, one was a younger son and one an elder son who lost his inheritance to his younger half brother, the son of his father's second wife.

In spite of the stable inheritance patterns of the quarter-*zemljaks* over this period there was considerable change in the size of their landholdings. Three families (including two in which women inherited) lost some land, and two others lost almost all their land. Other families may have sold and regained land, but since land loss is considered shameful, accurate reports are difficult to obtain.

Just as villagers are reluctant to discuss land loss, they are hesitant to state that they own more than the accepted average of a quarter *zemlja*. Nevertheless, it is clear that six of the quarter-*zemljaks* (including two of the three millers in this group) gained enough land to place them in, or close to, the half-*zemlja* category. These processes emphasize again the ever growing economic differentiation within the village.

While a quarter *zemlja* is considered the village average, it has been inadequate in most periods of Žerovnica history to support the family and produce money for taxes. Not only did peasants seek additional income in trade, forestry, wood carting, and smuggling; the poorer quarter-*zemljaks* were often specialists as well. Thus this group included another smith and a tailor, both of whom had married into the village, and a cobbler born in the village who had married an inheriting daughter. In several families the wife also earned income by working as a seamstress.

## Larger Holders
### Four Families in 1850

This group included one family with three-eighths of a *zemlja*, and three half-*zemljaks*. All the *gospodars* in 1941 had inherited their houses and land; two were eldest sons, and the other two were younger sons. None of the houses in this group changed family line from 1850 to 1941. One of the *gospodar*s left the country, but rents his land; one was forced to relinquish some of his land to a contesting brother, but remains a large holder; and the other two continue to work their original holdings. Since six quarter-*zemljak*s gained additional land during this period, by 1941 the group of large holders had grown from four to ten (but this includes two millers who had other assets in addition to land). No one in the village, however, including members of this group itself, readily asserts that there are more than three or four large holders. Reflecting village equalitarian ideals, spending patterns did not distinguish the larger landholders from the better-off quarter-*zemljak*s. Only the millers were differentiated by a more affluent life-style. Leaders were drawn from the stable quarter-*zemljak*s and half-*zemljak*s living in the central village. For example, the elective position of head of the village council was filled for three generations by one quarter-*zemljak* family line. This group of landholders also supplied the leaders of village social activities and voluntary societies.

The half-*zemljak*s and the more stable of the quarter-*zemljak*s displayed the traditional and prestigious life-style of the village. House and land were located in the central part of the village and remained in the male family line. When possible, the eldest son inherited; secondarily, house and land went to a younger son. Dominant values held by this group were cultivation of the land and maintenance of the traditional social order. Individual initiative, competition for scarce economic means, and hard work were the recognized methods for achieving the desired goals, but the flaunting of success was not accepted.

FROM THIS analysis of the various strata in the village from 1850 to 1941 it is clear that the least stable group was that of the cottagers, who frequently were forced to sell their homesteads, sometimes even leaving the village, and who achieved little improvement in economic position throughout this period. The recognized specialists occupied a more secure economic position. Of the eight specialists, four, including two millers, gained landholdings. Generally speaking, the quarter-*zemljak*s retained their economic position. At least five of the thirty-seven quarter-*zemljak*s lost land, but in the majority of cases landholdings remained stable, and six of the quarter-*zemljak*s enlarged their holdings. This does not mean that land was not often mortgaged, and possibly lost and regained. The five millers who became sawmillers showed the greatest improvement in their economic situation. Finally, excepting the cottager families, we find that of the forty-eight *gospodar*s in 1941, twenty-five had inherited by primogeniture, nineteen were younger sons, and four had married inheriting women. Of the forty-eight houses, one had been abandoned (that of the church sexton, located near the church), and very few had changed hands. The conclusion is that in the period between 1850 and 1941, despite two depressions and a major war, the structure was a relatively stable one, although economic differentiation gradually increased. Most of the members of the large group of landholders owning from a quarter to a half *zemlja* and a small group of specialists maintained their way of life, while a group of cottagers were an unstable element.

# National Economic Measures and the Village: 1948–53

After the trials of World War II and the emergency postwar reconstruction measures, village life returned briefly to its traditional ways. Over a long period, and in spite of depressions, wars, and limited reforms, the internal village structure, although constantly changing, had maintained its basic forms. However, the contemporary socioeconomic structure of the village has been and is being affected by revolutionary changes arising out of the relation of the village to the larger, national context.

In 1948 the federal government decided to collectivize agriculture through the formation of working co-operatives (*kmetijska obdelovalna zadruga*–KOZ), similar to the Soviet kolkhoz, to which peasants would relinquish ownership of their land, implements, and livestock. The program to achieve what was termed the socialist transformation of the village was pushed so rapidly that by 1951 there were 6,797 working co-operatives controlling 2.3 million hectares, over a fourth of the total cultivated area in Yugoslavia.

Even at the height of the early collectivization program, however, only a small percentage of Slovene land was affected. In Slovenia, according to official sources, state farms controlled only 8.8 per cent of cultivable land in 1949, and 11 per cent in 1951.[12] During this period the landholdings of working co-operatives rose from 3.6 per cent to 7.2 per cent.[13] At the same time, private landholdings were reduced from 87.16 per cent to 81.8 per cent in Slovenia, while in all Yugoslavia only 64 per cent remained private by 1951. In 1952 the national harvest was catastrophic, falling to the lowest peacetime level since 1920 and amounting to only 40 per cent of the prewar average and half the level of 1948.[14] As compared to the Yugoslav prewar annual export of about 500,000 tons of grain, and to the 1948–51 wheat import average of 100,000 tons, wheat imports in 1952–54 rose to an annual average of 700,000 tons.[15]

In a decree of 30 March 1953, which constituted a de facto recognition of the failure of the collectivization program then operating, members of working co-operatives were given the right to withdraw their land and livestock. (In fact this right had always been theirs, and some had withdrawn from 1950 onward, but many had been refused permission.) Most of the co-operatives were dissolved, and by 1958 Yugoslavia had only 507 working co-operatives, with a total of 216,000 hectares. General co-operatives (supply and marketing organizations) then numbered 5,630 and owned 203,000 hectares.[16] Immediately after the decision in 1953 to permit peasants to withdraw from the working co-operatives, a new land reform provided for the expropriation of cultivable landholdings in excess of ten hectares. (In exceptional cases owners were allowed fifteen hectares.) By 1954, 268,954 hectares throughout Yugoslavia had been expropriated under this law and distributed to the working co-operatives that survived and to state farms and general co-operatives.[17]

Although the inhabitants of Žerovnica were not affected by the land laws of 1945 and 1953 limiting the size of private holdings, since no one held more than the maximum allowed, they were directly affected by the early program to organize working co-operatives, and in 1948 approximately ten villagers joined a working co-operative. Others resisted, although some report that considerable pressure was exerted upon them to enlist. Members pooled their land for joint use, shared machinery, and were paid according to work performed. It was their right to withdraw and take back their land when they wished. All agree that this venture failed. The dispersed landholdings of the co-operative's members presented an insoluble problem, and attempts to consolidate the holdings by land exchanges met with little success. Furthermore, shortages of machinery and volunteers caused members to lose enthusiasm and drop out.

During this period rural craftsmen and specialists were also urged to form their own co-operatives. Three cobblers from Žerovnica joined a co-operative with seven cobblers from Grahovo. A general crafts co-operative called the *obnovitvena zadruga* (the repair za-druga), in turn united all smaller co-operatives of cobblers, tailors, carpenters, and builders. A craftsman who served private individuals received a certificate for reimbursement by the co-operative. Some individuals were simply assigned to this co-operative because of the shortage of skilled labor for rebuilding the villages.

After the war, wood for reconstruction was provided from the nationalized forests. A major project was the construction of a community center (Co-operative House), situated on the road between Grahovo and Žerovnica. It was to provide Žerovnica and surrounding villages with recreation facilities including a gymnasium; storage space for fertilizer, machinery, and supplies of the agricultural co-operative; a post office; a general store; and housing for the employees of the marketing co-operative in Grahovo. Today its facilities consist only of a few apartments, a general store, a post office, and a hall where occasionally a movie is shown.

Enthusiasm for participation in revolutionary institutions dissipated as the problems grew, and by the early 1950s peasants were repeating a familiar cynicism: "The peasant works for everyone but himself." Žerovnica returned to its former methods of cultivation but not to its old ways of marketing agricultural, forestry, and craft products. The agricultural co-operative was dissolved, and the supply and marketing co-operative (*zadruga splošnega tipa*) in Grahovo became the primary outlet for Žerovnica products, replacing all traditional modes of transaction. The general crafts co-operative, too, was dissolved, and factory products began to replace those of local tailors, cobblers, smiths, and weavers. After the period of government-supported postwar reconstruction, during which carpenters had been busy replacing with tile thatched roofs that had burned, building activities slowed to such a pace that carpenters found little employment. Most peasants began to repair their own houses when resources and time permitted.

## The Evolution of the Working Co-operative after 1953

After 1953 efforts to collectivize were not abandoned. Although official policy accepted the continuation of private cultivation on limited landholdings, collectives continued to expand, frequently at the expense of the private peasant. Private enclaves partially surrounded by collectivized land were subject to the "rounding off," or enclosure, process (*arondacija*). According to law, a peasant whose land was incorporated into socialized farms through *arondacija* was to be given land of equal quality in exchange or, if this was not available, land of a different quality or cash compensation.[18] By the latter part of the 1950s socialized farming, expanding by this new method, had increased in significance.

The evolution of the working co-operative since the late 1950s has been one of the most significant factors affecting private farming in Slovenia. The working co-operative has become a complex economic enterprise that shares few characteristics with the early, voluntary co-operative of the postwar village. A large administrative staff and full- and part-time agricultural workers are employed, all of whom, theoretically, are members of the co-operative and share in the system of workers' self-management. The economic activities of the co-operative have been widely extended to include the operation of stores and minor industrial enterprises, as well as experimentation with, and the development of, modern mechanized farming methods. A Yugoslav economist writing in 1964 calls the relation of the co-operative to the private peasant a new form of collaboration, since most economic transactions in which the peasant engages today—the sale of his product and the purchase of fertilizer, seed, or machinery—are regulated by, and carried out with, one agent, the working co-operative.[19] According to this economist, the working co-operatives are solving many problems, including those associated with "the process of detaching the peasant from his land," and thus the peasant "is being gradually converted into a social producer."[20] By 1961, according to official sources, state and co-operative farms accounted for 27 per cent of the total land area in Slovenia.[21] However, included in this figure is a relatively high proportion of forest reserves as compared to cultivated fields.

The constitution of April 1963 did not introduce basic changes in the legal status of agricultural land or in the rights of the private peasant. The rights of the government or of agricultural organizations regarding rounding off, as well as commassation (a related form of obligatory redistribution of land) were outlined.[22] According to a report of 1968, "Throughout the postwar period the prime objective in the development of agriculture has been to strengthen the socialist sector as the principal factor responsible for the promotion of agricultural production and the socialist transformation of the countryside. In addition, the gradual integration of small-scale private farming with socially-organized production through cooperation between smallholders and the socialist sector, has also been a means of transcending private property in Yugoslav society."[23]

In spite of such orthodox views, however, the general trend of the new constitution was toward administrative decentralization. Each administrative unit from the socialist enterprise to the *občina* and the republic has been encouraged to develop its economy in accordance with its own resources, with less support from external institutions.[24] While the new constitution did not offer significant legal concessions to the private peasant, since 1963 there has been a gradual lessening of the pressure upon the peasant village to integrate itself into socialist farming institutions. Thus the basic agricultural producer remains the private peasant.

# Changes Affecting the Village Economy since 1953

Since 1953, when intensive collectivization was abandoned, the most significant changes in the larger society affecting Žerovnica have been the virtual disappearance of many of the private markets for village products and services, the increased restriction on all forms of private enterprise, heavier taxes on peasant income, greater domination of the agricultural economy by the working co-operative, and the establishment of factories in rural areas where they would attract peasant labor. The peasant economy, equipped only with a nineteenth-century technology with which to exploit its restricted resources, has been forced to cope with this new situation without significant aid from the larger society.

In 1959, as a result of the consolidation of a number of small co-operatives that were limited primarily to marketing activities, the working co-operative (*kmetijska zadruga*) called Marof was formed. Located on the road from Grahovo to Cerknica approximately five kilometers from Žerovnica, its core land of 250 hectares was secured from a confiscated estate. The main house of the estate became the central working office for the co-operative, although official headquarters are located in the *občina* center of Cerknica.

Further consolidation of small co-operatives into larger units was carried out in 1962 and 1964. The Cerknica center then controlled all the co-operatives in an area that extended as far as the Lož valley. By 1964 Marof held only 500 hectares, but the total area under the administrative center at Cerknica amounted to 2,220 hectares. According to the goals announced in 1964, but already modified by 1965, Marof was to be expanded to 1,000 hectares, and the total consolidated holdings to 3,000 hectares. Half of all the new lands that the Marof co-operative planned to incorporate lie in the plain where the best of Žerovnica's land is. Another ambitious project of the co-operative and the *občina* was to drain parts of the lake in order to extend cultivated areas further. The recovered lake lands (some of which are owned by villagers) were also to be added to the area under zadruga administration.

In 1969, however, officials of the co-operative said that plans for expansion had not been pursued, for working co-operatives had had to retrench and economize. Only plans for draining the lake, supported by the *občina*, were still under active consideration.

Since 1960 Marof has become the official middleman, with whom the peasant lacks bargaining power, but to whom he is forced to turn not only for the sale of most of the village produce (milk, potatoes, cattle, and whatever other surpluses the village has), but also for the purchase of such goods as machinery, fertilizer, and seed. Formerly, village markets for cattle and other products, city markets for lumber, and smuggling across the Italian border all provided important sources of the revenue needed for paying taxes and purchasing products in short supply such as wheat and fodder or other goods not produced in the village at all. Today, however, few opportunities for the peasant to sell privately still exist. This situation has forced the village to move further toward an uneconomical specialization in hog breeding in order to sell the young pigs, for which there is still a demand on the shrinking private market. Because the state has not been interested in raising hogs, the co-operative has bought only full-grown animals for slaughter.

Perhaps as crucial to the village economy as the decline of private markets for the sale of livestock and other products have been severe restrictions on private exploitation of forests and the sale of lumber. Žerovnica still owns the two hundred hectares of forest land that were granted to the village in the nineteenth century, and people remember that the five peasants who owned sawmills powered by the Žerovnišča River were the richest villagers in the early twentieth century. Today, as the village economy becomes more subject to the demands of the nation, Yugoslavia's need for Slovenia's forest resources in her competition for world markets has priority over the needs of the traditional peasant economy.

Other forms of private economic activity, subject to increasing *občina* regulation and competition from socialist enterprises, have also rapidly diminished. The five mills were allowed to saw only a limited amount of private lumber until 1962. After that year only one of the five millers was able to work his sawmill uninterruptedly, and that was because he secured contracts with socialized enterprises. More recently restrictions upon sawmills have been relaxed somewhat, but private milling is no longer a significant activity. Private wood carting has been replaced by state trucking. Shop owners and craftsmen, who were denied various privileges, most importantly retirement insurance,[25] gradually abandoned their pursuits. Inn owners who continued to cultivate their land lost their licenses.

The primary solution to the peasant's perennial problem of insufficient cash has come to be employment in the furniture factory in nearby Martinjak, combined with crop cultivation. This is least difficult for peasants having little land or for larger families that can spare one worker for eight hours a day. The factory grew out of the small prewar furniture factory, Premrov, and is a part of the modern furniture enterprise Brest, which has its main factory in Cerknica and a second branch in the Lož valley. Martinjak is three kilometers from Žerovnica, within commuting distance by bicycle, motor bike, or motorcycle. Thus, for the first time a relatively reliable source of nonagricultural income has become available to all villagers.

## The Village, the Co-operative, and the Factory

While the confusing early postwar years were dominated by emergency measures, experiments, and failures, by the later 1950s the new society had begun to assume a more definite direction. It brought changes in the social systems even of peasant villages like Žerovnica that succeeded in maintaining their land and enough of their labor force to continue their traditional farming activities and many of their traditional ways.

The two external institutions that impinge most directly upon village life are the working co-operative, Marof, and the furniture factory, Brest. While these two institutions threatened to deplete village land and manpower, the two primary assets of peasant society, they also opened up new sources of income that were urgently needed when traditional opportunities for economic activity rapidly disappeared. Of the new economic activities, it is necessary to distinguish at least four kinds, bringing markedly different kinds of rewards in power and prestige: (1) employment as an unskilled farm laborer for the co-operative, paid by the hour; (2) employment as a skilled factory or white-collar worker in a local socialized shop; (3) employment in the administrative bureaucracy of the socialized enterprises of factory and farm, sometimes leading to employment by the *občina* as well; and (4) other forms of economic collaboration in which the socialized enterprise awards contracts to individuals—for example, to sell tractors or saw lumber or sell insurance.

The relationship between the village and the co-operative farm at Marof defies easy definition. While some village lands meet Marof territory in the lake and during haying time the co-operative's tractors are in view on the far side of the lake, the Marof complex of buildings is not within sight of Žerovnica. Whereas employment in the factory is not without prestige, although some half-*zemljak*s would like to manage without it, there is hardly a status lower than that of farm laborer for the co-operative. Villagers believe that it is manned by itinerant field hands from Yugoslavia's poorer southern republics and its administrators are largely drawn from urban centers.

When asked whether people from Žerovnica were employed by Marof, villagers almost invariably answered no, frequently commenting that Marof pays less than the factory and requires a longer work week. However, our survey of employment in 1965 revealed that eight villagers were working for the co-operative or had worked for it for various periods since its inception in 1959. Three *gospodar*s had worked as field hands for several years. Of these, two held almost no land and one owned less than a quarter *zemlja*. In addition, five individuals had been employed by the administrative offices of the co-operative. Three of these had formerly been landless specialists; one became the director of the co-operative for a brief period shortly after it was formed, and one worked there for a few years as a technician. Two others, members of the younger generation, a son and a daughter of well-off peasants, were able to pursue advanced training, and they now work in the accounting department of Marof.

Another form of involvement with the co-operative occurs when a peasant leases land to it. Peasants assert that very few in the village have been so unfortunate as to lose their land to Marof under the terms of the standard contract, which stipulates that for a ten-year rental the peasant will receive the nominal fee of 4,000 dinars a month.[26] According to our findings, four families in the village lost land to the co-operative, but in all cases exceptionally severe circumstances were responsible. In one case a widow with small children had been forced to abandon her land, but hoped to recover it for her married son, who would soon retire from factory work. In a second case a *gospodar* whose wife and son were killed in the war gave up his land and moved to the house of a married daughter in a nearby village. He still retains a few strips, which he carefully cultivates, and he deplores the lack of interest of his factory-employed grandson, who is ignorant of the location of the original land of his family. In the third instance a young man whose parents died found employ-

ment in the *obČina* and surrendered his land to Marof, but he hoped
to retrieve it upon his marriage. In a fourth example, mental disability
deprived one family of all field workers.

Thus the involvement of villagers with the co-operative through
employment or leasing of land has been limited. Nevertheless, one
need not be long in the village to sense the co-operative's omnipres-
ence. When questioned about their future, villagers commonly re-
plied with a shrug, followed by a significant, "We do not know what
Marof will do"; and some added, "Perhaps they will take our land."
Yet today villagers are more confident that the co-operative will not
have the economic means to expand. Villagers frequently criticize it.
Some compare the socialized system unfavorably to the peasant economy and point to newspaper reports of co-operative losses. They explain that while the peasant works all day, the co-operative employee
works only eight hours a day. One villager remarked that when it
rains during haying time, Marof hay is left to rot in the fields. Others
commented upon the large administrative staff that the co-operative
must support. Many complain about its right of *arondacija*, which
they understand to mean that if an individual wishes to sell his land,
he must offer it to the co-operative first, and that if the co-operative
wishes to exchange some of its land for private land contiguous with
its own fields, the peasant must comply. One quarter-*zemljak* said:
"They take the fields and then give us rocky ones. My neighbor received less land than Marof took in exchange; for one large piece he
got many small ones." A half-*zemljak* maintained that the co-operative gives up either stony land, which cannot be worked with machines, or land near the forests, where deer, bear, and badgers eat
the crops. Several *gospodars* complained of the co-operative's failure
to make fertilizer available to the peasant at a low price. As one villager pointed out, only the co-operative has chemical fertilizer, and
therefore it is not necessary for them to sell it cheaply.

While Marof is viewed by the inhabitants of Žerovnica as an un-
friendly presence, the factory commands more positive, yet ambivalent, attitudes. Although landowners fear the loss of their sons to
industry, at the same time the factory provides them with a new and
far superior source of cash. It is much easier to work in the factory
for a few years, in order to avoid debts and even accumulate some
savings, than to emigrate to a foreign country and leave those at home

to maintain the fields without the help of a *gospodar* or able son. With mounting taxation and increasing prices for products on the consumer market, the peasant has become ever more dependent on intermittent factory employment combined with field work.

Until 1965 Brest and all other factories in Slovenia, it is said, were ready to accept new workers. Full employment was accepted by villagers as an incontrovertible feature of the new economy. Moreover, retirement with full benefits (80 per cent of the wages, villagers said) is awarded to those who complete a designated period of factory employment, thirty years in 1965. Those unable to complete the mandatory period by retirement age receive proportionally less in social security benefits. Former partisans may retire earlier. Villagers reported that retirement age for partisan men in 1965 was fifty-five, partisan women fifty, and nonpartisan men sixty and women fifty-five.

Factory wages before taxes and social security payments were approximately 30,000 dinars a month in 1964, and 40,000 to 45,000 dinars in 1965. In the summer of 1964 one skilled worker with twenty years of employment received from 19,000 to 20,000 dinars after deductions. Former partisans are again privileged. Government subsidization of their salaries guaranteed, in 1965, a monthly minimum of 59,000 dinars before deductions. The six-day week and eight-hour day were in effect at Brest until 1965.

By the summer of 1965 changes in the national economy threatened the new security offered by the always available factory job. In line with provisions in the new constitution, in July 1965 central planning and government subsidies for socialized enterprises were decreased in favor of local autonomy. A currency devaluation changed the dinar-dollar ratio from 750:1 to 1,250:1, in order to move the dinar toward convertibility as a hard currency. Prices were allowed to rise by 30 per cent and incomes by 23 per cent. For the first time since the war peasants were threatened with unemployment, because some factories, forced to compete without subsidies on the international market, faced liquidation, and every Yugoslav was affected by rising prices.[27] Thus in 1965 villagers began to fear that Brest would lose its international furniture markets. At least ten *gospodars* spontaneously mentioned the threat of unemployment. Many stated that the government now believed too many people were employed in industry and would like the peasants to return to the land. One *gospodar* said, "My son is in the army. Who knows if there will be factory jobs when he returns. The peasants will be first to be let off because the peasant has somewhere to go." Many had heard of dismissals in a plastics factory in a nearby valley. When every other Saturday was changed to a non-working day at Brest, some pointed to this as an advance, although wages seem to have been lowered correspondingly; but others saw the shorter working hours as a sign of impending unemployment. The confidence in factory employment as a reliable alternative for villagers was deeply shaken.

In 1969 this crisis in confidence had not subsided. Villagers reported that factory employment had become more important in meeting the rising cost of living. They said that every house that did not have a worker in the factory was waiting for such a job to become available, and that more villagers were employed in the factory than ever before. However, villagers complained that there were not enough jobs available. Everyone continued to fear that in case of an economic crisis or war the factory would close down, bringing unemployment to the village. In 1965 some villagers believed that families with a quarter *zemlja* and with no more than four members in the household, three of whom were good workers, could manage without factory work. By 1969, however, most did not believe that this would be possible, since prices had continued to rise, as had taxes. However, all agreed that only the young can combine the long hours of factory and farm labor. Many remarked that for the landholding peasant, seasonal factory work in the winter would be preferable to year-long employment, since there is always free time in winter; but there has never been such an arrangement. While all pointed to the retirement benefits that are available to factory workers but not to peasants, no one believed it possible for a peasant to work the required number of years in the factory and also farm the land.

The greatest praise for the factory came from the landless or nearly landless villagers. One disinherited brother commented, "I do not envy my brother [a landholder in the village]. It is better to be in the factory. The land brings too much work and too many taxes." However, all those who held land believed that the peasant worker was better off than the landless factory worker because the latter could not fall back on the land in case of need or unemployment.

The richer peasants, who needed the factory least, most directly denigrated factory employment. A half-*zemljak* remarked, "No one works in the factory in this house. If that happened, everything would be finished. No one would be left to work the land." Such half-*zemljaks*, who can boast that they work the land without sending a son to the factory, express an ideal that few can realize. As attractive as are its monthly wages and other enticements—among them cheap credit for rebuilding and modernizing houses, retirement benefits, and awards for faithful service—the factory implicitly threatens the peasant way of life. Almost all landowners commented that should their heirs permanently desert the land for the factory, when the *gospodar* became too old to manage alone, the land would have to be abandoned to the co-operative.

In the summer of 1969 two representative village spokesmen commented upon the significance for the village economy of the relation between cultivation of the land and work in the factory. A quarter-*zemljak* in his middle thirties, who had been a village leader for a decade and who had worked in the factory for many years, put it this way: "I have lived through one war. For three years we had no bread. After the war I worked as a bricklayer. I worked all day for five kilograms of flour. So we think, if we have land, at least we will have milk and potatoes—at least we won't be hungry."

The most respected village elder elaborated on this theme: "We work in the factory so that we *can* continue to hold onto the land, and we hold onto the land because no one knows what is sure. It may be hell but we still hold on. If we did not have the factory, life would be bad. Now at least the young people live well, but the old ones suffer because they have so much work. It used to be that the old could stop working and the young could take over, but now the old must work the land while the young go to the factory." His wife added, "Yes, you are right, but it is exhausting for the young also, for they both cultivate and work in the factory. It is all right while the old are here to help, but when they are alone and we are gone, how can they do it?"

To clarify the relation of the village to the factory, the employment status of every villager was documented, and some were asked to estimate the number of factory workers in the village. In 1964 and 1965 most estimates ranged from fifteen to twenty villagers in the factory, although some guessed less than ten. Villagers often added, by way of comparison, that in Martinjak and Grahovo one person in every house was a factory employee, far more than in Žerovnica. In fact, village estimates were below actual figures, reflecting, it seems, the belief, or hope, that factory work was not then indispensible in Žerovnica. In 1965, according to the survey, twenty-four individuals (including seven women) from twenty-one families worked in the factory. In addition, one villager worked in a factory in Ljubljana and returned only for weekends. By 1969 more villagers were working at Brest, and estimates of their number ranged from thirty-five to forty.

Table 8 presents the findings of official statistical surveys of the

TABLE 8

*Population Supported by Various Occupations in Žerovnica, 1953 and 1961*

| | 1953 | | | 1961 | | |
|---|---|---|---|---|---|---|
| Occupation | Workers | Depend-ents | Total | Workers | Depend-ents | Total |
| Industry | 12 | | | 24 | 16 | 40 |
| Farming | | | | | | |
| (peasants) | 130 | | | 83 | 88 | 171 |
| Building | 2 | | | 3 | 6 | 9 |
| Trade, or stores | 4 | | | 2 | 1 | 3 |
| Crafts | 4 | | | 3 | 4 | 7 |
| Banking and | | | | | | |
| insurance | — | | | 1 | 3 | 4 |
| Health and | | | | | | |
| social services | 1 | | | 1 | 3 | 4 |
| Administration | 4 | | | 2 | 2 | 4 |
| Transportation | — | | | 2 | 1 | 3 |
| None | 1 | | | 12 | 3 | 15 |
| Unclassified | | | | | | |
| or unknown | 2 | | | 4 | 0 | 4 |
| Total | 160 | 115 | 275 | 137 | 127 | 264 |

SOURCE: Geographical Institute of the University of Ljubljana, unpublished data.

village economy in 1953 and 1961. It cannot be ascertained whether these figures are entirely accurate. The decline in the number of peasant cultivators shown can be attributed to several factors: the decrease in village population, the increase in factory employment, and the change in the age structure of the village. Thus twelve individuals are listed as inactive or too old to work in 1961, while only one is so listed in 1953. However, the number in 1953 must have been larger. Tables 9–15 (pp. 113–29) employ a combination of criteria in addition to occupation to aid in an understanding of the structure of the various strata and groups in the village today and of their relations to each other and to the world outside. The data in these tables were gathered in personal interviews with one or more members of each family.

## Social and Economic Strata Today

In determining the strata in the village, data for the year 1965 are used, but when additional information gathered in 1969 is relevant, it is included. The first step was to find out how many families live in Žerovnica. In 1850 there were sixty houses, one of which was subsequently destroyed. Of the fifty-nine houses in the village in 1965, four were unoccupied,[28] and the data cover just fifty-five, each owned and occupied by one family, with two exceptions. In one house a young man whose father is landless rents an apartment, and he and his wife work in the factory. There are no other similar cases, although in the past young couples sometimes rented temporarily. This couple is omitted, since they consider their residence temporary. One house is entirely rented. Its owner, a half *zemljak* who emigrated to Australia, rents his house and land to a village family who are permanent members of the village community. Four of the fifty-five houses are occupied by only one generation.[29] Each of the remaining fifty-one houses is occupied by a nuclear or an extended family, a few of which include one collateral relative.

Of the fifty-five households, in 1965 there were nineteen in which no members had outside employment. The other thirty-six households included forty individuals who were working for outside employers and seven who had retired from such employment. These seven received retirement insurance gained from combinations of partisan activity, work in the early postwar co-operatives, and government or factory service. Several of them drew only partial pay because ill health had forced them to retire early.

In order to isolate the strata in the village today I have divided the fifty-five households into four general categories and a number of subcategories on the basis of two intersecting criteria: type of employment (factory work, other extravillage employment, cultivation of the land), and size of landholding (little or none, quarter *zemlja*, half *zemlja*). The four broad categories and their subcategories are:

1. Factory workers, landless or nearly landless
2. Factory workers, quarter-*zemljak*s
3. Families having no outside employment
   a. Quarter-*zemljak*s
   b. Half-*zemljak*s
4. Families having outside employment other than factory work
   a. Landless or nearly landless
   b. Quarter-*zemljak*s
   c. Half-*zemljak*s

Crosscutting the fourth category is a small additional category that may be called the new elite. The criterion for membership in this category is the special status achieved by a few who have found their way into the administrative or political bureaucracy of the *občina*, factory, or co-operative farm. The internal structure of this small new group, as well as its role in the growing factional divisions in the village, demands separate analysis.

The first three broad categories approach true groups composing relatively stable strata that still reflect some aspects of the traditional village structure, even though all strata today are in the process of extensive change. Thus these three categories recall the earlier division of the village into cottagers and specialists, quarter-*zemljak*s, and half-*zemljak*s. On the other hand, members of the fourth category are not a unified group. The three subcategories appear to have little in common except that from them, and only from them, are recruited members of the new stratum that is beginning to compete with the traditional leading group for elite status.

For each component family in these various categories the follow-

ing characteristics, which bear importantly on the economic functioning of each household, are noted: (1) the amount of land owned,
as reported by the *gospodar;* (2) the family status of each outside
worker; (3) the length of time employed; (4) the number of persons
residing in the house; (5) the number of children in the family; and
(6) the number of generations in the family. Further, each household,
and each category insofar as it reflects an internally organized group,
is considered in relation to its social rank and power in the village.
While the traditional ranking in the prewar village was easily cor-
related with ownership of land and mills, and with participation in
local social and political life, today new criteria related to new forms
of involvement with the larger society must be considered in analyzing the village hierarchy. Some attributes may signify high rank to
those who identify themselves with the older system and low rank
when evaluated by those who identify themselves with the new. For
example, the prestige of land ownership is challenged by new forces,
while the new status of government employment is disparaged by the
old system. These differences all contribute to attitudes of ambivalence and sometimes hostility on the part of some villagers toward
one another. In order to discover to what extent traditional ranking
is maintained and to what extent new criteria are employed, we asked
each *gospodar* to evaluate his particular way of life in relation to alternatives taken by other villagers: Was farming, factory labor, or
another kind of employment the most desirable and why? Was the
retention of land an advantage or a disadvantage? The data concerning each family in the various segments are presented in tables 9–15.[30]

## Landless or Nearly Landless Factory Workers

In the village of 1850, comprised of sixty houses, there were nineteen
landless families, which I divided into two classes: the poorer cottagers and the better-off specialists. In the 1965 village, of fifty-five
houses, there were eighteen landless or nearly landless families, which
also may be divided into two classes: families whose *gospodar* or chief
support worked in the factory (table 9) and those whose *gospodar* or
chief support had outside, nonfactory employment (table 14). In general, all the landless show greater upward mobility than formerly. The
position of the landless factory workers can be compared to the posi-

tion of the more stable members of the cottager and specialist classes of the prewar period. However, differences are more significant than similarities.

Of the nine houses listed in table 9, two are occupied by members of one three-generation family that split because a widow (family 6) with little children was forced to turn her quarter *zemlja* over to the

TABLE 9

*Families With Little or No Land Chiefly Supported by Factory Employment: Nine Families in 1965*

| Family | Land-holding (ha.) | Outside Worker(s)[a] | Years in Factory | House-hold Members | Children | Generations |
|---|---|---|---|---|---|---|
| 1 | 0 | *Gospodar* Wife[b] | 20 | 5 | 3 | 2 |
| 2 | 3 | *Gospodar* | 20 | 5 | 2 | 3 |
| 3 | 5 | *Gospodar*[c] | ? | 5 | 3 | 2 |
| 4 | 0 | *Gospodar* Wife Son | 20 ? 2–3 | 4 | 0 | 2 |
| 5 | 0 | *Gospodar* | 10? | 1 | 0 | 1 |
| 6 | 0 | Daughter | 8 | 2 | 0 | 2 |
| 7 | 0 | Widow | 10–15 | 3 | 0 | 2 |
| 8 | 2–3 | *Gospodar*[d] | 15 | 3 | 1 | 2 |
| 9 | 2–3 | Wife | ? | 2 | 0 | 1 |

SOURCE: Interviews.
[a] Factory workers at Brest unless otherwise indicated.
[b] Sews for Marof occasionally.
[c] Works in factory in Ljubljana.
[d] Retired in 1965.

co-operative. Her married son (family 4) moved from the small and unimproved house of his birth to a rented house. Unencumbered by land, he worked in the factory from 1945 on. With the aid of factory wages gained by his wife and son, and after 1965 by a second son as well, he earned enough money so that by 1969 he had enlarged his mother's house. He planned to move his family back there in the future. His family was the only one with more than two members working in the factory. By 1969 this *gospodar* was said to live better than others in the village because so many of his family earned factory wages. Yet, he planned to reclaim his mother's land, to which he was heir, when the contract with the co-operative expired in 1971, since he believed that his sons must cultivate their land after factory hours like all the others. He also will cultivate the land after 1971, and claim retirement benefits as a disabled veteran.

Two of the landless listed in table 9 are disinherited sons who were reduced to the cottager class shortly before the war. They exemplify the traditional role of nonpartible and single inheritance in creating a landless group within the village. One, a deviant isolated both by the force of cultural rules and by idiosyncratic factors, was an eldest son. He explained that his mother died shortly after his birth, and after his father's death his stepmother preferred her own eldest son. As a result, this younger half brother inherited the land, while he, the eldest, was forced into the specialist class and, more recently, into the factory. Implicit in his explanation was his feeling that a birth defect that left him handicapped also had contributed to his ill luck. By 1965, however, he had radically improved his economic position, having worked in the factory for over twenty years, thereby benefiting from bonuses and awards for long service. His ambivalent attitude toward peasant life led him to frank, even hostile discussion of internal village problems. With the exception of two doctrinaire village ideologists, to be discussed as members of the new elite, no other individual so readily described factional splits in the village. The position of this individual illustrates one modern process that encourages divisiveness in the village. While traditional tensions between competing brothers were once contained by the integrating institutions of a more stable community, today they may be reinforced by tendencies in the new society that reward the landless but deprive the landed. Thus today a disinherited brother may find ways to challenge a community that he believes rejects him.

All households listed in table 9 are small. Only three have five members, one has four, and the remaining five have from one to three members. Only one family includes three generations. From the perspective of traditional criteria, which are still important, the members of this group retain a low social rank, although successful landless factory workers command greater prestige than did prewar cottagers, wage laborers, and poor specialists. Yet landlessness is viewed as particularly disadvantageous for those who do not have an occupation more skilled than a factory job. However the three men who have worked in the factory since the war (families 1, 2, and 4) are recognized as having a superior position.[31] Aided by credit from Brest, one of these modernized his house; in 1965 his kitchen had the only electric stove in the village and new kitchen cabinets. He installed modern plumbing and blasted the rock beneath his house to build the only basement in the village. A second family had a far more elaborate radio than did most villagers and in 1965 owned the only television set in the village (by 1969 there were several more). These villagers accept the values of the technological society more readily than do the landowners. Nevertheless, while uninterrupted factory employment is a distinct advantage—which the landless, unburdened by the chores of cultivation, can achieve more easily than the peasant—in this group few asserted with much conviction that their position was better than that of the landowner.

## Quarter-Zemljak Factory Workers

There were twenty-eight quarter-*zemljak*s in the village in 1965 as compared to thirty-seven average holders in 1850. While the average holders of 1850 were considered as one group, landholdings within the group varied. However, in the modern village the situation is far more complex. Thus I have divided the quarter-*zemljak* families of 1965 into three groups: those with one or more factory workers (ten families), those with no outside employment (twelve families), and those with other forms of outside employment (six families). The quarter-*zemljak* factory-working families approach most closely the traditional average holder, while the quarter-*zemljak*s without outside employment today correspond to the traditional poorer average holder. This is true because those with no outside employment are in this situation not by choice, but because their families are too small to spare a factory worker. The quarter-*zemljak*s with other forms of employment are a heterogeneous group from the point of view of economic power and prestige.

Table 10 lists the ten quarter-*zemljak* families that included factory workers in 1965. In addition, approximately half the quarter-*zemljak*s with no outside employment in 1965 (listed in table 11) by 1969 had sent one member to the factory or planned to send a son to the factory. These families, although they did not have a member in factory

TABLE 10

*Quarter*-Zemljak *Families Having One or More Members in Factory Employment: Ten Families in 1965*

| Family | Land-holding (ha.) | Full-time Field Workers | Outside Worker(s)[a] | Years in Factory | Household Members | Children | Generations |
|---|---|---|---|---|---|---|---|
| 10 | 10 | 1.5 | *Gospodar* <br> Wife | 11 <br> 2–3 | 5 | 1 | 3 |
| 11 | 13 | 1.5 | *Gospodar* | 5–6 | 5 | 2 | 2 |
| 12 | ca. 15[b] | 2 | Unmarried paternal aunt | ? | 4 | 1 | 3 |
| 13 | 15 | 3 | Son <br> Daughter[c] | 2–3 | 4 | 0 | 2 |
| 14 | 13 | 2.5 | *Gospodar* | 5–6 | 6 | 3 | 3 |
| 15 | ca. 12 | 2.5 | Son-in-law | 5–6 | 5 | 1 | 3[d] |
| 16 | 9 | 2.5 | Son | 5–6 | 3 | 0 | 2 |
| 17 | ca. 15 | 1.5 | *Gospodar*[e] | 4 | 4 | 2 | 2 |
| 18 | 16 | 2 | *Gospodar*[f] <br> Son | ? <br> ? | 5 | 0 | 2 |
| 19 | 17 | 2 | Son <br> Daughter-in-law | ? <br> ? | 5 | 1 | 3 |

SOURCE: Interviews.
[a] Factory workers at Brest unless otherwise indicated.
[b] Reported as a quarter *zemlja*.
[c] Teaches home economics in Grahovo school.
[d] The eldest generation consists of the *gospodar* and his wife.
[e] Retired in 1965. With his former partisan activities this *gospodar* accrued twenty-nine years of service, although he worked only four years in the factory. He was a specialist and a younger brother, but acquired the family land when the elder brother died.
[f] Retired. A former partisan and a factory worker who also had accrued enough service to retire in the fall of 1965.

employment in 1965, must be distinguished from the poorer quarter-*zemljaks* (the remainder of those listed in table 11) who were too shorthanded to release a worker from the fields at any time for employment outside the village.

While all the families in table 10 combined factory work with cultivation in 1965, only three had succeeded in bettering their economic positions significantly. Two *gospodars* (families 17 and 18) are former partisans who were also active in the postwar experiments in craft zadrugas and accrued enough credit to receive retirement pay.[32] In family 10 a disinherited younger brother married a village woman with some land and succeeded in remaining in the factory long enough to save some money. Therefore he added a room to his house in 1965, tiled his kitchen, and installed modern plumbing, including a bathroom—all, as he reported proudly, with cash. Special circumstances aided him in this endeavor. Since his landholdings were smaller than a quarter *zemlja* and his wife's mother cared for the couple's one small child, both husband and wife were able to work in the factory.

The primary problem for these ten families is the shortage of field hands, for in only one of these families does there remain the necessary minimum of three full-time workers. When one essential worker gives eight hours a day to the factory, only four or five hours are left for the fields. Consequently, after a few years in the factory most workers are forced to return to the fields. Yet, this group averages larger families than does the landless group listed in table 9. Only one family has less than four members in the house, five have five members, and one has six. Five of the ten families include three generations. Although elders are listed as inactive in official statistics, the presence of a grandparent who is still able to look after children in a house where there are young ones is a distinct advantage, since a parent is then released for full-time field work. A grandmother also may prepare the meals.

The social rank of the families in this group corresponds approximately to that of the prewar quarter-*zemljak* group. Their views express the traditional peasant values in which retention of the land and the village way of life is of paramount importance. A leading member of this group is the former head of the village council, the last male representative of a family of political leaders in Žerovnica.

While his office has been sacrificed to recent administrative reorganizations, he is still addressed by the honorific tile *oče* ("father") and continues to exercise authority and command respect. As the custodian of historical documents he is the final authority on village traditions. Only families 10, 17, and 18, which have secured some economic advantages, express a somewhat more detached attitude toward cultivation of the land and village ideals.

## Families Having No Outside Employment

This category of nineteen households is divided into two groups that are far apart in social rank: those with a quarter *zemlja* or somewhat less (twelve families), some of whom are among the poorest families in the village today, and those with approximately a half *zemlja* (seven families), who may be compared to the traditional large holders.

### QUARTER-ZEMLJAKS HAVING NO OUTSIDE EMPLOYMENT

The twelve quarter-*zemljak* families with no outside employment (table 11) represent the weakest sector of the quarter-*zemljaks*, for their manpower resources are critically limited. Members of this group are pulled between two poles. Those who can hope to send one individual to the factory will probably move toward the core group of quarter-*zemljak* factory workers, while those who do not succeed face the prospect of losing control of their land and even of selling their houses. By 1969 some families of this group had mustered one member to work in the factory. A departed son or daughter returned, or a younger son or daughter became old enough to work in the factory. However, the situation of the families with only one child or no children at all remained critical. No household in this group can provide more than two and a half field workers. Two families cannot cultivate their fields themselves and must rely on help from others. The fate of one of these (family 31) is to many older peasants an omen of their impending future. The *gospodar* is a former miller who lost the right to work his mill in 1961 and whose sons departed for other occupations. In 1969 his wife had died. Old and crippled with arthritis, he lives alone, but he guards his fields and

TABLE 11

*Quarter*-Zemljak *Families Having No Outside Employment:*
*Twelve Families in 1965*

| Family | Land-holding (ha.) | Full-time Field Workers | House-hold Members | Children | Generations |
|---|---|---|---|---|---|
| 20 | 15–16 | 1.5 | 5 | 3 | 2 |
| 21 | 16–18 | 2.5[a] | 3 | 0 | 2 |
| 22 | 15 | 2[a] | 3 | 1 | 2 |
| 23 | 14 | 2.5[a] | 3 | 0 | 2 |
| 24 | ca. 15[b] | 2.5 | 3 | 0 | 2 |
| 25 | ca. 15[b] | 0.5 | 4 | 2 | 3 |
| 26 | ca. 15[b] | 2 | 2–3 | 0 | 2 |
| 27 | 17 | 2 | 5 | 1 | 3[c] |
| 28 | 14 | 2[d] | 4 | 1 | 3 |
| 29 | ca. 15[b] | 2 | 5 | 3 | 2 |
| 30 | 16 | 2 | 7 | 4 | 2 |
| 31 | ca. 15[b] | 0 | 2 | 0 | 1 |

SOURCE: Interviews.
[a] Family expected to send one son to work in the factory soon.
[b] Reported as a quarter *zemlja*.
[c] The eldest generation consists of the *gospodar*, his wife, and his sister.
[d] The *gospodar* worked in the factory for a few years until the shortage of help forced him to return to the fields.

will not surrender them. "Rather a sparrow in the hand," he remarked, "than a pigeon on the roof." A neighboring first cousin cultivates his fields for half of the produce. A daughter from a nearby village helps him tend his house, which still contains some fine old furniture. Spacious but in bad repair, the house stands at the far end of millers' row in greater isolation than the others. The mills and water wheel are beginning to deteriorate, but the *gospodar* recalls better times when his mills worked day and night, and a large family filled the house. An independent and proud man, who can relate tales of feudal days told him by his father and grandfather, he was decorated for heroism by the partisans, but he has not found a role in the village today. Peasants often comment on the sad fate of this miller and indicate their admiration for his refusal to give up the land. He is frequently compared favorably to another old *gospodar* who was once much respected in the village. Because his wife and son were killed in the war, he gave his land to the co-operative and left for a neighboring village, where he is cared for by his daughter. Paid what villagers consider only a pittance as rent for his land, he spends his time in the inn, recalling better days.

In the second family without field workers (25), a young woman with small children was widowed, and she and her mother-in-law and children must depend on the aid of neighbors.

Most *gospodar*s in this group stated that their income, unsupplemented by factory wages, was insufficient to meet heavy taxes. Consequently, as compared to the peasant-workers, these peasants are forced to sell proportionately more lumber, cattle, or pigs in order to satisfy the tax collector, and yet they cannot keep out of debt. Again the view was expressed that only a young man is strong enough to combine factory and field work. With considerable pessimism concerning their lot, many remarked that the quarter-*zemljak* unable to work in the factory holds the most difficult position in the village. Yet, when the *gospodar*s who seemed unable to keep up their land were asked if they might relinquish it for work in the factory, all firmly rejected this alternative. A frequent response was, "And if the factory closes down, what then? And if a depression comes, what would we eat?"

As one would expect, these quarter-*zemljak*s average smaller families than the quarter holders with one or more members in the factory. Half of the twelve households have three or less members. Furthermore, only three include three generations, and one household is limited to one generation. Clearly this group more than any other has been affected by family disintegration, the most severe threat to the landholding villager.

The quarter-*zemljak*s with no outside employment have various social ranks. They include two former millers (families 30 and 31) whose status was once high but who lost their right to saw lumber, as well as some of the most impoverished families, who retain the land but no longer have the ability to work it to full capacity. Yet perhaps two-thirds of this group still retain the traditional social rank of the quarter-*zemljak*, which is superior to that of the landless factory worker.

Thus I conclude that most of the quarter-*zemljak*s in the village (those listed in tables 10 and 11), whether they have worked in the factory or not, have held to the peasant outlook that values cultivation over other occupations and distrusts the promises of security offered by the factory. A partial exception is the group of three peasant-worker families (10, 17, 18) who by virtue of either partisan activity or long factory service or both have gained a superior economic position. For most landowners the factory remains a secondary form of employment that provides cash for unreasonable taxes and, in good times, for some of the products of the industrial society such as motor bikes, motorcycles, radios, and new farm equipment. Combining factory work and cultivation is looked upon as a necessary sacrifice, made by the peasant in order to save his land.

HALF-ZEMLJAKS HAVING NO OUTSIDE EMPLOYMENT

In the 1850 village there were four large landholders, and by the postwar period there were ten. However, in 1965 there were only nine, since one of the owners had left the village and rented his land to relatives. I divide the nine families into two groups, those with no outside employment (seven families) and those with nonfactory employment (two families). While the latter group includes only two families, it is an important exception to the generalization that most half-*zemljak*s still express, and by example represent, traditional village ideals. Therefore these two families are discussed with the other families having nonfactory employment.

The seven large holders listed in table 12 spurned factory employment in 1965, although by 1969 some of them who could spare a worker had accepted factory employment. However, the shortage of field workers has become acute for this group. For larger holders a minimum of four workers is necessary; yet in 1965 three of these seven families had only three field workers, and the rest had even fewer.

These families are somewhat larger than families of the landless and quarter-*zemljak* factory workers previously considered. All except one include five or more members, and four of the seven include three generations.

With the former village head, who owns a quarter *zemlja*, this

TABLE 12

*Half-*Zemljak *Families Having No Outside Employment: Seven Families in 1965*

| Family | Land- holding (ha.) | Full-time Field Workers | House- hold Members | Children | Generations |
|--------|------|------|------|------|------|
| 32 | 21 | 2.5 | 5 | 2 | 3 |
| 33 | 28 | 3 | 4 | 0 | 2 |
| 34 | 21 | 2 | 5 | 1 | 3 |
| 35 | ca. 30[a] | 2 | 5 | 3 | 2 |
| 36 | ca. 30[a] | 3 | 5 | 3 | 2 |
| 37 | ca. 30[a] | 2.5 | 6 | 1 | 3 |
| 38 | ca. 23[b] | 3 | 7 | 3 | 3[c] |

SOURCE: Interviews.
[a] Reported as half a *zemlja*.
[b] Reported as ⅜ of a *zemlja*.
[c] The eldest generation consists of the old *gospodar* and his wife.

group of half-*zemljak*s occupy, as they did in the prewar period, the highest social rank in the village and continue to represent the traditional ideal. The former miller (family 32) is a partial exception, since the millers have always occupied a position somewhat outside the traditional village structure. Forebears of four of the seven families of this group were half-*zemljak*s in the nineteenth century, and two others were among the larger quarter-*zemljak*s during that period. The miller's large holdings were acquired only in the interwar period. While this group enjoys the highest prestige in the village, from the point of view of power its position is contested by the new elite.

In discussions of village history and customs, the views expressed by this group of half-*zemljak*s were less affected by rejection of the past and anxieties concerning the future than those of other groups. Furthermore, attitudes toward them expressed by other villagers included both envy and admiration. Few villagers wished to recognize that there were now ten, not four, half-*zemljak*s, yet they admitted the superior position of the large holders. When discussing the difficulty of surviving without supplementary income from factory work, many villagers excepted as a matter of course the three or four, as they said, more powerful peasants who owned more land and could manage without outside work.

## Families Having One or More Members in Nonfactory Outside Employment

This final category of seventeen households includes nine that have little or no land, six quarter-*zemljak*s, and two half-*zemljak*s. Seven of these seventeen households, drawn from all three groups, will be considered from another standpoint, since it appears that, to a limited extent, they form a new elite by virtue of the participation of their *gospodar*s, to varying degrees, in the power structure of the larger Slovene society.

### THE NEW ELITE

All seven *gospodar*s in this group have participated in the administration of the co-operative, the factory, the *občina*, or a socialized enterprise. Two own a half *zemlja* (table 13), three are nearly landless (table 14), and two own a quarter *zemlja* (table 15). For the first time the criterion of land ownership does not appear to be useful in isolating a segment of the social structure. Nevertheless, a closer examination suggests that those who have found their way into the new group are drawn primarily either from the former landless specialist class or from the class of rich peasants with large landholdings; none were drawn from the quarter-*zemljak* class that composed the core of the traditional village. While two *gospodar*s of the new group do hold a quarter *zemlja*, in the prewar period one was a miller and the other operated a successful machine repair shop; thus both had additional assets.

This group reveals a further kind of heterogeneity, for it cannot be assumed that participation in the new power structure of the larger society necessarily implies similar ideological commitments. Only three of the seven *gospodar*s are strongly committed to the tenets of the new society. They are landless former specialists who rose to prominence through activity in the partisan army, which in turn opened up to them channels to new kinds of employment. Clearly, the landless peasants, who occupied the lowest social rank

TABLE 13

*Half-*Zemljak *Families Having One or More Members in
Nonfactory Outside Employment: Two Families in 1965*

| Family | Land-holding (ha.) | Full-time Field Workers | Outside Worker(s) | Employment |
|--------|--------------------|-----------------------|-------------------|------------|
| 39 | ca. 30[a] | 4[b] | *Gospodar* | Sawyer for Brest |
| 40 | 34 | 3.5–4 | Brother[c] | *Občina* admin. |
|    |    |      | Son | Marof admin. |

SOURCE: Interviews.
[a] Reported as half a *zemlja*.
[b] Includes one nonresident relative.
[c] Retired.

in the prewar village, had the most to gain from the new social order. Nevertheless, even in these three cases there are significant differences in the kind of roles chosen in the new society. Two of these individuals approach the stereotype of the revengeful former member of the exploited classes who joins the new in-group. Anxious to seal his security, such an individual may volunteer for assignments in which new allegiances take precedence over personal attachments or traditional loyalties. Thus the two individuals in question have informed on respected villagers, which has inevitably brought bitterness and factional divisions. For example, one of them reported a violation of hunting regulations by another villager, such a denunciation bringing a reward. The accused, who declared himself innocent, believed that the informer himself was a secret violator of the same regulation, and he in turn accused the informer. He said that villagers expressed their hostility by spitting on the informer's door. In an earlier case, shortly after the end of the war, the other doctrinaire villager reported to officials that a highly respected village elder refused to deliver his compulsory quota of agricultural products. This incident has not been forgotten.

During the war, while the partisans dominated the village, there were conflicts between them and the Domobranci, but except for some extreme wartime acts, these conflicts were expected and, to a certain

| Years Employed | Household Members | Children | Generations | New Elite |
|:---:|:---:|:---:|:---:|:---:|
| 4–5 | 5 | 1 | 2 | x |
| 2 ? | 5 | 0 | 2 | x |

degree, have been accepted. However, there is no such tolerance for individuals guilty of peacetime acts that appear traitorous to the village, and Communist ethics, insofar as they justify such behavior, are rejected. Consequently, two individuals, formerly without status but representing power in the village today, are avoided, feared, and regarded with contempt by many villagers. This factional split—covertly expressed by villagers' remarks and gestures, and by their avoidance of the two men—was commented on openly by a few individuals. Furthermore, the two *gospodar*s in question were themselves among the most enthusiastic volunteers for interviews. No other individuals so clearly rejected the peasant outlook.

The third ideologically committed villager, who also rose from the landless class through the partisan army to participation in the governmental administration, is respected, although not fully accepted by most villagers. He is descended from a talented family—his father was the village musician and a storyteller, and his brother, who has left the village, is a successful writer. He exemplifies the potential artist and intellectual who could not hope to realize his talents under the old system. He sees the present society, which has offered him new opportunities, as his benefactor, but his values have prevented him from selecting roles that could be interpreted as contrary to traditions of village solidarity. Nor does this *gospodar* so inten-

TABLE 14

*Families with Little or No Land Chiefly Supported by Nonfactory Outside Employment: Nine Families in 1965*

| Family | Land-holding (ha.) | Outside Worker(s) | Employment |
|---|---|---|---|
| 41 | 1 | *Gospodar*[a] | Field hand, Marof |
| 42 | 0 | *Gospodar* | Field hand, Marof |
| | | Wife | Worker in general store, Grahovo |
| 43 | 0.5 | *Gospodar* | Road worker |
| 44 | 0 | *Gospodar* | Road worker |
| | | Wife | Factory worker |
| 45 | 0 | *Gospodar* | Technician, Marof |
| 46 | 3 | *Gospodar*[a] | Marof official |
| 47 | 6 | *Gospodar* | *Občina* official[b] |
| 48 | 1–2 | *Gospodar*[a] | *Občina* official[c] |
| | | Son | Factory worker |
| 49 | 6 | Wife | Postmistress |

SOURCE: Interviews.
[a] Retired.
[b] Formerly worked as a salesman of government insurance.
[c] Had served for one year as director of Marof.

sively reject the peasant values. His close friendship with the priest and his participation in religious activities distinguish him and his family both from the two other ideologically committed *gospodars* and from many other nonpolitical but irreligious villagers.

The four other members of the new elite are two quarter-*zemljaks* who entered the postwar period with additional assets and two half-*zemljaks*, one of whom, a former miller, also owned additional assets. The miller and one of the quarter-*zemljaks*, now a salesman for a socialized enterprise, have become the village entrepreneurs, and their life-styles express affluence. The miller owned the only automobile in 1965 (by 1969 there were two) and employs the only hired laborer

| Years Employed | House- hold Members | Children | Genera- tions | New Elite |
|---|---|---|---|---|
| 9 | 4 | 2 | 2 | |
| ? | 4 | 2 | 2 | |
| ? | | | | |
| 20 | 4 | 1 | 2 | |
| ca. 10 | 5 | 2 | 3 | |
| ? | | | | |
| ? | 1 | 0 | 1 | |
| ? | 3 | 1 | 2 | X |
| ca. 0.5 | 6 | 3 | 2 | X |
| ? | 3 | 0 | 2 | X |
| ? | | | | |
| 15 | 5 | 3 | 2 | |

in the village. His house is large, in good repair, and more formal than other village houses. He is the only villager who meets guests in a carpeted main room, not in the kitchen. The salesman has a modern kitchen and the largest house in the village. His more cosmopolitan outlook reflects his occupation, which requires him to travel throughout Slovenia. All four of these *gospodars* continue to participate in village life and are respected by the villagers. While many envy them, we did not observe signs of hostility to them. The two richer men represent the "uncommitted new class," which values professionalism over ideology; the other two appear to be trying, perhaps successfully, to join this stratum.

TABLE 15

*Quarter-*Zemljak *Families Having One or More Members in Nonfactory Outside Employment: Six Families in 1965*

| Family | Land-holding (ha.) | Full-time Field Workers | Outside Worker | Employment |
|---|---|---|---|---|
| 50 | 16 | 2 | Son | Truck driver in winter |
| 51 | ca. 15[a] | 1.5 | Son | Field hand, Marof |
| 52 | ca. 15[a] | 1.5 | Daughter-in-law | Seamstress, Cerknica |
| 53 | ca. 15[a] | 3 | Daughter | Accountant, Marof |
| 54 | ca. 15[a] | 2.5 | Son | Tractor salesman |
| 55 | 12 | 2 | *Gospodar* | Sawyer for *občina* |

SOURCE: Interviews.
[a] Reported as a quarter *zemlja*.

LANDLESS OR NEARLY LANDLESS FAMILIES HAVING
NONFACTORY OUTSIDE EMPLOYMENT

Of the nine families in this category, I include three among the new elite (see table 14). Workers in the other six have found various kinds of employment—at Marof or as road workers, and one as postmistress. With the exception of the postmistress, members of these six families occupy the lowest rank in the village. Landlessness was always a shameful state, and when combined with unskilled wage labor it remains without prestige. Road workers and Marof field hands can be compared to the prewar cottagers who worked on others' land and broke rocks. Villagers with little or no land can improve their status only through long factory service (see table 9) or through entrance into the governmental bureaucracy. The remainder of the landless class with nonfactory employment continue to occupy, as they did before the war, the most undesirable economic and social position in the village hierarchy.

| Years Employed | Household Members | Children | Generations | New Elite |
|:---:|:---:|:---:|:---:|:---:|
| ? | 2 | 0 | 2 | |
| 2 | 6 | 3 | 3 | |
| 1–2 | 4 | 1 | 3 | |
| 1 | 5 | 0 | 3 | |
| 0.5 | 6 | 2 | 3 | x |
| 0.5 | 5 | 2 | 3 | x |

QUARTER-ZEMLJAKS HAVING NONFACTORY OUTSIDE EMPLOYMENT

The six quarter-*zemljak* families who have one member in outside employment but include no factory workers are a varied group (table 15). Two of them rank with the new elite. The poor quarter-*zemljak* (family 51) who is a Marof field hand occupies a rank lower than that of a peasant–factory worker. Another family is still stigmatized for its active participation in the antipartisan movement during the war. One family is left with only two members. Finally, one of this group (family 53) approaches the ideal village type. An industrious cultivator and old-time settler, the *gospodar* manages his household without recourse to the factory. His family has three field workers. While the eldest son plans to remain a peasant, a daughter holds a good position in the co-operative administration and a son is learning to be an automobile mechanic. These four quarter-*zemljaks*, then, range from a rank just above the poorest landless to close to highest in the village, demonstrating once more the deep inroads on the traditional village structure effected by influences from the outside world.

THE STRUCTURE of the modern village, then, retains some significant but limited parallels to that of the prewar peasant village. Some of the landless unskilled workers who were once members of the cottager class employed as day laborers are today field hands for the cooperative or road workers. This group continues to occupy the lowest social rank in the village. Some of the landless factory workers bear comparison to the former specialist class. The quarter-*zemljaks* who can afford to send one family member to employment outside the village for intervals when necessary compose, as they did before, the core of the village. But the means of gaining additional revenue have changed. Temporary emigration, wood carting, and smuggling have been replaced by the more freely available opportunities in the new industry. The half-*zemljaks* having no outside employment in 1965 (some of whom now send one family member to the factory) still occupy the top of the traditional hierarchy.

There are, however, sharp contrasts, as well as parallels, to the past village structure. Three of the five millers, once among the village rich, have lost their prewar economic status, as has also the owner of the inn. Furthermore the traditional structure has been challenged by the growth of a new group whose power derives from sources outside rather than inside the village. The more powerful institutions of the larger society present their greatest rewards to the landless peasant (frequently the disinherited brother) who may choose to become a fully insured factory worker or a member of the new administrative class. Furthermore, some of the members of the richest stratum, composed of quarter-*zemljaks* with additional assets, and larger landowners, find it profitable to lend their skills to the new bureaucracy. In contrast to the landless and the rich villagers, however, the quarter-*zemljaks* who are the core of the village are barred from many of the benefits of the new society because they cannot continuously sell their services to the new labor market. Thus traditional conflicts between historical economic and social strata are intensified by the contemporary situation, and allegiances formerly only threatened become in fact divided.

# III

## THE PEOPLE AND
## THEIR INSTITUTIONS

# 6

## *The Village Economy*

THE ECONOMY of Žerovnica is based, as it has always been, on crop cultivation and animal husbandry, but landowners have always had to secure additional income from trade and wage labor. Today, however, with the disappearance of craft production and the decline of independent markets, and with the development of the co-operative farm and the factory, the village has become more dependent on the vicissitudes of national economic policies.

Although the average landowner holds approximately a quarter *zemlja*, ideally fifteen hectares, only two or three of these are cultivable by animal-drawn plow; moreover, there is insufficient land for pasturing cattle. Yet most villagers have remained landowners, although economic differentiation has grown. The amount of land held is not entirely indicative of the wealth of a peasant, since the land varies greatly in quality, the flat areas near the lake being the most desirable. Land near the forest is stony and hilly; there wild animals eat the harvest, and crops are subject to rust (*rja*). And while the dryer lake areas provide good hay, the flooded areas offer only sour grass. The older landed families control the more desirable areas, while the cottagers have obtained only marginal land.

Not only land is in short supply but manpower also. The population of the village declined by approximately a fourth from 1868 to 1962, and at the same time the age structure of the village shifted, so that many more old people and fewer younger ones are a part of the village today. Furthermore, the young now attend school for longer periods, and many of those who remain in the village after completing school spend the larger part of their day in factory work. At the same time, technological improvements and mechanization have been limited and have hardly compensated for the decrease in manpower available for agricultural tasks. All landholding villagers including the half-*zemljak*s, except for the few who have joined the new elite,

are confronted with the basic problem of subsisting under these difficult conditions. Consequently, they must work arduously and for
long hours.

A villager may welcome an opportunity to break the routine of
the workday by talking to an inquiring ethnologist, but he continues
his tasks as he converses. On a Sunday or a rainy day, or in the late
evening after the chores are done, a peasant family may congregate
around the kitchen table, relax, and join in a heated conversation.
Then Turkish coffee, plum brandy (*slivovka*), sausage, bread, and
pastry are pressed on the visitor as the *gospodar* leads the discussion
and the wife, grandparents, and sometimes the children add their remarks. But leisure is a rare aspect of peasant life. Peasant attitudes
toward the relentless demands of the workday are characterized in
two remarks: "If we want to eat honey we have to work hard," from
a woman departing for the fields, and "Doing things slowly, you get
further," from a leading village elder. The remarks pose the peasant's
old dilemma of how to meet both his own demands and those of the
outside world. The pressure to do both is increasing, as villagers are
tempted by the products of the industrial society, visible in the win-
dows of the socialized stores in Cerknica, and as they must meet the
growing demands of the state, which sees the peasant with ambivalence, not only as a source of labor, goods, and taxes, but also as a
social anachronism that perhaps might best be taxed out of existence.
The peasant can either work harder or continue at his traditional pace
and eat less. Both alternatives are tried, but no one knows which
technique is better.

# Agriculture

## Crop Rotation

For as long as villagers can remember, the village-wide crop rotation
system, or *kolobarjenje*, has been the basis of cultivation. According
to legend the system was established when the descendants of the
twelve founding families divided each of the seven village complexes
into twelve equal parts. Each family then owned one-twelfth of the
village land—a full *zemlja*, composed of seven fields, one in each of

the seven complexes—and each family participated in the crop rotation system. Later, it is said, with partible inheritance, fields were subdivided until each villager owned only a quarter *zemlja*, composed of one or two narrow strips in each of the seven complexes.

Grafenauer describes the system under Maria Theresa as based on a three- to four-year rotation with fallow. Beginning under Joseph II, and increasingly by the early nineteenth century, the practice of leaving land fallow was replaced by fertilization and the introduction of new crops such as clover (*detelja*), maize (*koroza*), and potatoes (*krompir*). These crops were planted on a given strip of land in alternation with grain. In the later nineteenth century crop rotation became even more variegated.[1] The system has worked well for Žerovnica, peasants point out, because village land is not dispersed but composes one unit surrounding the village. Except for lake hay land and forest land, all village land was traditionally included in the rotation system. The village plan calls for crop rotation in a seven-year cycle. Thus the fields around the village are divided into seven complexes. Three complexes are devoted mainly to wheat (*pšenica*), with part of this land reserved for oats (*oves*) and rye (*rž*), and one complex is given over to barley (*ječmen*). In the nineteenth century buckwheat (*ajda*) and millet (*proso*) were often substituted for some of these grains, but millet is not cultivated today, and buckwheat is less important than it was earlier. Two complexes are devoted to potatoes and one to clover. After the July harvest of wheat and barley, the summer crops of beetroots (*pesa*) and turnips (*repa*) are planted on part of this area. In the nineteenth century maize was added to the potato fields, and other vegetables, such as beans (*frižol*), cabbage (*kapusta*), carrots, and beetroots were also gradually added. The latter two vegetables are used primarily for pig feed. Flax (*lan*) was part of the early crop rotation system, but it was abandoned by the interwar period. Wheat, once the basic crop, is now challenged by potatoes but remains more important than maize. Many remark that the summers are too short and too wet for wheat, frequently causing the stand to be only half as thick as it should be. Finally, more clover for cattle feed is grown today because more and more cattle are sold on the market. In short, each of the seven complexes is planted to the following seven-year succession of crops: potatoes, wheat (turnips in summer), clover, wheat, potatoes, barley (beetroots in summer), wheat. The crops encircle the village in this order, and each successive year each crop is located in the adjacent complex. Potatoes are followed by wheat and barley in the cycle since these grains are planted in fall after the potatoes are harvested in late summer.

Today all peasants buy some chemical fertilizer, which they add to animal manure, but few can afford as much as they need. For a quarter *zemlja*, 1,000 kilograms of fertilizer is considered a minimum, but some villagers assert that 2,000 kilograms are necessary. One of the better-off quarter-*zemljak*s, who owns six or seven head of cattle, reported that he bought 1,800 kilograms in one summer and could have used another thousand. With more fertilizer, he said, he could have raised the productivity of his land sufficiently to support three more head of cattle. All villagers complain of the high cost of chemical fertilizer (from twenty-five to forty dinars per kilogram in 1965) sold to them by the co-operative. Some peasants buy seed from Marof when they run short, but it is considered expensive, and most obtain seed from their own harvest.

Villagers are proud of their system of co-operative plowing, made possible by the crop rotation system, in which two neighbors with contiguous fields planted to the same crop plow these fields as though they were one. Plowing is done in rows parallel to the four sides of a field, working in an unbroken furrow from the outside to the center. At the center is a ditch that is not cultivated.[2] When two fields are plowed as one, the area of the wasteful central ditch is considerably reduced.

Until the interwar period, all those holding sufficient land participated in the crop rotation. However, the present-day shortage of field workers has forced some families to turn over more fields to hay, and some families who lost land during the depression were forced to withdraw partially from the system. If one walks the land, it is easy to see these exceptions. A strip of wheat may be isolated by other crops, and some plots may be uncultivated or given over to hay.

Some landholders are prevented from participating by the location of their holdings. An example is an elderly *gospodar*, formerly a cobbler and a member of the cottager class, who was gradually able to buy six hectares of land, only one of which is plowable. In 1965 he owned scattered plots in Grahovo, Lipsenj, and Žerovnica, and clearly he could not take part in the crop rotation system. A factor that is said to have contributed to the dispersal of some holdings, preventing their integration into the rotation system, is the interference of Marof. A few families, because they lack field workers, have been forced to rent their land to the co-operative for ten years. Furthermore, the co-operative, with its right of *arondacija*, has in certain instances insisted on land exchanges disadvantageous to the peasant, who, finding that he no longer owns plots in each complex, may decide to plant only three or four of the crops—perhaps clover, potatoes, and maize—of the variegated system.

In spite of these irregularities, which are bringing a slow disintegration of the traditional crop rotation system, it is still the basis of agriculture in the village. Praise of the system is unanimous. Even peasants whose landholdings are too small and scattered to be fully integrated into the cycle commend this practice, and all villagers express pride in the fact that theirs is one of only two modern examples of a village-wide crop rotation system in all of Slovenia, the other, they say, being Dolenja Vas pri Ribnici.

The system of crop rotation is supplemented by the cultivation of individual small vegetable and flower gardens alongside each house and orchards of apple, pear, and plum trees behind each house. There is no attempt to spray the fruit, for villagers say that the altitude is high enough to prevent fruit pests. Apples are stored in barns all winter. Some fruit is made into marmalade, and most families make fruit brandies; beans, cucumbers, and beets may be pickled. When villagers who seemed to have more fresh fruit than they could consume were asked whether they sold their surplus, they all agreed that there were no buyers. There was, in fact, little interest in making better use of the fruit harvest. A number of peasants keep bees for honey.

## Technology

Until about thirty years ago a wooden plow with a factory-made metal plowshare (*na pol lesnji plug*, or half-wood plow), was in general use (fig. 9). In 1965 all villagers owned metal plows, drawn by oxen or horses. However, two villagers continue to use their half-wood plows, which they believe to be superior to the modern metal

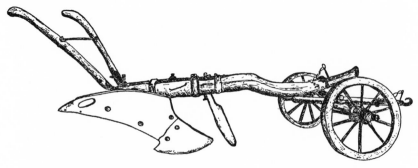

FIG. 9. *Half-wood plow*

plow because they are lighter, turn the earth more effectively, and are easier for the oxen to pull. A wooden peg harrow was still in use in 1965.

The richest miller (a half-*zemljak*) bought a secondhand tractor for half the price of a new one, which would have cost, it is said, 2,600,000 (old) dinars. However, since the miller's land is divided into three separate parcels, he could not plow with the tractor and has employed it to power his hay-loader (a blower that throws the hay to the upper barn floor). Another tractor was owned by a member of the new elite who sells them for a socialized enterprise. He, too, was unable to use his tractor for plowing because his land is dispersed.

Until after World War II most mowing was done with a scythe, although a few villagers had animal-drawn mowing machines, and the ox- or horse-drawn wooden carts in which the harvest was transported from the fields had wooden wheels, which were gradually replaced by metal-rimmed wheels. After the war approximately twenty villagers, or over half the landholders, used American-made, animal-drawn mowing machines (*kosilnica*), most of which were obtained from Germany. The other villagers continued to rely on hand scything or on help from a neighboring owner of a mowing machine. The richest miller bought a motorized mowing machine in the early 1960s at a cost of 750,000 dinars.

Perhaps six peasants owned hay-blowing machines in 1965; until 1967 the others were forced to use a pitchfork to throw the hay into the loft of the barn. Potato diggers, which are attached to the animal-drawn mowing machines, were generally owned. One peasant, a half-*zemljak*, owned an electric motor that he used to power his hay-blower. This completes the list of privately owned mechanized farm machinery in 1965, most of which was obtained after the last war.

In the Austrian period each household threshed grain in the thresh-ing room in the barn. Three or four people, each wielding a threshing stick (*cep*), beat the grain. Nostalgically, many recall the "*pica poca*" that resounded through the village at threshing time. In the interwar period some peasants used hand threshers and others occasionally employed itinerant workers who received 25 dinars a day. Because millet and buckwheat were too fragile to be threshed by beating, groups of girls and boys would stamp on it barefoot. After the threshing there were parties and dancing, with food and drinks.

Grain was winnowed by tossing it into the air from large cane baskets. Later, a hand winnowing machine (*trier*, after the German trademark) replaced this traditional hand labor. The winnower is one of a few pieces of equipment remaining in the village that were once owned communally by the farmers' co-operative (*kmetijska podružnica*). This organization was formed in the Austrian period and had thirty members in the village in the interwar years. Other communal equipment from the co-operative includes a fruit press and a manure pump. The co-operative's small thresher is now pri-vately owned, and unavailable to villagers. The peasant owner ex-plained that if he rented it out, he would be obliged to pay more taxes than he could afford on his income from the machine. After the last war the village acquired another type of hand-turned win-nower (*pajtel*), which is now used for small quantities. It sorts grain into three sizes and separates it from the chaff (fig. 10).

By 1965 most threshing and winnowing had become partially mechanized, since a Marof-owned threshing machine, produced in prewar Czechoslovakia, had been made available to the villagers and at threshing time was stationed in Grahovo. In 1965 villagers paid thirty-two dinars an hour for its use, the average family requiring at least four hours for threshing grain. Five adults and one child are needed to operate the thresher: two women feed the grain into the top of the machine; one man loads the straw that falls from the thresher onto a cart; and one or two women stand on top of the cart stamping down the straw. Meanwhile the grain flows into sacks from

FIG. 10. *Hand winnower*

an opening underneath the thresher. A child ties the sacks, and the chaff blows to one side. At threshing time in Grahovo debris fills the air, and the noise of the thresher reverberates throughout the village. An atmosphere of hustle and urgency prevails. The road from Grahovo to Žerovnica is lined with wagons coming and going, and peasants try to thresh as rapidly as possible in order to cut costs. Marof itself, equipped with combines, does not use this cumbersome and awkward piece of equipment.

Milling of flour by village millers is now generally supplanted by the service of the Cerknica state flour mill, where villagers take their grain in exchange for flour.

Beginning in 1967 an important change took place in the agricultural technology of the village. By the summer of 1969 approximately half the village households had acquired new gasoline-powered mowers. In addition to mowing, the new machine can cut and bind the grain, saw wood, sharpen knives, power the hayblower, spray, and rake. Villagers had bought these machines in Italy for 9,500 new dinars (950,000 old dinars). They said that except for plowing, the machine could do almost anything, and thus the work load was greatly alleviated. There were still only two tractors in the village.

It was not the co-operative or any other form of governmental aid that made it possible for the peasants to finance this new equipment. And factory wages alone did not suffice. The cash came primarily from an unpredictable event that was fully exploited by the villagers, demonstrating again their ingenuity and perseverance in battling for a greater share of the limited goods available. In the spring of 1965 a severe storm damaged a large part of the peasant forest. At that time villagers looked upon the storm as a calamity. However they undertook to log in the ravaged areas, to saw the salvaged timber in the village mills, and to sell the lumber wherever they could for a price, they said, that was 50 per cent higher than the average. In this they succeeded, although official regulations continued to prohibit the private sawing of lumber for any purpose except home use. However the storm created its own imperatives, and the *občina* decided to overlook village expedients. As one villager said: "Now all the millers saw wood although it is not allowed except for private use, but when the storm came they had to allow it, or the wood would have rotted; now the sawing just goes on."

By the spring of 1967 the villagers had earned enough from the sale of wood to begin to buy the new mowers. They also bought new carts, lighter than the old ones, that can be hauled by one rather than two oxen. They are used primarily to carry fertilizer to the fields. By 1969 half the villagers owned these two new kinds of equipment. In addition, the new cash supply had been used to buy such modern kitchen equipment as washing machines and refrigerators.

An important consequence of the introduction of the motorized mower has been the further disintegration of the crop rotation system. Less land is being devoted to grain and more to clover for cattle feed because the motorized machine can cut the clover in a day and turn it over the next day. While some villagers had not decreased their wheat cultivation, there was general agreement in 1969 that since more villagers combine factory and cultivation, wheat takes too much time to thresh and mill, and thus an increase in animal fodder is more profitable for the village. A leading village elder, asked to assess the shift in the agricultural economy, commented, "It depends on how you take it. After all you can buy bread. So now we are turning more toward cattle and pig breeding."

## Some Examples of Cultivation

As the following examples indicate, most families work alone or with the help of a relative or friend in the labor of cultivation. These descriptions reflect the situation and equipment of 1965. Families that have motorized mowers can harvest grain and hay more quickly and with fewer people.

A peasant departs for the fields at seven o'clock with his ox-drawn cart loaded with manure. He spreads the manure over his field and plows it. He then takes a long pole sharpened at one end and digs it into the ground at intervals of approximately one foot. His wife and daughter follow and set beetroot plants into the holes.

Oats are to be harvested, and a group of five—the *gospodar* and his son-in-law and daughter, who live with him, and two other women, one a relative and one a friend—depart at two-thirty in the afternoon with a mower pulled by two oxen. After fifteen minutes they reach a strip of approximately 11 by 100 meters. The *gospodar* leads the oxen as they draw the mower along the long edge of the strip, and the son-in-law sits on the mower and flattens the oats with a wooden rake. After reaching the end of the strip, the mower returns to the other end and begins again.[3] The women follow and, with the help of sickles, gather the oats together into bundles (*snop*), which they bind with two lengths of oat stalks (*proveslo*). On each field length there are approximately thirty piles of oats to be bound. Groups of eight bundles are then piled together in conical structures (*stavka* or *rastava*) and left to dry in the fields for one week. At four o'clock the work on one strip is completed. A similar procedure is used for wheat. However, barley is stacked on an *ostrnica*, a tall pole made from a tree trunk with stumps of branches protruding, where it dries for several weeks.

When haying, a *gospodar* and his son leave at seven in the morning with their ox-drawn mower. The *gospodar* also brings his scythe, for the hilly areas, a sharpening stone, and a wooden rake. A walk of fifteen minutes brings him to what was the communal pasture, where his strip of hay land, seventeen meters by twenty, is identified by a stone marker. The *gospodar* paces off his land and marks the end with a branch. By eight o'clock the strip is mowed, and the son leaves to cut hay for relatives nearby while the *gospodar* continues to scythe the borders by hand for another half hour. At eleven the *gospodar* will come back to turn the hay, and the next morning he will load the hay on his cart, bring it to the village, and throw it up into the barn.

Lying about three kilometers from Žerovnica are the village's 225 hectares of the 2,345 hectares of lake land. Formerly, before cattle were stalled, they grazed on these fields in August after the haying. The July wind that sweeps across the broad, flat lake basin, bending the stand of hay, is refreshing, in contrast to the dusty air of the village, with its closely placed houses and animal sheds. Breughel-like, peasant families with oxen, horses, and carts can be seen in the distance descending from the surrounding villages; little children, women, and grandparents ride on carts and carry implements, while the *gospodar* leads the team. In view are the Marof tractors, which are harvesting the hay on the far side of the lake. Often the lake ground is soggy, and draft animals become stuck in the mud; sometimes they are injured or even killed. All the varied grades of hay in the lake are used: the wettest (the most sour) provides cattle bedding, while some of the dryer hay can be used for fodder. One *gospodar* remarked, "The hay gets weaker as we get further into the lake, but God knows it's all important." A peasant who owns five hectares of lake land, which is somewhat more than the average, estimated that with good weather he can cut, rake, and load his lake hay into the barn in one week's time.

In harvesting potatoes, typically, a *gospodar* and his son, and perhaps two women helpers, work together. After the greens are scythed and put aside for compost, a potato digger, which uncovers every other row of potatoes, is attached to the mower and the potatoes are unearthed. The following day, the potatoes are loaded on carts by the *gospodar* and his son, and the alternate rows are dug. In two full working days one strip of potatoes, covering approximately 1 per cent of a hectare, can be harvested, yielding 100 kilograms of potatoes. After the potatoes have been piled by the side of the house, the whole family spends many hours sorting them according to size and quality.

## Animal Husbandry

All villagers except those with very little land have always owned cows, oxen, and calves, and some have owned horses. Sheep were also once kept by some, but today they are found only in the more mountainous areas. Before 1915, when part of the common pasture was divided (the remaining portion was divided in 1925), animals were pastured communally. From 24 April to 25 July they were kept in the enclosed pasture. After the July harvest they were let out on the cut hay land of the lake and the stubble of the fields, although tramping on the fields packed down the soil. The three village herdsmen (for horses, cows, and young cattle, respectively) were often indigent village elders who were fed in turn by different families.

Peasants seem to agree that the division of the common grazing ground was profitable, since it resulted in more fertilized fields for crops and hay. They explain that they have neither land to spare for pasture nor manpower for herding cattle. However, the wisdom of stalling the cattle all year is questioned. While some believe that dry hay is preferable to fresh grass and that stalled cows provide superior milk and better meat, others say that pasturing would improve the health of the animals. Villagers stated that it was illegal (in 1965) to own bulls and that artificial insemination was always employed for cattle breeding, although at least one family reported that they kept a bull.

Villagers said that although cattle breeding was being encouraged, the number of cattle had declined since World War II. In 1965 three head of cattle (cows, and oxen or horses) were considered a minimum for quarter-*zemljaks*. Only nine villagers owned no cattle. The richer quarter-*zemljak* owned from four to five head of cattle; half-*zemljaks* and a few other peasants owned from six to nine. At least eighteen peasants owned one or, more likely, two horses, and an equal number owned oxen, generally a pair, although sometimes only one. Horses, frequently decorated and to a limited degree a sign of wealth, are of greater value to the peasant than oxen. They require only one driver while oxen require two. They are better suited for work and less expensive to feed. Furthermore, horses can be sold more easily and may also be exported to Italy for slaughter. While the peasants sometimes slaughter oxen for meat, the meat is of poor quality. All families had chickens, a few raised rabbits, and some kept pigeons for pets.

The postwar trend toward specialization in raising and selling young pigs has caused them to rival cattle as Žerovnica's most important livestock. In 1965, with a few exceptions, every family with a little land, even those who did not own cattle, owned from three to four pigs. The time-consuming chore of preparing the feed for the pigs, delegated to the women, involves the preparation every other day of a mixture of milk, boiled potatoes, grain shells, beetroots, turnips, and sometimes carrots and barley, which is then cooked in a large kettle over a special stove (*kuhinja*) in an outbuilding usually adjacent to the cattle barn (fig. 11).

FIG. 11. *Pig-feed stove*

## Hunting and Fishing

Traditionally villagers hunted and fished with relative freedom. Under Austrian rule three counts controlled the lake, and fishing rights were rented to villagers. When the lake began to dry up, in early summer, fish were caught by nets strung on frames, or with circular bottomless baskets thrown over the fish, which were then removed by hand. Women recall catching crabs and taking them in large tubs to Trieste to sell. The crayfish were so large, one villager remembers, that they were sent to Vienna, to the emperor. Hunting bear, deer, and small game was also traditional and was enjoyed but, unlike fishing, was never important economically.

Fishing, which was once a village-wide activity, is now officially restricted to those who pay a fee. In 1965, according to villagers, this privilege required payment to the fishermen's society, the central offices of which are in Ljubljana, of 5,000 dinars a year or 1,000 dinars for a few days. According to the rules of the society, fishing is restricted to Tuesdays and Fridays, and hook and line is the only equipment allowed. Since enforcement of these regulations is difficult, villagers continue to fish when they can with whatever equipment they possess (including baskets or nets) and are rarely apprehended, but the fishing in which all traditionally took part as the lake water receded is no longer a part of village life.

Hunting is another activity that is affected by a conflict of interest between the state and the peasant. The forest reserves, which are inhabited by wildlife including deer and bear, attract tourist hunters, who are a source of hard currency. In 1965 a license to shoot one bear was said to cost the foreign tourist the equivalent in hard currency of 50,000 dinars. Hunting by Yugoslav citizens is strictly regulated. Only those who join a hunters' club (*lovča družina*), at a reputedly high fee, have the legal right to hunt. Villagers asserted that, according to regulations, three hunters together may keep no more than one deer a year and that other deer shot by peasant hunters must be turned over to the state. Bears may not be hunted under any conditions. Should bears damage the crops, as they frequently do, particularly in the higher mountain villages, a peasant may demand compensation from the government; he risks a fine of 300,000 dinars (in 1965) if he kills a bear.

Needless to say, the state has not entirely succeeded in restricting hunting, particularly for the highly valued venison in an area where meat is expensive and scarce, and hunting traditions are strong. Yet hunting, which was a general pastime enjoyed by all, is no longer an important part of village life.

# The Yearly Round of Activities

In early March, if weather permits, villagers clear the fields. Then plowing proceeds, and maize, oats, potatoes, cabbage, and other vegetables are planted. By May villagers are occupied with weeding and hoeing. As the winter supply of wood disappears, more wood is brought in for summer fuel.

June and July are among the busiest months. In June, hay and clover are harvested, and in July the lake hay, barley, and wheat are harvested as well. Some villagers fish as the water recedes. Activities continue to press in August. Wheat and barley are threshed; beetroots, potatoes, turnips, and carrots are harvested; and potatoes are sorted by size and quality. The second stand of hay in the main hay fields is cut. At the end of August forestry work begins and fruit is gathered.

In September and October harvesting of potatoes, maize, beans, beetroots, turnips, and cabbage continues, and the villager plows the fields on which he will plant fall grain. Wheat and barley are planted in the plots where potatoes were harvested earlier. Lumbering is a constant occupation.

In winter (November through February) peasants chop and prepare wood for fuel or sale, clean and repair tools, dig up rocks in the fields, care for the livestock, slaughter pigs and make sausage, and repair house interiors. Villagers are busiest from March through November, but even in the winter months the day is full.

# The Division of Labor within the Family

The division of labor by sex was far more clearly defined in the early village than it is today. Women traditionally carried the main burden of the field work. They sometimes cut hay with a sickle, and they raked it; they dug up the potatoes, which even today, with the help of an ox-drawn potato digger, is a time-consuming chore; they planted, weeded, and hoed, and generally cared for the crops throughout the year. Men scythed, fed the cattle, and plowed, but they spent much of their time on other jobs, such as carting wood, working in the forest, and repairing tools and buildings. In addition to their field work, women made the everyday clothes and linen for household use. Flax, wool, and sheepskin were the main materials. The flax was whitened by drying it in the sun, then beaten, spun, and taken to a weaver. Each family had a spinning wheel (*kolovrat*). In Žerovnica only one woman owned a loom (*statve*). In the interwar years most families continued to spin enough flax for their own linens, but store-bought cloth was used for clothes, and today the home industries of spinning and weaving have all but disappeared.

Women also prepared all the food. This task has changed little today, although now some bread and other food is bought. Traditionally, flour was ground at the local millers, and bread was baked in the brick ovens at home.

Today the division of labor varies with individual circumstance. Men frequently combine factory work with farming, and sometimes women also work in the factory; because all families are shorthanded, work is assigned to whoever is available. In the earlier days, when the *gospodar* departed for several years' work in a foreign country, a brother, the father of the *gospodar*, or another male member of the enlarged family remained at home. Today the *gospodar* may be the only adult male in the household, so that some women whose husbands work in the factory are forced to assume more responsibility for the field work than formerly. Moreover, widows who are left entirely without male helpers may be forced to rely on neighbors for help.[4] On the other hand, in one family in 1965 the wife worked as a local civil servant, while her husband remained at home and cared for their small fields and their young children.

Most villagers say that today the fields are worked by men and women together. Nevertheless, certain traditional divisions of labor still obtain whenever possible. Men continue to mow and to feed the cattle. The plow, pitchfork, axe, and scythe are never used by women. Men, on the other hand, milk cows only in an emergency. One well-to-do *gospodar* remarked that while his father would never have prepared the pig food, some men in the village now occasionally must do this. In addition, men sell pigs, a chore that frequently requires traveling, are responsible for any other village trading, work in the forests, repair tools, and sometimes rebuild or enlarge their houses, barns, and other buildings.

Women continue to milk the cows, care for the pigs, cook, and care for the children, in addition to hoeing and weeding in the fields. Today most women have foot-pedal sewing machines. Cloth in bolts may be procured in stores in Grahovo and Cerknica for everyday clothes, but men's clothes and women's more formal clothes are usually bought. Generally, two pigs a year are slaughtered, and women prepare ham, sausage, and salami for family consumption. Except for the families who have recently acquired washing machines, laundry remains a time-consuming weekly chore assigned to the wife or her daughter. The clothes are soaked and rubbed with soap, then carried to the river, where they are beaten and rinsed; then they are taken back to the house and boiled over the kitchen stove. Finally they are rinsed again in the river and hung to dry.

Women agree that their work was more strenuous in former days, when there were more children to care for and when families lacked such labor-saving devices as mowers, potato pickers, wood-burning stoves, and sewing machines. Nevertheless, while chores may be somewhat easier, the hours of labor continue to be long, since women now have so few helpers. When grandparents are living in the household, they and the older siblings may take over much of the care of the infants and small children while the parents are in the fields or at the factory. Old people, however, continue to help in the fields as long as they are physically able to do so.

By 1969, with the additional income gained from the sale of timber after the storm of 1965, about half the villagers had bought washing machines imported from Italy. About one-third of the villagers had refrigerators in 1969, while in 1965 there were only two. Few had bought electric stoves because they are considered to be too expensive to operate, particularly since water for cooking pig food is kept boiling on the wood stove for much of the time.

## The Men's Workday (Summer 1965)

On a typical day the *gospodar*, his son, and perhaps his aging father rise at four in the morning, feed and water the cattle, and then depart for the fields. When the pressure to harvest hay is greatest, field work may start at three o'clock. Those who do not own mowers and must cut hay with a scythe may leave for haying even earlier in order to scythe when the grass is still wet with dew. If beetroots are to be planted, everyone begins work before dawn, in order to plant when the ground is still wet.

Workers return from the fields for breakfast (*zajtrk*) between six and eight o'clock, then go back to the fields until noon. On less busy days some return at nine or ten for a second breakfast (*dojuž-nik*) of bread, sausage, and wine or tea. More frequently, *gospodar*s take some refreshment with them to the fields.

After the noon meal the *gospodar* and his male helpers may toss hay into the loft of the barn with pitchforks and then return to the fields. The *gospodar* or his son returns to the village to feed and water the cattle at four o'clock. If there is time, there is an afternoon snack (*malica*) consisting of bread, marmalade, and wine. Then the men depart for the fields again, where they may remain until nine, when they come home for the evening meal, after which the men's day generally ends.

## The Women's Workday (Summer 1965)

The wife is aided, if she is fortunate, by female helpers who are a part of the household. They arise at four with the *gospodar* and milk the cows. The morning milk is collected by a designated woman in the village and sent to the co-operative. The wife and her helpers then light the stove, feed the pigs, clean the house, and prepare breakfast, which may be simply substitute coffee (*kava*)[5] and bread, or may include also *žgance* (a porridge consisting of potato flour or corn flour and water, which is fried in fat for half an hour and then eaten with sugar, milk or *kava*, or fat). By seven or eight o'clock the wife and those of her helpers who are not occupied with the care of infants leave for the fields to weed and hoe. At ten or eleven the wife returns to prepare the main meal (*kosilo*).

The noon meal begins with soup, usually made of noodles and vegetables, although once or twice a week it may include meat. A salad of cabbage, beets, or beans, prepared with garlic, pepper, oil, and vinegar, and a serving of potatoes (either boiled or fried in pork fat) or another starch completes the meal. On rare occasions meat (beef or pork) may be served as a separate dish. Bread is rarely eaten at noon.

In the afternoon the wife or a female helper milks the cows for the family needs, places the milk in a can of cold water, prepares and cooks the feed for the pigs (this chore is carried out every other day), and feeds the pigs; then she and the other women of the household return to the fields. Later, women may help load hay into the barn, after which the wife prepares the simple supper (*večerja*), served at nine o'clock. Supper usually consists of what is left over from the noon meal, potatoes, *žgance,* and a salad. After supper the wife and her helpers must put the children to bed, clean the house, perhaps wash and iron, and prepare for the next day. At eleven, often long after the *gospodar* is asleep, the wife retires. One woman remarked, "Five hours' sleep is enough for us. We are accustomed to it."

In the winter months the workday is shorter and there is more time to sleep. Women have time to sew, gossip, and listen to the radio. Men repair houses, construct new buildings, and repair tools. During these months the evening meal is served earlier, perhaps at seven, and the day closes.

## Local Trade and Industry

Village-wide and regional markets, which once dominated local trade forms, are infrequent in Slovenia today, although this is not true in all areas of Yugoslavia. Because the sale of young pigs is one form of trade that can be carried out privately, between individuals, hogs now rival cattle in importance in the village economy. Economists in the co-operative farm expressed concern over the decline in cattle production and the substitution of hog raising. This is an increasingly pressing problem because Yugoslavia depends on beef exports and consequently finds beef in short supply at home.

Since pork is the most popular meat in Slovenia, the co-operative farm paid peasants well for hogs. In 1965 a hog brought 50,000 to 80,000 (old) dinars. However, villagers have found it more profitable to sell young pigs to other peasants to raise and fatten, and Žerovnica has become a center for this trade. Villagers say their sows have the largest litters, and since a sow litters twice a year, a fortunate family may sell eight piglets a year and slaughter two. When times are good, peasants come to Žerovnica from the Lož valley and nearby Croatia to buy, as they did in the summer of 1964. However, the next year peasants began to curtail some purchases because of rising prices, and fewer pigs were sold. One villager complained that while he could have sold a piglet for 12,000 dinars early in 1965, by June of that year he was forced to accept 6,000 dinars. The co-operative also bought fewer hogs in 1965. That summer, in contrast to the previous one, villagers had to search out their customers. Calling on a village family one evening at seven o'clock, we found the *gospodar*'s wife and daughter worriedly awaiting the return of their husbands. The *gospodar* and his son-in-law had departed at four that morning with a horse borrowed from relatives in a neighboring village and a cart loaded with six small pigs. Around eight o'clock, as night was falling, the two men wearily returned with two pigs as yet unsold, although they had searched the neighboring villages for buyers from dawn to dusk.

While the peasant may sell cattle to an individual for his own use, his only other legal outlet for cattle is the co-operative farm, which acts as a middleman. The co-operative exports the best cattle to Germany and Italy, and releases only limited numbers for domestic consumption. In no case can the peasant initiate his own sale directly to a socialized store. In 1964, villagers said, the co-operative paid from 250 to 360 dinars a kilogram on the hoof for young cattle, but the price was said to have risen to 450 dinars in 1965. One *gospodar* reported that he received 150,000 dinars for a year-old cow weighing 350 kilograms, but that he was obliged to put the entire sum aside to pay his yearly taxes. Officials described a bonus plan, initiated in the spring of 1965, that offered tax reductions to peasants who sold cows and calves to the co-operative farm, but villagers seemed to have little information about the new regulations.

Other products sold to the co-operative include potatoes, which only the rich peasants who have a surplus can supply. In 1965 villagers said that potatoes brought only thirty dinars a kilo. Occasionally the co-operative buys some sour, but never sweet, hay, and it buys milk regularly. In 1964 the co-operative paid forty-three dinars a liter for milk, and was reported to have sold it for eighty dinars. In 1965 the price paid to peasants rose to fifty-eight dinars. The co-operative profits from the marketing of milk, one villager explained, because although it must pay its workers hourly wages, peasants' labor is uncompensated. The woman who collected the village milk received one dinar a liter for her effort. Some peasants sell honey to an enterprise in Ljubljana (Medex), which, in turn, exports it.

The five millers in Žerovnica were permitted to continue sawing wood after the war, for their services were needed in the rebuilding of the devastated areas. Later the three smaller mills were closed, then opened again and permitted to operate until 1962, when it was decided that only the Brest enterprise might operate a sawmill. One *gospodar* explained that Žerovnica had been selling a large amount of wood to Brest at 9,000 dinars a cubic meter for logs and 39,000 dinars a cubic meter for sawed boards. Clearly, he concluded, Brest could economize by sawing its own boards. The halting of the sawmills meant hardship for the village and an economic crisis for the millers, who were permitted to saw only for their private use. Even this required permission from the *občina* and the payment of high taxes amounting, according to one miller, to 2,400 dinars a cubic meter in 1964. The miller was forced to secure a second permission if he wished to sell his sawed lumber to Brest, but the taxes on such sales were said to be so high as to be prohibitive.

However, in November of 1962 the richest miller obtained the right to service Brest directly by renting his mill to that enterprise, although he did not regain the right to sell wood. Consequently villagers in a wide area, as far as the Lož valley, who wish to have their lumber sawed for use in home construction employ his services. The villager pays Brest directly for this service, and Brest in turn compensates the miller. It is reported that in 1964 the fee was 2,400 dinars a cubic meter. In addition, the peasant was obliged to pay an equal amount to the *občina* as a tax on the miller's services.

In 1965 the second largest miller, who had suffered considerably from the three years' shutdown of his mill, received permission to saw for the *občina*. However, only in the winter and the fall does he have enough water power to operate. On a summer afternoon in 1965 the scene at millers' row, beside the river, reflected the contrasting fortunes of the five millers. At the site of the largest mill the river is dammed up, causing it to widen greatly. Three large water wheels were turning at this mill, which also utilizes additional power from turbines. A hired helper, the only one in the village, was in the distance, working the miller's large fields. The miller's automobile, tractor, and motorcycle were in view, as was his well-kept, unattached barn—far larger than others in the village and housing nine head of cattle. A villager arrived with several large logs chained to a low cart pulled by two oxen. In businesslike fashion the miller's son measured the logs and helped the peasant unload them onto rail carts. They were then rolled over metal tracks into the busy sawmill, and the peasant departed for his fields. The four other mills along the stream were quiet. (By 1969 limited circumventions of the sawing regulations were beginning to be overlooked by officials, although the regulations themselves remained unchanged.)

Restrictions on lumbering also affect the peasant's use of his forest land. Before logging, the peasant must receive permission from the *občina*. Permission to cut a limited amount of lumber for his own use in repairs, and for firewood, is routinely granted, but before cutting wood for new buildings or for sale the villager must submit plans for approval. The trees that may be felled have been previously marked by a government forestry agent (*logar*). Later the agent returns and measures the stacked wood on which the wood tax is based. Then, if the peasant has permission to saw wood for his household needs (for this purpose he is allocated two cubic meters a year), he takes those logs to the village sawmill. If he sells lumber, it must be left unsawed, unless he wishes to risk a heavy fine. Officially Brest is the only agency that may buy the peasants' lumber, and other buyers of village lumber must secure permission from the *občina*, which is rarely granted. Villagers explained that Brest does not wish to compete for lumber. They said in 1965 that a few years earlier, before this restriction went into effect, buyers from other factories sometimes came to the village and offered prices as high as 25,000 dinars a cubic meter for logs, while now villagers were receiving only 10,000 to 15,000 dinars a cubic meter from Brest for logs delivered to the factory. Villagers reported that sawed lumber, if they were allowed to sell it, would bring 50,000 dinars a cubic meter. One young *gospodar*, a quarter-*zemljak*, complained that even if he sold and delivered twenty cubic meters of logs a year at a price of 10,000 dinars a cubic meter, he would barely have enough left over, after paying a wood tax of 2,000 dinars a cubic meter, to pay his annual property tax, which amounted to some 150,000 dinars in 1965. According to his calculations, furthermore, every time he sold a cubic meter of logs instead of sawed lumber he suffered a significant loss, even allowing for a 30 per cent loss from waste in sawing and a 6,000-dinar tax on the sawed boards, since a cubic meter of sawed lumber would bring 30,000 dinars as compared with 8,000 for logs.

In 1965 few villagers understood or accepted the goal of the state, to conserve Slovenia's greatest resource, its forests, and to utilize them for export. Underlying this program was the assumption, stated by officials in 1964 but qualified in 1965, that by right the forests belong to the state, rather than to private individuals, and that consequently the correct program was one of gradual advancement toward nationalization. In 1965, while increasing control and exercise of the right of *arondacija* for forest lands continued to be the official position, the provisions of the new constitution protecting private property were held to rule out direct confiscation. The threatening question of nationalization of the forests was so laden with tension that, with few exceptions, villagers avoided it even when confronted by direct questions. When asked, "How important is the forest to you?" they answered:

"Most important [Največ]. It is not subject to weather. It is always there."

"The peasant cannot exist without the forest. It is the source of his repairs and of cash."

"We could not live without the forest. Everything is small in comparison. We would have to sell thirty head of cattle to make up for what we earn by cutting the forest."

"The peasant who has forest land breathes easily."

Another *gospodar* (who may be rated as an uncommitted member of the new elite) concluded with the following rarely stated thought: "The next step is that they will take the forest away. Officially it will remain private, but the government will cut it with its own equipment and its own workers, and pay the peasant the price it thinks is right. The peasant will only be permitted to help in lumbering for wages. He will lose the right to sell his wood, and all he will be able to do is harness his horses and drive the logs where they tell him to take them."

In the summer of 1969 no significant changes had been made in official regulations bearing upon private exploitation of the forests, yet, as evidenced during the sale of the storm-damaged timber, enforcement had become less strict. Officials of the co-operative farm said that they and others would like to see the peasants given greater latitude in the use of their forest lands, and it was said that this question was then under discussion by the government. In Žerovnica people said that no villager was observing the restrictions against selling of timber. In fact, by 1969 not only the millers, but other peasants within the central village, owned saws and prepared their own boards for sale to factories in the area, thereby circumventing the Brest monopoly. For example, a plastics factory sent trucks to the village and openly bought wood. Villagers believed that existing regulations would be modified. While the richest miller was still the only large timber salesman in the village, other peasants were earning money by this means and intended to continue to do so.

## Inns, Stores, and Local Prices

The typical Slovenian inn is a simple gathering place, perhaps the large front room of a house equipped with long tables and chairs or benches, where drinks and food are served. Some inns also have rooms for rent. In the evening young people frequent the inn, singing and dancing to the music of a local accordion player. Because it is illegal today to own land and also operate an inn, there are far fewer private inns in the peasant villages than formerly.

Žerovnica had two inns during the interwar period. The one at the north end of the village, called Under the Willow Tree (Pod vrbo), included a general store carrying food and other small items. A second inn was in the center of the village. Only one inn survived into the postwar period, and in 1957 it lost its concession. Neighboring Grahovo had six inns before the war, of which only one remains, but the inn in Lipsenj still operates and also serves Žerovnica.

Villagers complain that they miss the two former inns where they used to gather and talk, and that a stranger cannot find board or lodging in the village. The loss of the general store was also regretted, and in 1965 the village representative to the *občina* applied for permission for a new general store that would fall under the administration of the large, diversified socialized trade enterprise Škocjan Rakek, located in the area of Cerknica. The *občina*'s approval was conditioned upon the village's showing that the projected store would be self-supporting and could be housed in a facility provided by the village. A year later permission was granted, and a small general store was established in a large house next to the bus stop at the entrance to the village. This was the same house that once had lodged the main village inn. Today the new establishment includes a modern small buffet with tables and a bar, where sandwiches, hard and soft drinks, and coffee are served, and an adjoining room with a small food store. Villagers are proud of their new cafe, but it has not replaced the traditional, more spacious inn, with its relaxed atmosphere.

In the interwar period there were two bakers in Grahovo, but they abandoned this occupation, since at the time bakers did not qualify for state retirement pay. Grahovo also had a butcher shop and two stores that sold food and general provisions. After the war a small general store called Jezero was opened in the community center on the road between Žerovnica and Grahovo. It is the store most frequented by villagers. A second store, controlled by Škocjan Rakek, opened in Grahovo in 1954. A butcher shop in Grahovo, private until 1962, is administered by Marof. For other purchases, villagers in Žerovnica and Grahovo must take the bus to Cerknica, where there are a one-story department store, a general store, a coffee shop, a butcher shop, and a vegetable and fruit store, all belonging to Škocjan Rakek, as well as a bakery that is still private. The baker frequently runs short of bread, but villagers prefer his bread to that sold in the socialized stores.

Villagers say that they buy little at stores. Until recently most families have made their own bread, supplementing it by occasional purchases from the store. Although villagers lack fruit and vegetables in the winter months (except for stored apples, marmalade, and pickled vegetables), they rarely buy fresh fruit or canned products. They regularly purchase salt, sugar, rice, macaroni, spaghetti, oil, vinegar, chocolate, matches, substitute coffee, and real coffee, which is so expensive it is bought only in very small quantities. Villagers sometimes run short of grain and are forced to buy flour. Some can afford to buy beef once or twice a week, but others rarely eat it. Sugar is considered very important, and children are frequently given bread sprinkled with sugar. One villager remarked that in prewar Yugoslavia sugar was a luxury and that if she bought half a kilo, she kept it all year long. Now villagers can buy sugar in bulk and like to buy large quantities. For example, two *gospodars* shopping at Jezero, when offered a ride home in our Volkswagen microbus, took advantage of it to buy fifty kilograms of sugar and several very large bags of flour. Jezero was stocked with the following kinds of provisions in 1965: food, kitchen equipment, small farm equipment, cotton cloth, work clothes, and such miscellaneous items as ballpoint pens, paper, and rope.

PRICES OF ITEMS REGULARLY PURCHASED, 1965 (in old dinars)

At Jezero

| *Food* | *Dinars/kg.* |
|---|---|
| Bread (dark) | 104 |
| Bread (white) | 122 |
| Cheese | 1,280 |
| Chocolate | 800 |
| Coffee | 2,800 |
| Coffee substitute | 600 |
| Flour (white or corn) | 124 |
| Lard | 580 |
| Lemons | 300 |
| Macaroni | 200 |
| Oil | 396 |
| Rice | 1,800 |
| Salami[a] | 1,300 |
| Salt | 60 |
| Sugar | 219 |
| Tea[b] | 1,800 |
| Vegetable fat or margarine | 520 |
| Vinegar | 150 |

| *Other items* | *Dinars* |
|---|---|
| Cigarettes (20) | 55–100 |
| Detergent (1 kg.) | 800 |
| Laundry soap (1 kg.) | 300 |
| Matches | 15 |

| | |
|---|---|
| Printed cotton cloth | |
| (1 m., 80 cm. wide) | 400 |
| Rope (1 kg.) | 800 |
| Woman's nylon slip | 1,820 |
| Work shirt | 1,700–1,900 |

### At the Butcher Shop in Grahovo

| Meat[c] | Dinars/kg. |
|---|---|
| Beef | 950 |
| Pork | 950 |
| Veal | 1,000 |

### Major Purchases Made in Cerknica

| Item | Dinars |
|---|---|
| Cart with rubber tires[d] | 300,000 |
| Secondhand animal-drawn mower[e] | 150,000 |
| Ox | 450,000[f] |
| Cow | 200,000[g] |
| Horse | 400,000–500,000 |
| Motor bike | 150,000–240,000 |

[a] Salami is sometimes bought in the summer, when peasants run out of meat from their own slaughtering.

[b] Peasants frequently make linden blossom tea and rarely drink regular tea, which they call Russian tea.

[c] There has been a steady rise in meat prices in recent years. For example, beef is said to have cost 300 dinars a kg. in 1950, 600 dinars in 1960, and 800 in 1964. The prices of other kinds of meat rose correspondingly.

[d] Carts formerly were made by the peasants themselves, but to-day when an old cart can no longer be repaired, a new one is bought.

[e] A new mower with a motor cost 600,000 dinars.

[f] This may be compared to the lower price villagers reported paid by Marof: in 1965, 450 dinars a kg.; in 1963, 360,000 dinars for two oxen.

[g] Price depends on age of cow.

## Levels of Living

Differences in wealth were reflected in the early village by the amount and quality of land and the number of animals owned, by the possession or lack of other assets, such as sawmills, and also by the character and size of houses. The houses of the sawmill owners contrast sharply with other village houses, having larger ground plans and two full stories, and being more elaborate and more formal. One has richly carved beams on which the date 1843 appears. Some of the millers' houses are furnished with fine old heirloom furniture. The inn owner and a few of the larger landowners also have houses larger than most others in the village.

On the other hand, the typical early village houses were simple and small. A stone house near the village, constructed in 1721, is an example of the type of house usual in Žerovnica until after World War I. The stone walls are perhaps seventy centimeters thick. The house is one and a half stories high, the upper story, reached by a ladder, being simply an unfinished attic under the thatched roof. There is no cellar under the stone floor of the two rooms. In the kitchen there is a raised hearth on which burnt an open fire (*ognišče*), vented by a hole in the ceiling. The smoke finally escaped through the thatched attic, where meat was stored. From poles over the open fireplace, pots for cooking were hung. The second room, the traditional main room, in which the *gospodar* and his wife slept, was heated by a large tiled stove located in the center of the house and opening into the kitchen. In winter the top of the stove was a favorite place to sit and talk or do chores. In addition there was a small storage pantry (*shramba*) for potatoes and a larder (*špajs*). Up to a hundred years ago oil lamps were rare, and houses were lit by a simple torch.

Many village women recall the misery of cooking in a smoky kitchen over an open hearth, for most Žerovnica houses did not have a wood-burning stove for cooking until after World War I. In the typical house the main room was heated by a tile stove, as it still is today (see fig. 12); the second floor was not finished, and boys slept in the barn in the hay. Village elders joke about the greater freedom boys had before there was room for them to sleep in the house. Tile roofs date from after World War II. Some of the poorer villagers still live in two-room houses with unfinished second stories.

The most important of the factors that since the war have lessened the incidence of severe poverty and altered the traditional patterns of economic stratification are the new kinds of opportunities available to members of peasant families. As Wolf has noted, one prerequisite for far-reaching change in peasant societies is "some kind of frontier which can serve as a safety valve for populations displaced from the land. . . ." Such a frontier can be geographical, as it was for Žerovnica in the nineteenth and early twentieth centuries, when surplus population emigrated to new lands, or it can be occupational, as it is for the postwar village.[6] Now factory jobs and opportunities for specialized training draw from the village not only the excess population, but also a significant number of the youth who are still needed to work the land as long as the village remains at its present technological level. Today, except when local factories curtail employment, villagers no longer need think of emigration. If they do leave, it is only to go to Western European countries for short work periods in order to profit from the hard currency and higher wages gained there.

For all these reasons the several economic strata that composed the prewar village have been subject to a certain leveling in the postwar era. Some members of the poorer strata have been enriched by participation in the expanding industrial and administrative complex. Moreover, the loss of young people needed to work the larger holdings, and regulations against private enterprise have impoverished some members of the formerly richest strata, the half-*zemljaks*, the millers, and owners of private shops and inns. Yet economic strata still obtain in the contemporary village, and, moreover, significant differences are developing between the most successful members of the growing new elite and the average villager. While near starvation and extreme poverty no longer exist as a general village phenomenon, landholding *gospodars* whose families do not include factory-age workers and who may be old, sick, or shorthanded cannot take full advantage of the occupational frontier. Furthermore, few landholders can work a sufficient number of years to obtain retirement insurance. The usual pattern is to spend a few years in the factory to meet debts and mounting expenses, and then to go back to the fields.

Today, as in the past, in spite of some economic gains most villagers assert that they are poor and overworked; their problems are intensified by the increasing demands of the tax collector and the shortage of

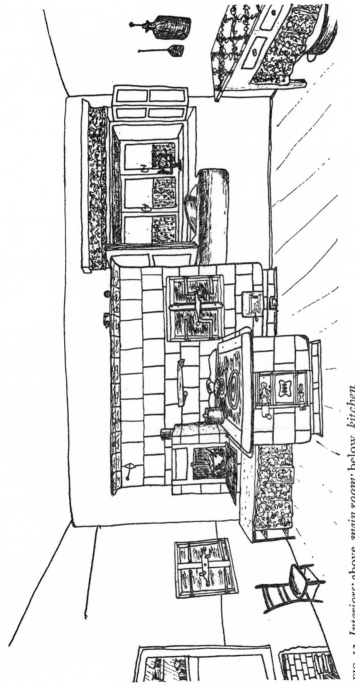

FIG. 12. Interiors: above, *main room*; below, *kitchen*

field workers. A former miller remarked, "It would be all right, if one could work enough." A wife complained that she worked from four in the morning until midnight and that women must work as hard as men. Villagers often apologized for the ill repair of their houses; the plaster was frequently loose or had fallen off, revealing the stones beneath. "If we had more money and time, we would whitewash," they explained. In 1965 few peasants felt that they could afford fertilizer, machinery, or other agricultural equipment. Many said that the only food in sufficient supply was the potato, although all believed that they were better fed than formerly, when even bread was a luxury.

Yet in 1965 there was evidence of a measure of economic progress in the village (and by 1969 there were significant improvements). Almost all families owned radios in 1965, for which they paid 500 dinars a month in taxes. Many families had bicycles, although the price equaled one month's factory wage. Some twelve families owned *mopeds* (bicycles with auxiliary motors) that cost from four to six months' wages apiece; and one owned a motorcycle. Some families belonging to the small group of the new elite had modernized their houses by 1965. Three had installed plumbing, two had purchased refrigerators, and one owned a television set. Some had adopted new styles of clothing. Men had abandoned the old straw hat, boots, and worn work pants for sport shirts, tailored trousers or blue jeans, and leather shoes. Some village women who had found jobs in the new administration wore urban styles rather than the traditional kerchiefs, dark printed cotton dress, aprons, felt slippers or boots, and heavy work stockings.

It is difficult to arrive at an approximation of peasant income, since very few *gospodars* were willing to give estimates. Often they blamed their inability to suggest a figure on the changes in tax levies. Others said that they never kept budgets. Some indicated that they must spend more than they earn, that the prices in the stores were rising, and that they obtained cash where they could, but that prices for young pigs and other village products were falling. One leading quarter-*zemljak*, who sends a member of his family to the factory for intervals when necessary, reported that he had been forced to sell one calf and two small pigs as well as some potatoes and lumber every year. He guessed that in 1965 the average peasant needed, and might obtain with luck, 400,000 dinars in cash for the year, of which he estimated one-third went to taxes. This did not include income from factory wages.

In 1965 there was a rise over 1964 in the purchase of durable goods in the village, and this process was accelerated in the years between 1965 and 1969. One of the motivations for purchasing refrigerators and bicycles, and investing in home improvements was fear of inflation and dinar devaluation, which did, in fact, occur. Some villagers feared that all dinar bills would be recalled and stamped with a value one-third below the original. Clearly, the peasant paid more for the products he bought in 1965, yet most said that their income did not improve correspondingly. Although factory wages rose, the market for village products fell. Thus, in 1965 the peasant was caught in the squeeze between inflationary pressures, from which he profited little, and his limited income. Still other problems within the peasant economy were the fundamental ones of debt, credit, and taxation.

It has always been a matter of pride in the village to avoid debt and to pay cash for all purchases. One villager, remarking, "We are tough peasants and would rather suffer than borrow," said that he had never resorted to borrowing for the rebuilding of his house but had paid for the job step by step; one year he bought bricks; the next year roof tiles; and the next year he planned to replace the straw roof on his barn. An urban daughter from Ljubljana, overhearing this conversation, added that in the city people buy on credit but that one must have a guarantor, at which the *gospodar* commented, "It is dangerous to be a guarantor. So dangerous that we say even a brother won't be a guarantor for a brother." Another almost landless, longtime factory worker boasted that he had installed a modern plumbing system in his house and tiled his kitchen, all with cash he saved or obtained by illegally selling his wood.

While the landowning peasant needs low-interest credit, little is available to him. Brest has offered credit only to long-employed factory workers, and although some said that the co-operative would grant credit, few were sure about this. One member of the new elite having close connections to the co-operative reported that horse-drawn mowers could be purchased from the co-operative with payments extending over one to three years, at 6 per cent interest. Co-operative officials themselves said that they were not equipped to offer the peasant credit at low rates, and there seemed to be no instance of a peasant being granted credit by this institution.

It was difficult to ascertain the degree of indebtedness in the village. The poorest peasants, who cannot work their land, can no longer turn to the usurer but eventually abandon their land to Marof and shift, if possible, to other occupations that were not available in the prewar years. The overwhelming problem, however, with which the peasant has few weapons to cope, is heavy and unpredictable taxation.

Officials said that each *občina* had the right to set the tax class of the land in its area, the classes ranging, at that time, from class one, taxed at the highest rate, to class four, taxed at the lowest or not at all. Criteria for classification were said to include proximity to state markets, transportation facilities, and configuration and productivity of the land. Žerovnica land was placed in class two in 1964, but was changed to class three in 1965. According to information from officials in 1964, peasant taxes were equivalent to 60 per cent of what was determined as the theoretical income of the land.[7] The officials estimated that a well-off peasant would pay from 200,000 to 250,000 dinars a year, which is not high, they explained, when compared with taxes of the western European peasant; if it seems high it is only because the productivity of the land is low.

An informed quarter-*zemljak* asserted that land taxes were actually closer to 75 per cent of the theoretical income established by the government for each category of field or meadow. In 1965 this *gospodar* paid a land tax of 125,000 dinars, based on a theoretical income of 164,000 dinars from his land. In addition, he paid special taxes on cattle and on other possessions: 2,500 dinars on his oxen; 1,000 dinars on a cart; 300 dinars on a dog; 15,000 dinars on his house; 27,000 dinars on cut wood—a total personal property tax of 45,800 dinars. Added to his land tax, this made a total tax of 170,800 dinars. Taxes are distributed, he believed, to the state and to the *občina*, and 20 per cent is allocated to health insurance, the only social security provision for which the peasant qualifies. (Villagers complain that health insurance pays only for about a half of hospital expenses.)

Although many villagers hesitated to reveal tax figures, some did divulge partial information, and seven besides the *gospodar* mentioned above provided relatively complete information for 1965. Two half-*zemljaks* reported taxes of 200,000 and 210,000 dinars a year, and five quarter-*zemljak*s reported taxes of 173,800, 160,000, 150,000, and two instances of 120,000 dinars. One landowner with considerably less than a quarter *zemlja* declared that his taxes amounted to 96,000 dinars.

Since, as one *gospodar* explained, the peasant is taxed on his theoretical income, rather than his real income, he must sell cattle, pigs, and wood for taxes. For nonpayment the government can confiscate a peasant's possessions, but this has never happened in Žerovnica, although villagers said that the government did seize an animal from a peasant in a neighboring village. Furthermore, the government branded the cow of one well-off quarter-*zemljak* in Žerovnica, identifying it as government property until that peasant paid his taxes.

The unanimous opinion in the village was that taxes were excessive. When asked, in 1965, how they would compare the old days with the new, at least twelve villagers spontaneously pointed to high taxes. Typical comments were: "The peasant works only for taxes"; "They kill you with taxes"; and "Today taxes are a hundred times higher than in prewar days." Several villagers admitted that they were in default of payment. One *gospodar* remarked, "What will come, will come. I have not paid this year." Another said he was 80,000 dinars in debt because of taxes. A half-*zemljak* complained that because he had a little more land, he had to pay higher taxes and thus was forced to sell more and more wood, cattle, and pigs. Another half-*zemljak* declared that, although he owned enough land and no one in his family needed to work in the factory, he could not secure sufficient cash to pay his taxes. A well-off quarter-*zemljak* stated that he wanted to buy some sheet metal for a hay-blower, since he owned a motor, but he would not have enough to do so if he paid his taxes. Many compared the peasant with the factory worker, whose taxes are lower. Although a peasant's land taxes pay for medical insurance, villagers resent the fact that peasants are excluded from retirement pay. One member of the new elite, a government worker, remarked that while he paid low taxes and was eligible for social security, his old father, a formerly landless peasant who now owned a few hectares, was burdened with heavy property taxes. He concluded that the full-time peasant will never be free of debt.

Taxes are collected four times a year, in February, May, August, and November. The unwelcome tax collector leaves a written bill, and the peasant pays by mail. The relation of the government official to the peasant was revealed in an incident that occurred as we sat in front of a village house talking to the elderly brother of a half-*zemljak gospodar* (this family, which has participated in the Marof administration, rates as among the new elite). We were interrupted by the arrival of a sportily dressed young man in city clothes who, holding a paper in his hand, approached the village elder and shouted brusquely, "Are you the *gospodar?*" The usual village politeness and restraint was replaced by a short "No!—in there," and the elder pointed toward the house. Nevertheless, the tax collector thrust the paper into his hand, saying, "Here, he owes something, go tell him!" The villager responded, "Go in and tell him yourself!" which the official did.

Few peasants offered explanations for the high taxes, but two villagers, one a quarter-*zemljak* and one a member of the new elite, said that they believed peasants were heavily taxed in order to force them to cede their land to the co-operative.

In 1969 most villagers stated that the period since 1965 had been one of improvement in spite of the fears they had frequently expressed in 1965. This was true even though there were no significant changes in official regulations, nor any increase in social security, technological aid, or tax relief. On the contrary, villagers reported that they were burdened with ever heavier taxes. Although village land was reclassified as in the fourth category in 1966, in 1968 taxes on land were raised. One villager stated that before 1968 a fifth land category was established that at first had not been taxed but that now was taxed at 5 per cent; and while the fourth category had formerly been taxed at 10 per cent, now it was taxed at 20 per cent. This step was taken by the *občina*, villagers believed, to compensate for local deficits. Villagers also stated that health insurance was less comprehensive than formerly and that prospects for retirement insurance had not improved. One *gospodar* concluded that social insurance for farmers was less adequate than ever: "I've heard it will be better for our children," he concluded, "but I doubt it." Taxes on wood were said to have increased ever since the sale of wood had begun after the storm of 1965. Most agreed that if peasants defaulted on tax payments, they were not prosecuted, although they sacrificed health insurance.

In 1969 villagers continued to face high taxes and inflationary prices, while the prices for peasant products remained low. Villagers said prices for cattle were depressed because of difficulties in the export market. Milk was sold only locally, and prices had not risen. Only the market for young pigs was subject to greater fluctuations, since channels remained private. In 1969, 150 new dinars was considered a good price for a pig. A village elder concluded that all prices had risen except those paid to the peasant, and he had to sell at low prices because Yugoslavia must compete for international prices for cattle.

Nevertheless, villagers believed that income derived from factory wages and sale of wood had improved their position as compared with four years earlier. They were proud that no one had been forced to sell land. The only exception, they said, was a woman eighty years old who lived on the hill. Because her son had died, and her other children had left for the factory, she sold her forest land to the richest miller and her farmland to a quarter-*zemljak* in the village. Otherwise, not one piece of land in the village had been sold. The sole absentee owner in the village, a half-*zemljak* who spent thirty years in Australia, refused to sell his land although many villagers wanted to buy it. A young village leader concluded, "This village does not sell! You can buy land in Grahovo, but if you want to buy one are of land around here you can't get it!"

An indication of better times in 1969 was the increase in technological products, including motorized mowers, new wagons, washing machines, and refrigerators, as well as five television sets and one additional automobile, a Volkswagen. Moreover, food was considered better. Stores were more plentifully supplied. Houses were in somewhat better repair. All agreed that without the factory, life would be difficult, but they believed that as long as the factory maintained its exports and did not decrease peasant employment, peasant life in Žerovnica could continue. The most enthusiastic views were voiced by members of the new elite. Thus a former member of the cottager class, who had been a partisan, had worked long enough in the government administration to retire. Now he lived on his retirement insurance and cultivated his few fields. "Everything is better now," he commented. "We have progress, peace, and freedom."

In spite of these more optimistic views and the general increase in morale caused by the introduction of a limited degree of mechanization, peasant landowners continue to struggle against heavy odds. The time-consuming chore of manuring and cultivating dispersed strips with an ox-drawn plow remains, and the shortage of field workers becomes ever more acute. A half-*zemljak* could not stop to talk to a visitor on a Sunday afternoon because the structure supporting his manure pile had broken. There was no one to help him, so he worked alone all Sunday. Another half-*zemljak* reported that because all his sons but one, who was ill, had left the village, he was severely burdened with overwork. Finally, there is the plight of aged peasants left without helpers to cultivate their land. "I am all alone," said the eldest miller. "My wife died three years ago. I would be better off dead. I wait only for Him. I am seventy-seven years old. Once I had twelve head of cattle. Now I have nothing. Some people have. Some people don't. The peasants in Yugoslavia have nothing."

The official view in 1969 was expressed in the remarks of a leading official of the co-operative farm. The peasant was not better off, he said. It was true that for a few years after the economic reforms, from 1965 to 1967, the standard of living for the peasant had improved. But in 1967 the situation stabilized, and since then had become worse because, he explained, the peasant increasingly felt the inflationary squeeze. The peasant was a victim of the market, he emphasized, for while prices generally were going up, the price of peasant products remained the same. Thus the dilemma remained unresolved, although some of its conditions had been altered and although some attempt at further reforms (discussed in chapter 11) had been made.

# 7

## Local Government and the State

### Prewar Žerovnica

The post-1848 village exercised a measure of local autonomy through an elected village council, which controlled local affairs. The council consisted of the village head (*podžupan*) and two other members, elected every three years. The carefully kept records of the Žerovnica village council begin in 1861 and continue until 1945. The first entry describes the construction of a road to the castle of Šteberk. Peasants with forests or fields in the Šteberk area were required to contribute six cartfuls of rocks, and others contributed three cartfuls. A decision is recorded in 1875 to fine individuals guilty of cutting wood in another's forest or harming another's field. In 1911, the records show, villagers went to court in Cerknica seeking legal aid to prevent landowners from driving Žerovnica cattle out of the lake pastures, and the village won its case.

These and other entries give some indication of the functions of the village council. In the spring there were always road repairs, and decisions had to be made concerning their financing, which required cutting and selling wood. Before the common pasture was divided, each peasant who had fields bordering on it was responsible for keeping his section of the fence in repair. On Sundays the village head inspected the fence to see that this obligation had been discharged. It was also his duty to collect taxes from those who sold cattle at the market and to designate market days. The village council also undertook various projects for village improvement. For example, it worked to introduce electricity and decided how the village was to finance this improvement, which was achieved just before the last war. At village meetings individuals were appointed to various posts, including those of herdsman, churchwarden, treasurer, and night watchman. The watchman patrolled the village, calling the hours and watching for fire and theft. The former village head believes that crime was never a problem in Žerovnica. Minor disputes concerning transgressions on others' property were heard by the village council and settled by the payment of fines. The village council also made arrangements for provisions to be donated to any destitute individuals within the village. Thus the regulation of day-to-day village life, social control, and even, to a limited degree, social welfare were a local village matter.

In the traditional administrative hierarchy the village council was subordinate to the *občina* council, which met in the administrative center of Cerknica. The *občina* council was composed of an elected head (*župan*) and delegates from the villages in the *občina*. The *občina*, which was considerably smaller than it is today, was in turn subordinate to the district, which also was smaller than districts today.

Villagers recall voting in national elections. The two main political parties in the village were the Liberal and the Clerical parties, but there were also some Peasant party members and a few Communists and Socialists. The patronage of the two village inns reflected strongly felt political divisions. One inn was a meeting place for Liberals and the other for Clericals, and villagers recall clashes and fistfights between members of different parties after a few drinks at the rival inns.

## The Developing Communal System

In the new Federal People's Republic of Yugoslavia, Slovenia became one of the six federated republics, each with a government of its own, although in fact power was based in the central government in Belgrade. Under the new, Communist administration the relation of the village to larger units in the political hierarchy underwent successive changes as the economic, political, and social institutions of the *občina*, the republic, and the federation impinged more and more directly on village life. In the early postwar period, before the reforms of the fifties again altered the relation of the village to larger institutions, local government was subjected to a strictly hierarchical organization. Elected people's committees (*narodni odbor*), the local governmental bodies, had only the powers granted to them by the federal government and were dominated by executive committees controlled by the party organization.[1] Although local voters' meetings, of all voting citizens, nominated the candidates for the people's committees, in most respects these meetings were only formal.[2] Few functions were left to traditional local governmental institutions within the villages, and the new compulsory delivery quotas and collectivization measures were imposed entirely from without.

In 1948 Yugoslavia broke with the Cominform and began to abandon the principle of centralism for that of regional autonomy. New institutions were designed to create a new kind of socialism based on decentralization and popular participation in public affairs at all levels.[3] In 1949 a series of laws and constitutional changes was initiated that eventually altered fundamentally the structure of local government. In that year the people's committees were given more authority; in 1951 the executive committees were abolished; and in 1952 the people's committees were given additional political and economic power. This trend culminated in the Constitutional Law of 1953, which gave to the people's committees (which then existed at the district, *občina*, and city levels) all authority not specifically reserved to the federal and republican governments. The people's committees then became "full-fledged local governments."[4]

During these years some unpopular policies were abandoned and economic enterprises were democratized. In 1950 legislation provided for the establishment of workers' councils in state enterprises; in 1951 the system of compulsory delivery of agricultural products was abolished; and in 1953 forcible collectivization was abandoned, and measures were undertaken to democratize the agricultural co-operatives by introducing forms similar to the workers' councils.[5]

The enactment of the Law on Organization of Communes and Districts of 1955 instituted the communal system. Since that time the terms *občina* and *commune* have been used to refer to the same territorial unit. However, while the term *občina* designated an administrative unit in prewar and early postwar Yugoslavia, according to Yugoslav scholars, *commune* implies a socioeconomic community as well: "It designates the socio-economic structure of basic local communities (communes and districts, the latter being groups of communes). The commune is the fundamental cell of the future socialist society . . . within which new socialist social relationships are being established on the basis of social ownership of means of production and, in rural areas, on different forms of socialization or co-operation and limitation of individual ownership of land among peasants."[6]

In the 1955 law the *občina*, or commune, was conceived as the basic political unit. The district was no longer to be a higher administrative unit but simply an association of theoretically independent communes.[7] One of the most important processes initiated by the law was a reduction in the number of local units through consolidation. The structure produced by the 1955 law reduced 4,519 separate administrative units to 1,479 *občina*s and 107 districts.[8] By 1 January 1963 there were only 40 districts and 581 *občina*s in Yugoslavia. Slovenia then had 66 *občina*s and 4 districts.[9]

Since the individual in the enlarged *občina* was remote from the center of power, other forms of local government were encouraged. Local or village committees were set up within the new *občina*s, composed of from five to nine members, some drawn from the people's committees elected in the *občina*, and a specific number elected at voters' meetings. These committees, like earlier forms of local village government, dealt with such matters as street repairs, electricity, and the upkeep of markets, cemeteries, and schools. They also could propose adoption of measures to the communal (i.e., *občina*) people's committee, which would decide whether to appropriate funds for the projects suggested and could "annul or abrogate any action which is unlawful or merely unjustified or irregular. The people's committee must provide the moneys required for the work of the local committees out of the communal budget."[10]

The voters' meetings, another instrument of local government, instituted after the war, increased in importance after the reforms of the early fifties. Composed of all voting citizens in small villages or urban centers, their functions were to discuss the work of the people's committees, make recommendations to the people's committees concerning policy, and nominate candidates for election to these committees, and to the republican and federal assemblies.[11] However, while the voters' meeting could make proposals, it had no power to enforce its views.[12]

A major innovation of this period was the introduction of worker representation in various levels of the government through the institution of councils of producers. After the adoption of the 1953 constitution (and until 1963, when the system was altered again) all representative bodies—from the people's committees of the commune and the district to the assemblies of the republics and the federation—were composed of two chambers: a council composed of delegates elected by the total voting population and a council of producers composed of delegates elected by workers in industry, commerce, and the crafts, and by peasants who were members of agricultural co-operatives.[13] Under this system full-time private peasants could not vote for members of the councils of producers. Furthermore, the number of deputies from agriculture depended on their " 'total social product,' based on somewhat arbitrary official price lists [which] tended to under-value agriculture's contribution and thus to reduce the number of deputies from agriculture on councils of producers." In 1954 in the Republic of Slovenia the council of producers had twenty-three representatives from industry and only two from agriculture.[14]

The reforms and developments of the fifties led to the April 1963 constitution of the Socialist Federal Republic of Yugoslavia. The constitution articulates many principles that had already been established by law, but it also makes certain important changes. It gives a far more detailed definition of the commune, using the term *občina* in the senses formerly implied by both *commune* and *občina*. The name *people's committee*, given to the governing bodies of the commune, or *občina*, and the district, is abandoned for the term *assembly* (*skupčina*). The governing body of the *občina* becomes the communal assembly (*občinska skupščina*), and that of the district, the district assembly. It was felt that the term *assembly*, which had previously been used only for the governing bodies of the republics and the federation, would suggest the broader self-governing role of the communal body.[15] The constitution eliminates the councils of producers. In the communal assembly this council is replaced by a chamber of working communities, in which there is wider and fairer representation, since the number of deputies is based solely on producer population and is not related to "social output."[16] However, only peasants who work in an agricultural co-operative may vote for members of this chamber, so discrimination against peasants, while lessened, is not eliminated.[17] The other chamber of the communal assembly continues to be elected directly by all citizens.[18] The members of the communal assemblies elect members of district, republic, and federal assemblies from lists nominated at voters' meetings. Some members of the Federal Assembly are elected both by communal assemblies and by electors in constituencies.[19]

The greatly increasing political autonomy of the communes in the years after 1950 is reflected in article 73 of the 1963 constitution, which states that "self-government by the citizens in the commune is the political foundation of the uniform social-political system."[20] However, the accompanying evolution of economic independence for the communes was more complicated. Under the laws of 1952 and 1953, the people's committees had been given wide economic powers. In the decentralized economic system they were "the basic units in formation of the economic plan and the chief initiators of new enterprises. Since there were no limits on the authority of the people's committee to tax enterprises, once federal and republic obligations were met, the local units were financially autonomous." After 1955, while the communes continued to be thought of as financially autonomous, their right to impose unlimited taxes on the income of economic enterprises was curtailed, but in 1959 a law was passed increasing their taxing power.[21]

According to Fisher's recent study, the predominant philosophy during the period from 1956 to 1963 was that "each commune had the right, in theory, to expect a living standard comparable with the most advanced areas of the country."[22] The trend was to encourage the commune to work out its own development plans within the framework of the policies of the federal government.[23] In carrying out their tasks of self-government, as outlined in the constitution of 1963, "the communes independently pass their own laws, create their annual plan . . . and budget, and set specific sums aside for various special funds." Moreover, the commune "independently establishes and distributes its own income. Communes with insufficient means for their tasks . . . are guaranteed additional funds from republican and federal sources."[24]

Since 1963 it has become apparent that the effort to establish economic independence and economic equality among the communes has generated new problems. As Fisher has pointed out, the commune, averaging 135.9 square miles and 15,000 people in 1961, frequently proved to be too small a unit for effective planning.[25] Investment funds tended to become "compartmentalized" in the hands of local administrative and political bodies, and it was possible for communal taxes to increase communal resources at the expense of local enterprises.[26] Intercommunal economic projects and rational economic integration had not proceeded efficiently enough. Since 1963 the view has increasingly been adopted that "each republic or commune should develop its economy in accordance with existing natural, financial, and local resources with only moderate and reasonable support from external (federal and republic) institutions."[27] Federal legislation in 1964 again reduced the communes' taxation of factories and thus gave factories greater freedom in working out their own economic plans. As a result, Fisher concludes, "commercial and industrial enterprises make their own investment decisions, while local (communal) administration is expected to improve the over-all climate and attractiveness of the area for business expansion. Communal investment is limited to noneconomic or social overhead items such as roads, schools and utilities."[28]

The role of the peasant within the evolving communal political and economic system is ambiguous. While the peasant sector of Yugoslav society remains large and of fundamental economic importance, there is little discussion concerning the contribution of the peasantry to the new system. Yet 90 per cent of the agricultural area of Yugoslavia is privately owned.[29] In 1965 peasants represented slightly over half the total population of Yugoslavia.[30] While many of this group are peasant-workers (in 1960 peasant-workers represented 45 per cent of the total labor force of the socialized sector[31]) it is not clear that they identify their interest with the enterprise in which they are employed. Thus Fisher notes that typically "peasant-workers remain a group apart from other workers and only seldom do they participate in the 'political process,' in 'management' of the factory through the workers' councils."[32] The question remains, How does the peasant, as peasant, participate in the new self-governing communes, the most significant units in Yugoslav society? Indeed, while the strengthening of the *občina* means an increase in local autonomy from the national and urban point of view, for peasant villages it has meant a loss of their traditional, although limited, political autonomy. The commune exercises total discretion in taxing the income, land, and other possessions of the peasant. Even the agricultural co-operative, which once evinced some interest in joint ventures with the peasant, now must think of its own economic survival, since no longer is the commune directly responsible for the economic development of the enterprises within its area. Finally, the peasant does not participate equally in the electoral process, for, unless he is employed by one of the socialized enterprises, he cannot vote for the chamber of working communities of the communal assembly.

## Postwar Žerovnica

During the early postwar years village political life was disrupted by the attempts of the state to collectivize and to impose compulsory delivery quotas on agricultural producers. After 1953, when villagers began to return to their traditional ways, they were still forced to sell most of their produce to state-run co-operatives, and it appeared that the village had irrevocably lost many of its former functions. Just what has happened to village political life during the postwar years is difficult to ascertain, for while villagers are well informed about the prewar village government, only a few can explain the many changes since the war. Few knew the names of delegates to village or *občina* committees or assemblies, and few were interested in attending village meetings. "We are no longer interested in village affairs," said one leading half-*zemljak*, "because it is all decided in the *občina* anyway, and our delegate can only say yes, yes, and nod his head, or out he would go." A well-off quarter-*zemljak* said he believed that there was some kind of elected village government but he was not interested in it because it could not do anything. A poorer quarter-*zemljak* said that he had been village head for six months immediately after the war but that he did not understand anything about the postwar village administration. While he thought there was a village council, he was not sure. There was one before the war, he said, but it was arranged otherwise now.

From reports of the few *gospodars* who had been active in village administration since the war it was possible to reconstruct the story of village political life. It was clear that the old prestige awarded those active in village affairs had disappeared. The delegates themselves expressed little faith in their own effectiveness.

Toward the end of the war the former village head was re-elected, but after a few months he resigned, for reasons of health, he said. For several years the person occupying the position of village head, still referred to as the *podžupan*, changed frequently.

At some time during the postwar period the village government became known as the regional or village committee (*krajevni* or *vaški odbor*). After 1955, under a strengthened and enlarged *občina*, the village committee was regularly elected and was composed of five members including a chairman and a treasurer. It also included the delegate to the *občina*, who was elected jointly by the inhabitants of Žerovnica, Lipsenj, and a few nearby villages and who attended the monthly meetings of the *občina* council. At first, village meetings were held approximately six times a year in the largest house, in the fire house, or sometimes outdoors near the *balina* field. The *občina* representative chaired the meetings, explained the latest views of the *občina*, and led discussions concerning village affairs such as forestry regulations, road repair, the construction of a water pipeline, and a projected general store. All adult villagers were invited in a written announcement passed from house to house. However, in 1964 villagers thought that at best one member of each house attended. Meetings had become less frequent, they said. A *gospodar* who had served as a representative to the *občina* in recent years commented, "Not everyone attends village meetings—earlier more went—now less go. Development goes by its own ways." Others agreed that the village committee lacked the power to carry out its wishes. Perhaps its last accomplishment of great interest to the villagers was the laying of the water pipeline from Grahovo in 1963, paid for by the contribution of a set amount of wood from each family that could afford to help.

Since 1965, in line with the provisions of the new constitution and new legislation, village committees have been replaced by larger administrative units. The six villages of the local school district (Grahovo, Martinjak, Bločice, Bloška Polica, Lipsenj, and Žerovnica), have been grouped into a new unit, which is administered by a regional community (*krajevna skupnost*) based in Grahovo. The regional community is composed of a chairman from Grahovo and one or two elected representatives from each village. To this body are delegated local functions formerly reserved to the village committees. A representative of the village government, asked whether he approved of the consolidation, answered, "Yes and no—it is good for the *občina*, but it is not good for the village. Everyone pays taxes to the *občina*, and now the *občina* can unite funds from several villages for larger projects for one village." And he added that he feared this might cause conflicts between villages.

Village meetings still take place, but their functions are limited, and local village government in the traditional sense no longer exists. There is no village head responsible for the welfare of the village community, nor is there a local law-enforcement officer to replace the former village watchman. Villagers say that illegal acts do not occur in Žerovnica. However, it is the custom to lock doors of houses and tool sheds when families depart for the fields, and to close the gates to the front gardens. "It's just our habit," villagers remarked. Minor disputes over boundary lines are the most frequent cause of conflict between families, but they are easily settled. On the other hand, disputes within families over land inheritance may become serious enough to result in legal action. While these disputes are rarely mentioned, we knew of two court cases between brothers, one of which had been settled only shortly before our stay in the village.

The Cerknica *občina* has been greatly enlarged since 1937. In that year the area of the *občina* was 7,089 hectares, and the population was 3,558, living in eleven villages. In 1954 the Cerknica *občina* had expanded to an area of 8,187 hectares, with 3,459 inhabitants, and it included three additional villages. Since 1961 the *občina* of Cerknica has included 48,215 hectares and 14,230 inhabitants, living in the villages of five former *občinas* and some of a sixth.[33]

Žerovnica elects one delegate to the *občina*. He attends the meetings in Cerknica of the *občina* assembly, where he may discuss new village needs and such problems as the relationship of the peasants to the *občina*. The present representative is also a member of the *občina*'s Council on Internal Affairs (*Svet za notranjske zadeve*), concerned with such matters as traffic, fire, and safety. In 1965 he was paid 700 dinars a meeting for transportation.

Villagers pointed out that the *občina* is poor. It has no large industries or mines, but only a factory for plastics at Lož and the Brest furniture plants at Martinjak and Cerknica. Its population consists primarily of peasants. Yet its administrators, who are increasingly responsible for decisions relating to village life, are detached from the peasant view. "Our landholdings are so small here," remarked a leading official, "that peasants work in the factory and then return home in the afternoon to use their little plots as recreation."

The *občina* of Cerknica forms a part of the district (*kraj*) of Ljubljana, which is administered by a regional legislature, or district assembly (*okrajinska skupčina*), the members of which are elected by the *občina* assemblies within the district. Over the regional legislature is the Assembly of the Republic of Slovenia (*republiška skupčina*), and over it, the Federal Assembly (*zvezna skupčina*) in Belgrade, some members of which are popularly elected. A politically active *gospodar* said that candidates travel throughout the republic and speak in Cerknica. "Everyone votes," he commented. "It's our duty, but no one has to vote." However, when asked if villagers were interested in politics, he answered, "No—peasants think only of work."

In 1965 national political organizations represented in the village included the Fighters Union (Zvezek Borcev), a partisan organization that had, it was said, five local members, and the Socialist Union of the Working People, to which perhaps one member per household belonged. However, the effect of the latter organization on village life did not appear to be significant. The state continues to exert, as it always has, its military authority, and in 1965 every young man was required to serve eighteen months in the armed forces.

There are ten state holidays: New Year's Day (two days), 1 May (two days), 9 May (Victory Day), 4 July (Partisans Day), 22 July (Liberation Day), 1 November (Memorial Day), and two days toward the end of November celebrating Constitution Day. But these holidays are poorly observed by peasants, who feel that they are not sufficient cause for halting work in the fields. For example, in 1965, Partisans Day (Den Borca), which memorializes events in the memory of most villagers, was recognized by the placing of a flag over the partisan monument in Žerovnica. At eight in the morning no other signs of celebration in the village could be seen. Peasants were working in the fields, and women were washing clothes in the river. However, since Partisans Day is also Homecoming Day (all factories are closed), there was evidence of preparation for visitors, and city people began to arrive, noticeable for their automobiles and urban clothes. At nine o'clock marchers in a partisan parade, including one villager, arrived by bus in Grahovo, and they marched through the village to the music of an accordion. Barely noticed by the villagers of Grahovo, the paraders did not turn off on the road to Žerovnica, and after the march they were picked up by the bus, which continued along the main road. In the larger urban center of Cerknica flags were out, a small band played, and a wreath was laid at the partisan monument. But only a small and apathetic group watched. In the evening, however, a district-wide picnic in the woods was well attended by young people, mostly factory workers, who arrived on motorcycles and motor bikes.

# 8

## Social Aspects of Village Life

### Family Relationships

Much that will be said in this chapter about family relations in the postwar village is implied by observations in the preceding chapters relating to changes in the family structure and the ever greater impingement of the outside world on the family. The traditional large and extended family gradually declined until, by 1965, four of the fifty-five households in Žerovnica were reduced to one generation and only nineteen were still composed of three generations. The preponderance of two-generation over three-generation households is greatest among the poor families. Thus in 1965 the landless or nearly landless villagers who depended on outside employment (eighteen families in all) included only two families with three generations in the household; of the quarter-*zemljak* families with no outside employment (twelve in all), only three were three-generation households. Few families still included collateral relatives of the *gospodar*, and the average number of children in a household was small.

The decline in the number of generations as well as in the number of children has weakened the family both as an economic unit and as a social unit. No longer can it send members to outside employment and at the same time have sufficient numbers at home to work the land without the aid of mechanization. No longer is it effectively controlled by patriarchal authority and a qualified form of primogeniture.

Traditional tensions between brothers, growing out of the resentment of the disinherited and competition over land, still affect the relations between numerous households in the village. In 1965 there were four cases in which a brother of the inheriting *gospodar* was also a *gospodar* in Žerovnica. Severe hostility in one case was revealed by the frank remarks of the disinherited brother. In the three other cases relations clearly were strained; the brothers rarely mentioned each other, and when asked about their relatives in the village, their remarks concerning their brothers were abrupt and brief. In a fifth case two brothers who maintained separate households in the village were both without land, since it had been surrendered to the co-operative by their widowed mother. Relations between them appeared friendly. However, the elder was reclaiming the land for himself. In addition to the five pairs of brothers there was a pair of disputants consisting of an aged *gospodar* who was the inheriting, though younger, son and the widow of his disinherited brother. The two occupied houses next to each other. While the widow inherited village land herself, an earlier court dispute over her husband's right to acquire a portion of the land that had been bequeathed to the younger brother had caused relations between these houses to be ruptured completely. Although the houses stand within a few feet of each other, there was no communication between them. Finally, in a seventh case, one *gospodar*, a large landowner, died without leaving a will and thus laid the basis for a family feud. The younger son, disinherited in the settlement, contested the decision and succeeded in winning some land. As a result, the elder son severed relations with his brother, who moved just outside of the boundaries of Žerovnica but maintained his newly gained land in the village.

In relations between the younger generation of brothers, however, competition for land ownership is no longer the dominant theme. The eldest son may decide that he prefers to leave the land for the factory or pursue another occupation. Frequently a son who inherits and remains at home may resent what he considers to be the more privileged position of his brother, who can receive more training at school and who may become a skilled worker or perhaps even follow a profession.

The *gospodar* today fears that he may be deserted by all his children, and, indeed, in 1965 there were two village households where only the older generation was left. Sometimes one daughter will remain at home while the sons depart. The *gospodar* may then hope to gain a satisfactory son-in-law to carry on his homestead. One leading quarter-*zemljak* was confronted with such a situation when his only son and elder daughter forsook the village for the city, leaving the younger daughter at home. The latter married a man from a nearby village, and he moved into her household. Since the son-in-law wished to remain a peasant, the *gospodar* had a male successor; but he sadly observed that after his death, when his son-in-law became *gospodar*, a new surname would designate the family inheriting his homestead. The imminent conflict between the younger generation and the land-holding *gospodar*s is expressed by such pessimistic remarks from the elders as "Only those between forty and sixty want to stay on the land. The younger ones all want to study"; and "It looks bad. From 1948 to 1952 they pushed the peasant too hard, and the younger ones began to leave."

In order to illuminate this problem, in 1964 we asked landowning parents what plans they had for their children's future. Parents whose children were still small responded vaguely. However, all parents who were interviewed, whether their children were infants or approaching maturity, expressed fears concerning the future. Parents frequently emphasized their faith in professional training as offering the greatest security for their children, while unskilled factory labor was generally considered too vulnerable to economic crises.

According to the data gathered, in 1964 there were in the village thirty-six young people (twenty-two girls and fourteen boys), from twenty-three families, who were from fifteen to twenty years old. Of these, four were still completing the eighth grade, two girls were prevented by illness from pursuing further training, and only two boys (born in 1944 and 1947) were planning to remain peasants. Of the remaining twenty-eight, four were working in the factory, and twenty-four were being trained for special skills in the factory or elsewhere, or had recently completed this training and were beginning their careers. No one was attending a gymnasium for further academic work.

Among the boys, four were training in Cerknica or Ljubljana to become automobile mechanics, one was a bricklayer's apprentice in Cerknica, several were receiving training in various furniture production skills in Martinjak, and one had joined the administration at Marof. Among the girls, three were training in Cerknica or Ljubljana to become dental assistants, and three more were studying in Ljubljana, nursing, teaching, and agronomy, respectively. Three girls were training to be seamstresses in Cerknica, and two had gone to other villages to receive training as salesgirls in food stores. Of the young people who are pursuing, or have already completed, specialized training, approximately a third are from landless or nearly landless families having outside occupations, one-third from quarter-*zemljak* families, and one-third from half-*zemljak* families. Thus, land ownership does not seem to be a factor in the ability or willingness of the older generation to support the younger ones in their ambitions to attain skills beyond those of peasant or factory worker. Some young people receive financial aid for education from the *občina* or the factory, but most families must bear these expenses themselves. One family said that board, room, and tuition for their daughter, who is studying in Ljubljana, amounted to 11,000 dinars a month. Typically, the young person lives with a family and works while studying. Generally a sibling remaining at home contributes his or her factory wages to meet the educational expenses of the brother or sister.

In answer to the question, "Do you believe that one son will maintain your land?" thirteen landholders gave concrete answers. Only three believed that no child would stay at home to carry on the farm. Two of these held a quarter *zemlja* or less, and one held a half *zemlja*. The situation of the half-*zemljak* exemplifies the problems for families today. In 1964 this *gospodar* said that while his elder son was an automobile mechanic and his daughter was learning to be a seamstress, his younger son, who would shortly enter his teens, would remain on the land. "An auto mechanic and a seamstress will always be needed," he said, "but a factory worker can lose his job." A year later, however, he said that his younger son had decided that he also wanted to leave, to get advanced training. "It is difficult for peasants," his wife commented. "Their children go away and there is no one to help them." The elder son, present during the conversation, explained: "They [the government] changed their minds too late. We would have stayed if they had helped the peasant earlier with credits, fertilizers, and machinery."

One of the two quarter-*zemljak*s who believed their children would not remain peasants explained that his son was learning to be a locksmith and that each must choose what is best for him. He concluded, as did so many others, that no young person wanted to work the land.

Of the ten *gospodar*s who expressed confidence that one of their sons would remain and work the land, six were half-*zemljak*s and four were quarter-*zemljak*s. The ambivalence evoked by this question was shown in a conversation with one well-off quarter-*zemljak* who commands great respect. He said that his youngest son was preparing to be an automobile mechanic and his daughter to be an accountant, but that his eldest son, in his late teens, would remain a peasant. "Everyone wants his children to be educated," added the wife, "so that they have better bread than we, so that they do not suffer so much." The wife believed that only her family and two others in the village could boast that one son would stay at home helping his father to maintain the land. "All the rest will go away and study," she predicted. "But maybe some will return when the parents no longer can work. Farming is for old people." During this conversation, which covered many subjects, the inheriting son listened, but made no comment.

Another villager, a half-*zemljak*, said that his younger son and daughter would receive additional training after eight years of primary school in Grahovo, but that his older son would become a peasant. "He likes it," said the father defensively. "He prefers our twelve head of cattle to 25,000 dinars in the factory." (This claim exaggerated the *gospodar*'s cattle holding and understated factory salaries.) "We gave him his choice," the *gospodar* stated, and then added, "If our son did not stay on the land—what would we do?" Recalling the case of the *gospodar* who was forced to leave the village and give his land to the co-operative, he concluded, "With no sons remaining I would share a similar fate."

Another half-*zemljak*, whose sixteen-year-old son did not want to become a peasant, said that he hoped his other son, then four, would decide to remain on the land. Two widows who were left with a quarter *zemlja* expressed more emotional and less pragmatic aspects of the relation of the inheriting generation to the land. "I won't sell the land," said one, "because my son loves the land." Another said that before her husband died, he instructed her son (now a young man) to take care of his mother and above all not to sell the land. She confided that while she loves the land, her only son does not. Nevertheless, he had just given up a good job, although he would like to return to it. "Now," she said, "he is just a peasant." She concluded, "He will marry a girl from Žerovnica. Then she and I will farm, and perhaps my son can again combine his former position with cultivation." On another occasion her son said that during his mother's lifetime, at least, he would abide by the old tradition of his village, which says that when the father dies the family must not allow the land to go to pieces.

In the summer of 1969 the eighteen-year-old daughter of a half-*zemljak* reported that she had been waiting for one year for a factory job and thus had been forced to remain at home and work in the fields, although she would prefer to go away and work. Her older sister had been able to attend a special school for dental assistants because she was supported by her elder brother, who had worked in the factory. However, now he was in the army, so there was no one to pay for the younger girl's training. After his army service he would return, she predicted, and work half time in the factory and half on the land. A young man of eighteen, whose parents owned a quarter *zemlja*, complained in 1969 that all his friends had left the village, but that he was forced to remain at home, since a disability kept him from a factory job. But, he predicted, when parents get too old, the children will go back and take over the land. Either they will take turns or one child will return permanently.

It is clear that the fears of most elder *gospodar*s were greater than the situation warranted. In 1965 only two families were left entirely without help by the younger generation.[1] In other families the moral imperatives of the traditional society continued to bind at least one child to the homestead. However, one cannot predict how long this tradition will maintain itself. As the younger generation directs its aspirations outward from the village, the older generation can find a measure of comfort in identifying with the success of children who leave peasantry for careers in the new society. And, in fact, parents often boast of the achievements of an absent child, whereas boasting about oneself is always avoided. But the success of those who leave, if it consoles the elders, also threatens the peasant way of life.

Women are also affected, though perhaps not as directly, by changes in the traditional family structure. Women who marry into the village from outside are less apprehensive of a dominating mother-in-law than formerly. An older woman recalled that when she came to the village, she cleaned, fed the pigs, and milked the cows, while her mother-in-law cooked and took care of the children. "We understood each other quite well," she remarked. "I obeyed her, but when we didn't get along, well, it was not so good." At meals the wife still serves the family and only eats afterward. One woman joked, "When everything gets cold, the wife gets something too," and another added, "If anything is left for the wife."

In spite of the differences between generations, respect for elders is still strong. During discussions younger members of the family sometimes added contradictory information to remarks of the *gospodar*, but the *gospodar*'s views generally prevail; we never observed a son or daughter openly flouting the *gospodar*'s authority. Traditional respect is illustrated by forms of address, which are, however, undergoing some changes. According to tradition, members of the older generation are addressed by the polite second person plural pronoun, *vi*. When an elder is referred to in the third person, the verb must be in the third person plural. These rules are generally observed and are also followed by wives when referring to or addressing their husbands. Older wives may refer to or address their husbands by terms signifying father (*ata, oče*). In fact, all older people may be called father or uncle (*oče* or *stric*), which are understood as honorific terms.

Today, however, some younger people address their fathers or fathers-in-law with the intimate pronoun, *ti*, and use the second person singular of the verb. In one family the father asserted that the children always say *vi* to parents, but the daughter reminded her father that she employs *ti* when addressing him. One *gospodar*, commenting on the more frequent use of *ti* today, observed, "After all, the father is closest to you." He added, "It does not depend on whether you use *vi* or *ti*. It is a question of attitudes and relationships." One woman in her thirties reported that she asked the younger children to continue using *ti* after her marriage, although traditionally a married woman is addressed as *vi*, but that the children refused.[2]

## Social Activities

For as far back as can be traced Žerovnica has been linked structurally to the world outside, yet the early village exhibited a number of characteristics that have been ascribed to closed corporate peasant communities as described by Wolf.[3] Such traditional communities, which may once have been held together by kinship ties, tend to re-

strict membership to those born within the community and are frequently endogamous. Land, which may have been communal in the
past, is exploited by a traditional technology. It is scarce and is rarely
sold outside the community. Within the context of the poverty of the
community, class differences may exist, but they are limited by general disapproval of conspicuous consumption and by such leveling
mechanisms as periodic reallotment of land. Since such communities
are not fully self-sufficient, individuals must buy goods not produced
in the village; cash needed to meet levies from the outside such as taxation is gained from the sale in planned markets of products in which
the community specializes, from part-time wage labor, and by other
means.

There does not seem to be any evidence that land was redistributed
in earlier times in Žerovnica, but the early village community did
possess enough of the other characteristics to give it, to a certain degree, "the form of a corporation, an enduring organization of rights
and duties held by a stable membership."[4]

In societies that are corporate, peasants tend to form organizations
of a sort called by Wolf "polyadic, horizontal many-stranded coali-
tions." A many-stranded association is formed between persons who
share many interests; it is polyadic if it includes more than two persons or groups, and horizontal if it involves peasants with peasants,
rather than with superior outsiders.[5] In Žerovnica the firemen's association, created in the early twentieth century, is the only recent organization exhibiting these characteristics, although earlier organizations may have taken similar forms. The firemen's association united
many villagers, all peasants, in a voluntary association that became the
focus for various village-wide cultural and social activities. Its decline
in the modern period followed the fading of other traditional aspects
of village social life, including local government, village markets, the
enlarged family, and many associated characteristics.

The villagers of Žerovnica formed their own voluntary fire brigade
(*Prostovolno gasilno društvo*) because the nearest one, in Cerknica,
was too far away for village safety. Records were kept from its
founding in 1907 until 1957, although after World War II its activities
declined sharply. Grahovo considered joining and sent delegates to
the first meeting, but a chairman from Žerovnica was elected, so out-
raging the delegates from Grahovo that they withdrew. The villagers

from Žerovnica decided to raise enough money to purchase their own equipment; thirty Austrian kronen were to be contributed by each of the half-*zemljak*s, twenty kronen by each quarter-*zemljak*, and ten kronen by the smaller owners. In 1909 a horse-drawn fire pump and fire hose arrived and, in a celebration in which other villages participated, were tested against the equipment of Cerknica and Grahovo, and found superior. A committee was then elected to oversee the construction of a building to house the equipment. In 1910 the building, with the names of the brigade's first members engraved in the stone wall and covered with glass, was completed, and blessed by the priest in a village ceremony. The society held regular elections of officers, and members obtained uniforms and hats in which they paraded at Easter and other holidays. Its members—men, women, and young people—grew to nearly fifty and undertook the duty of fire watching for the whole area. The organization was affiliated with the national fire brigade organization of Slovenia and received awards for superior service.

The society began to organize dramatic productions, the first presented in 1926. A small admission was charged for performances in the firehouse attended by villagers from the area. Villagers from the Lož valley and Dolenje Jezero also offered productions in Žerovnica. In winter, members designed and built stage sets, made costumes, and studied scripts obtained from the school in Grahovo. Generally the plays dramatized local historical or legendary events or traditions, in which hunters, counts, or smugglers often figured. Performances were always occasions for a *veselica*, a celebration with food, drink, music, dancing, lotteries, and games. Just before the last war the society obtained a motorized pump. During the war the society was dissolved by the Italians, and in 1952 it reformed in a joint association with Grahovo. Until 1957 it continued to participate in dramatic performances in Grahovo and take part in *veselica*s.

Although fires are now rare and the village is no longer entirely responsible for fire control, the firemen's association has not dissolved. Nevertheless, the young people have lost interest in this society, and it therefore no longer gives plays. It was said in 1965, however, that the society still had thirty members, that meetings were sometimes held, and that occasionally a *veselica* was held to raise money to maintain the horse-drawn, motorized pump.

In 1969 a new village project was under way. The second floor of the firehouse had become the location for a social center that would replace the prewar inn. Village boys, who volunteered their services in the construction of the center, said that it would be equipped with a record player, Ping-Pong table, television set, radio, and chess set. The young people said that all would be welcome to use the center simply as a place in which to congregate and visit. It was being financed by the *občina*, the factory, and the village, through a regional lottery. One villager donated honey. Brest gave furniture, and a plastics factory gave prizes and money. The village also raised money from a large *veselica* celebrating the fiftieth year of the village since the formation of the Yugoslav nation.

The *veselica* once was a part of many social events in the village. Wedding celebrations, often at the inn, might extend over three days. Tables were laid outside, and a band from Cerknica, as well as Žerovnica musicians, provided music. Threshing was another occasion for celebration. Religious holidays and market days provided further opportunities for the always popular *veselica*. Although the form has declined in importance, the 1969 *veselica* celebrating the village's fiftieth anniversary within the Yugoslav nation was considered a great success. Street dancing and feasting lasted through the night. A week later, when we arrived in the village, many signs of decorations and outdoor stands were still visible.

Villagers recall that informal visiting used to be more frequent than it is now. Women and children would gather for the evening, and, sitting on the large tile stove, they would relate stories and talk over village events while they knitted, embroidered, or sewed. Men sometimes congregated in a small room over one of the sawmills and spent the evening visiting. Some of them were known as outstanding singers and tellers of tales.

Today such traditional social activities are less important than they once were. Rarely in our many visits to peasant houses were other visitors encountered. The most frequent social events are visits of urban relatives on Sundays and holidays, and on birthdays. On summer evenings villagers sometimes sit outside, but the tendency is to remain on the bench in front of one's own house, or perhaps to converse casually with one or two neighbors. A *gospodar* with a quarter *zemlja* reported, as did many others: "For us there is very little time to visit.

We don't go anywhere. Since there is no inn, people visit less. Sometimes on Sunday relatives visit for an hour or so. Before the war there were bigger families and more helpers, and we had more time."

The wife of a quarter-*zemljak* recalled friendlier days: "I used to sit on the stove and tell stories to the children and talk to neighboring women. Now there is the radio. There is not much visiting any more. In our house no one goes anywhere. My husband is busy all winter long." The wife of a half-*zemljak* agreed: "In my youth we used to sit on the stove with girls from the neighborhood. We would knit and embroider, and my father would sing. Now I have no time. I work as much in winter as in summer." One woman said that she rarely had time even to visit her sister, who also lived in Žerovnica, directly across the road from her.

Villagers maintain that one traditional social form, the *kolina*, is still followed. When a pig is slaughtered, a family distributes some of the meat to relatives and friends, an offering that is reciprocated when those who receive these gifts slaughter their own pigs. The preparation and cooking of the sausage and other meat is carried out alone by individual families, but the offering of food sometimes involves feasts to which friends are invited. More frequently, however, feasts are not a part of the *kolina*.

Although there has been a marked decline in the frequency of informal social activities in the village, the tradition of hospitality remains strong. Visitors are always asked to come into the house and to sit around the kitchen table, where refreshments are invariably served. Guests are strongly urged to eat, to remain longer, and to return. "We like to talk," is a frequent comment.

Furthermore, relatives maintain that they help each other when in trouble. A villager generally turns to a relative rather than to a neighbor for favors or to borrow. For example, one villager, whose cow was sick, ran short of milk, and her daughter went to the far end of the village each day to fetch milk from an aunt.

Groups of boys and girls rarely play together in the village. Boys and men play *balina*, but girls do not. At ten o'clock one Sunday morning nine teenage boys were playing *balina*, while younger boys watched. Women and girls were at home or at mass. The *balina* court is a rectangular dirt field measuring about three by nine meters, surrounded by a foot-high wooden enclosure. Each participant rolls a large wooden ball, attempting to hit a smaller ball, as well as the other large balls belonging to the other players.

Girls and boys attend movies shown several times a year at the Co-operative House in Grahovo, and after they have completed primary school, they may participate in dances that are sometimes held at the inn in Lipsenj. Generally, however, social life in the village is still family dominated. While small children play in groups, a school-age teen culture, which can be observed in the more urbanized factory villages nearby, is not yet visibly a part of Žerovnica social life.

# 9

## Religion

THE SLOVENES are Roman Catholic, as are their Croat neighbors. Inhabitants of the eastern part of present-day Yugoslavia belong to the Orthodox church, while many Yugoslavs in the south profess the religion of Islam, a heritage from the rule of the Ottoman Empire. Thus religion is one more force for diversity and national feeling in the heterogeneous group of peoples that make up the federal republic of Yugoslavia.

### Prewar Observances

In every Slovene village there is at least one church, usually standing on the highest ground. Wayside shrines and mountaintop churches and retreats punctuate the rural landscape.

In 1791 Grahovo, which had been a part of the Cerknica parish, became the center of the subparish (*podružnica*) that included Žerovnica. Around 1860 the subparish became an independent parish (*župnija*) encompassing four villages: Žerovnica, Bločice, Lipsenj, and Grahovo. Its priests faithfully kept the church register, the sole record of vital statistics and landholdings until 1946, when civil records began to be kept. The earliest entries were in German, but by the mid-nineteenth century there were full accounts in Slovene, including date and place of birth, dates of baptism, marriage, and death, and size of the estate of the *gospodar*.

The parish was supported by a church tax (*bira*), administered by the village council. For a quarter *zemlja*, a peasant contributed thirty liters of wheat and thirty liters of barley. If he lacked sufficient land to supply wheat and barley, he could substitute money or wood. For failure to contribute, a person could be prosecuted in court, but villagers say this never occurred. The priest was paid by the state and also received remuneration from his parishioners for his various services—conducting religious education for children and officiating at masses and at baptisms, marriages, and funerals. Civil marriages were unknown before the war. Monthly confession and attendance at special masses in the Žerovnica church were compulsory for school children, and attendance at mass on certain days was also expected of adults. One villager recalled that in his childhood, at Easter mass, the priest distributed slips of paper to be surrendered at the next confession for other slips of paper of another color, thus enabling the priest to check attendance. If an individual could not turn in the proper slip, the priest would threaten to announce his name publicly. The religious calendar, the official Catholic one supplemented by many local saints' days, was full and well observed. Five regional masses were traditionally celebrated each year at the mountaintop pilgrim church of Sveta Ana (Saint Ana), on Križna Gora, which is a three or four hours' walk from Žerovnica. The road is marked by wayside shrines where worshipers once stopped to pray. Villages within a radius of forty kilometers participated. Next to the large church was a dormitory, now in ruins, that sheltered the pilgrims. Singing and praying at the mountaintop lasted through the night. All religious holidays were accompanied by dancing, feasting, and general celebration.

Around 1800 a German observer described these traditional ceremonies:

> However poor a village may be, its churches are usually clean, well-found and strongly built, especially the steeple. One church does not suffice for the village; many parishes have as many as seven or nine such temples, standing on mile-high mountains and dedicated to various saints. Yet as a rule such churches are visited only once a year. As there is usually no priest's house at the temple, all the vestments for the church ceremonies are carried up. On the feast-day the innkeepers set up in huts of branches or tents; there is a sermon and a feast, and then, since there is no shelter other than the temple of the Lord, all the faithful crowd into it together to spend the night.[1]

The writer decried this practice as licentious and believed that in deference to economy these superfluous churches should be closed, although he saw little chance of his reform being adopted.

# Postwar Observances

Government regulations in contemporary Slovenia have seriously curtailed the activities of the Catholic church, leaving it little power and few approved functions. According to law, a church is permitted to hold only three hectares of land. Some church forest land was therefore given to Žerovnica as communal village property. Civil marriage, unknown before the war, is now obligatory, and the religious ceremony is sometimes omitted. Civil divorces are now easily obtainable. The church has, of course, lost its right to collect taxes. Only on rare occasions is a priest in clerical garb seen on the streets.

The priest of the Grahovo parish continues to maintain the church records and to provide religious services: he officiates at masses, baptisms, and funerals, and offers religious instruction to children. Fees paid by parishioners constitute his income. The priest who served until 1965, a highly respected man on intimate terms with many of the villagers, celebrated mass on Sundays in Žerovnica as well as in Grahovo. In that year, however, he was transferred, against his own desire, and replaced by another priest, who because of ill health was unable to travel to Žerovnica for Sunday mass. Since 1965 mass has been said only in the parish house in Grahovo (the Grahovo church was destroyed in the last war and has not been replaced). Because few villagers wish to walk the kilometer and a half to Grahovo, attendance at mass and contact between the priest and the village has sharply diminished. In 1969 we learned that the parish had awarded sufficient funds to the Žerovnica church to rebuild the ceiling. Moreover, the *občina* had granted permission for the erection of a new church in Grahovo. The priest believed that this signaled a more tolerant attitude toward the church, and he also believed that there had been some increase in the participation of older people in religious activities over the previous four years.

In spite of the dwindling power of the Catholic church, it continues to be a significant moral force in the peasant life of Žerovnica, as is evidenced by the strength of certain rules of behavior, by the participation of many villagers in masses until 1965, and by their observance of religious holidays. However, because of official disapproval of religious activities and because peasants fear discriminatory treatment if they openly ally themselves with the church, it is difficult to obtain complete information on the subject of religion.

Villagers stated that all children are baptized. Godparents, frequently relatives, are designated, but their function is limited primarily to participating at the baptism and confirmation. Some village children are sent to the priest for religious instruction in preparation for first communion (*obhaja*) and later confirmation. At the age of six or seven, generally during the first year of primary school, these children meet the priest twice a week over a period of one year and are also expected to participate in Sunday mass. Three children from Žerovnica (from a total of seven between the ages of six and eight years in the village) were among nineteen in the parish who received first communion in 1965. Other village children of this age group may have received first communion the year before or after. A number of villagers asserted that most eligible children still receive communion. After the ceremony of first communion in the church the children gather in the priest's apartment for a small celebration, at which simple food is served. At home they are given a few presents, mostly sweets.

Every five or six years (formerly every year) there is a confirmation (*birma*) of children in Grahovo. In preparation they receive catechism lessons weekly throughout the school year until Easter and twice weekly thereafter until the day of confirmation. Four village children participated in these lessons in 1965, although there were twenty-three children in the village between the ages of eight and fourteen who may have been eligible for confirmation. Thus religious education after first communion, which most clearly conflicts with secular education, has almost completely disappeared. The school in Grahovo, situated directly across the square from the parish house, is the approved place for education of the youth, and many peasants are reluctant to flout state institutions by sending their children to the priest after first communion.

Most villagers asserted that in spite of the disapproval of the state young people continue to have religious marriage ceremonies in addition to the prescribed civil ceremonies. Divorce is permitted by civil law, but is still rare among peasants. There was only one in the village, and it was undertaken only after consultation with, and explanations to, the priest. While the priest accepted the extenuating circumstances, he nevertheless did not give his official approval. We did not observe any instances of civil funerals. Apparently most peasants want religious funerals, whether or not they participate in other religious forms.

The ceremony of Sunday mass fulfilled a significant role in the village until 1965, when masses were discontinued in Žerovnica. Since then the church, which formerly had been opened on Sundays, has remained closed, the keys guarded by a villager who still performs minor caretaking tasks. The interior of the church is vaulted by a light blue ceiling and has whitewashed walls that are hung with framed reproductions of religious paintings. Crystal chandeliers, candles, a carved altar, and the figure of the officiating priest in his vestments, as well as the sounds of the church bells and the choir, all contributed to an impression of the sacred, removed from life in the village below. The sexton's house, next to the church, was deserted for many years; in 1969 it was sold to a village family. Until 1965 it was the responsibility of one child to ring the bell in the church tower to call villagers to mass. The same child also wound the church clock each day.

While villagers do not observe state holidays, they rarely work on religious holidays or on Sundays unless there is an emergency, such as impending rain that forces them to bring in hay. When masses were said in Žerovnica, the church was filled to capacity—probably sixty to seventy persons. The majority of the churchgoers were women, children, and older men. Boys frequently spent Sunday mornings at the *balina* field, and many younger *gospodars* remained at home and relaxed. "God will forgive me!" one explained on a Sunday morning. "I am out of the habit, but I am friendly with the priest." His mother and his daughter were attending mass, but he and his wife did not join them. Women continued to wear kerchiefs in church, but young girls were bareheaded. While villagers were attentive during the ceremony, they did not always kneel or cross themselves, and few took the sacrament. In the sermons the priest frequently exhorted his flock to fulfill their religious obligations and related tales whose moral was the ill effects of irreligious behavior and indifference toward the church.

While more men than women have withdrawn from formal religious activities, many men regret the virtual disappearance of the church choir. Although singing is still a part of Sunday mass, there is no longer a formal choir that meets and practices regularly. How-

ever, the musically gifted priest of the Cerknica parish has attempted
to revitalize this form, an endeavor in which he has been highly successful, judging from a rehearsal of his male choir in Grahovo. Several young men from Žerovnica sang in the choir, which was composed for the most part of younger men. The repertory included folk
and religious songs, sung in harmony, to the accompaniment of a
harmonium. Villagers regret the general decline of musical activities
today and recall that on Saturday afternoons boys used to gather
under the linden tree and sing together, as girls listened. Weddings
also once provided opportunity for group singing.

Traditional religious holidays observed by the villagers include
Christmas, Mardi Gras (*Postni Torek*), Easter, Whitsunday (*Binkošti*), and various saints' days. There is also a special village holiday,
the Wednesday following *Binkošti,* a day of thanksgiving that Žerovnicans have observed since they promised to do so if rust would disappear from their crops.

One or two pilgrimages a year to the church of Saint Ana on
Križna Gora are still held, and we participated in one on Whitsunday
in June 1965. That Sunday, and the following Monday, few villagers
went to the fields, although all were under pressure to gather hay because several weeks of rain had set the agricultural calendar badly
behind schedule. We left the village by automobile at eight-thirty in
the morning with one village family, and in forty-five minutes we had
driven to the end of the road that climbs part way up Križna Gora.
From there we walked, joining many others from throughout the
area, who had started much earlier, since they walked the entire way.
(A few young people came on motor bikes and motorcycles.) The
empty shrines along the path were ignored. At the top of the mountain stands the imposing, old church, fronted by three large, primitive, carved crucifixes. Beside the church is a tall bell tower. A pano-
ramic view of the valley and the Cerknica lake may be seen from the
churchyard. Inside, the church was crowded with participants, all
standing pressed closely together, but after a while some of the men
went outside to talk and smoke, and children left to play. The sermon
exhorted the listeners not to forsake religion for technical gains and
to protect the aged, often left today without homes. Morality stories
pointed to the tragedy that might ensue if religion became a concern
of women only. After the ceremony families and friends gathered and

promenaded in holiday spirit on the church hill. Children climbed the tall bell tower, and boys rode motorcycles and motor bikes around the crowd. Finally the rain began, and the villagers dispersed to begin the walk home.

# 10

## The Life Cycle

### Birth and Early Childhood

While children are welcomed and a son is strongly desired, women are grateful for their knowledge of birth control, which frees them from the burden of frequent pregnancies and the care of many children. Furthermore, legal abortions are not difficult to obtain today. Although illegitimate births are recorded occasionally in the church records, undoubtedly they were more frequent than records indicate. Some *gospodars* speak freely of their own illegitimate children. One aged *gospodar*, a former itinerant musician and teller of folk tales, who is widely respected for his knowledge though he stems from the cottager class, is known by all to be illegitimate. We knew of one illegitimate birth in the village during the period of this study. The parents, both from Žerovnica, married subsequently. While the subject of illegitimacy is generally avoided, the occurrence of illegitimacy is looked upon as unfortunate but not tragic.

Peasant women work in the fields until shortly before the birth is expected. Prenatal care is available at the hospital in Postojna, about twenty kilometers away, and women may see doctors regularly, free of charge, after they are three months pregnant. Today the services of the midwife and neighbor in childbirth are replaced by those of the hospital in Postojna. Free postnatal care is provided by two doctors in Cerknica and supplemented by the visits of a nurse to the mother at regular intervals during the first few weeks after birth. The infant is inoculated against smallpox and given injections against diphtheria, whooping cough, tetanus, and polio within the first year, and his weight is regularly checked. Women return quickly to the fields after giving birth. For example, one young nursing mother worked in the fields throughout a long hot day two weeks after she had been released from the hospital following a Caesarean delivery.

Infants may be nursed for one year and are given a modern diet recommended by pediatricians. Milk is supplemented by fruit juice when the infant is three months old and by cereals at six months. Cereal is flavored with sugar and frequently with substitute coffee or chocolate. Colicky babies are given camomile tea. Often babies are given pacifiers. By the time an infant reaches one year he is fed from the family table, although he continues to drink milk from a bottle.

Toilet training is casual and does not begin before the age of fifteen months to two years. Mothers are not concerned over a child's progress in toilet training, and the advice they receive from pediatricians today reinforces this attitude.

Children are treated permissively and are comforted when they cry. They are never forced to go to bed, but play or remain with the family until they can no longer stay awake. They generally sleep with the grandmother or the parents while they are small. Later on, children may share a bedroom if there are enough rooms in the house, but they never sleep alone. Parents explain that the children would be frightened without another member of the family nearby. At bedtime an infant may be put into a long sacklike nightgown (*pindekle*), which is tied around the neck, thus restraining the arms, a practice that continues until the infant is one year old. Villagers explain that the *pindekle* prevents the baby from standing or falling and keeps him warm. Traditionally, the baby was also swaddled, except when being fed. While swaddling has been abandoned, many mothers continue to use the *pindekle*, although some have rejected it, saying it is not in accordance with the practice followed in the hospital.

Some infants have homemade playpens and walkers, and all have simple household articles that serve as toys. Children are kept near home until they are of school age, although after the age of four some wander fairly freely throughout the village. They are humored and treated with patience and affection; when they casually enter neighboring houses, as they frequently do, they are always welcomed. Discipline is not lacking, however; a child may be slapped for irritating behavior, may be sent to bed without his evening meal, or may be forced to remain at home when the parents depart for the fields. Teasing and frightening a child into submission is not uncommon. A mother may threaten, "Daddy will come [Ata bo prišel]!" and when the father arrives, the child may be made to kneel to ask his forgiveness. A father may threaten a child with a switch for crying and disturbing him but pay little attention to the cause of the commotion. On one occasion, as I attempted to photograph a child, he became frightened and began to cry. A woman passing by tried to appease the child by holding up an object. "Here is a sweet!" she promised. However, it was only a nut. Children are taught manners at an early age. A two-year-old child may be reminded to offer his hand and greet a stranger. A common request is, "Look into the eyes nicely [Lepo gledej v oči]."

By the time the children are of school age they run errands, go to the store for small purchases, rake the hay, and begin to help in the fields. Girls assist with the laundry, dig and peel potatoes, prepare beetroots, and watch the younger children. Boys bring in wood for the kitchen and take part in the heavier haying jobs. Villagers comment that children help less than formerly in the household and explain that it is because they all attend school regularly and become interested in their studies, school excursions, and affairs beyond village life.

Between the ages of five and twelve boys tend to play in groups. Girls also form groups, but less frequently. In summer, children play in the Žerovnišča River, and boys frequently drink the water although their parents forbid this, since the water is known to be polluted. Children also play simple games, such as horse and driver. When hungry, a child is generally given a piece of bread with lard, sugar, or marmalade, or he is given a boiled potato.

## Later Childhood and Adolescence

All village elders recall attending school for a number of years, and illiteracy has been unknown in the village for as long as can be remembered. School records have been kept since the founding of the first one-class, one-room school in Grahovo in 1888. Before that time, villagers say, a small school in Žerovnica was conducted by an old soldier in a rented house. With the founding of the school in Grahovo, an old man from a nearby village was employed as a teacher. The language of instruction was always Slovene, although during the Austrian regime, until 1919, German was taught as a foreign language. Shortly after the founding of the school, a second grade was added, and by 1899 a third grade. Enrollment rose from 180 in 1893 to 301 in 1910, but according to the school records at this time attendance was poor, for in addition to the problems of weather and health, children were kept at home to help in the fields, since emigration to America had caused a shortage of working hands. In 1913 a fourth grade was added, and in 1924 a fifth. Enrollment began to drop in 1924 and fluctuated between 225 and 250 during the interwar years, reflecting the smaller families of this period.

By 1937 the school district served by the school in Grahovo included Grahovo, Martinjak, Lipsenj, Bločice, Bloška Polica, and Žerovnica, as it does today. The fifth to the eighth grades now also include children from the village of Gorenje Jezero. Shortly before World War II medical examinations, including X rays, and immunization for diphtheria began to be provided in the schools for students. During the war years the school was disbanded by the Italians, although records continued to log the major events of the war in the area, and in 1946 the school resumed with only 150 pupils. It expanded in the postwar years to eight grades.

Village children begin school at seven years of age, when some also begin religious training in preparation for first communion. School attendance is now compulsory for eight years. Children walk to the local school in Grahovo. All pupils remove their shoes and put on slippers, according to Slovene urban custom, before they enter the classroom. Classes for the first three grades are held in the afternoon from one o'clock to four-thirty, and are interrupted midway by refreshments of cocoa and bread. Children in the upper grades arrive shortly before eight in the morning. At half past nine they are served a breakfast of bread and soup, and at one in the afternoon they are dismissed. Many parents complain about the expense of sending children to school—the cost of clothes, supplies, and books, and the charge, in 1965, of twelve dinars a day for the school meal—but most are proud of the local school and satisfied with the education their children are receiving.

The school is staffed by a director and six teachers. In the first grade, pupils are instructed in reading, writing, arithmetic, social studies, gymnastics, singing, and art. In the fifth grade, English, biology, home economics, and technical training are introduced. In the sixth grade children study history, geography, and Serbo-Croatian. Finally, in the seventh and eighth grades, geography, physics, chemistry, and political economy are added.

All children stand when the teacher enters the room. Discipline, however, is mild, and classes are not strictly controlled. Most children appear to like school. At the close of the term, toward the end of June, all children report to school to receive their marks. Those who have spent eight years in school may discontinue their education, although, if they have not passed all eight grades, they are permitted to continue in school. Often, however, parents will not allow their children to spend more than eight years in primary school. It is relatively common for a child to fail a grade, and children accept this fact without great concern or shame. After the marks are received, the children present flowers to the teacher and depart for the summer.

An important part of the school program are extracurricular activities. Movies on educational subjects or on subjects of national interest such as the partisans are sometimes shown at the community center. One excursion a year is planned for each class. In 1965 one group went by bus for a day's trip to a Slovene beach resort, for which each child paid 1,500 dinars and provided his own lunch. The most ambitious project during that year was a one-day trip to Venice for the oldest group, which cost each student 4,500 dinars. The bus left the village before dawn and returned that night. Thus some village children have traveled far more extensively than their parents. While village elders may have emigrated to foreign countries for employment, and many village men have served in the army, some women in the village have never been beyond Cerknica. Although some villagers go to Ljubljana on special occasions and, more recently, to Trieste for major purchases, the borders of Slovenia appear distant to most villagers, and crossing the frontier to a foreign country is considered a major event.

The school also operates a summer camp at Koper, on the seashore of the Istrian Peninsula, which may be attended by children in poor health. In 1965 four children from Žerovnica spent one month at the camp at a cost of 5,000 dinars each.

Clearly, the school is broadening the horizons of young people beyond those of their parents. To some young people graduation means the end of a liberating experience and a return to village life. To others it means the frightening prospect of moving to a city in order to enroll in a course of specialized training, in which competition is severe. It rarely means continuance of formal academic training in a secondary school. Thus at fifteen years of age village children face many of the problems of active participation in the adult world.

How few young people wish to return to traditional village life is indicated by school essays that one teacher, at our request, asked the children in his class to write on what they wished to do when they left school. Because only one teacher was interested in this project, participation was limited to fourteen children in the upper classes, of whom half were from Žerovnica and the remainder from the surrounding villages. Only one boy wrote that he wished to remain at home and become a peasant. Another boy was undecided about his future, and the other twelve students expressed definite preferences. Boys wrote that they wished to become teachers, automobile mechanics, or technicians; and girls, that they wanted to be dental assistants, seamstresses, teachers, or salesgirls at a general store.

The graduation ceremony itself suggests the seriousness with which the end of primary education is viewed by the pupils. During the last period of the day before graduation, eighth graders pass from class to class, singing a sentimental farewell song that they have composed. In 1965 they sang: "The morning has come / When I must leave you / Dear mother, father, and sister; / Nor shall I forget you, dear brothers, / You, I will sometimes remember. / I am not going far / Dear schoolmates, / I shall remain in my homeland. / Dear school and teachers / I am asking you all to let me shake your hands. / I shall keep a little memory of you. / I shall send you a white letter / A little one. / Yet, we shall never again be as happy as we were in school."[1]

Graduating girls sob, while boys are gay, as they sing their farewell song. Then all go outside and are seated for the ceremony. Other songs composed by the eighth graders are sung. Children present posters caricaturing the teachers, address speeches to each teacher, and offer them flowers. Seventh graders, in turn, respond with their speeches, asking to buy the eighth-grade class key, which lies resplendent on a flower-bedecked cushion.

In the afternoon, after the ceremony is completed, the graduating class holds a party, and dancing continues until ten or eleven in the evening, after which the girls, sobbing again, go home complaining that now they must leave their friends. Now boys too are sad as they hear the final speech of their teacher, who concluded in 1965, "Wherever you go, to cities, to the gymnasium, remember, my door is always open to you in Cerknica!"

## Young Adulthood

The crucial transition from high school to work in the fields or to a few years of specialized training and then work in town or city presents a less severe conflict for boys than for girls. Boys, although they wish to leave the village, are willing to commute from village to factory. Girls however are more rebellious. One eighteen-year-old girl who had spent several years in Ljubljana studying to become a dental assistant and had returned to the village to visit her parents, owners of half a *zemlja*, explained to our daughter the attitude of many village girls. They prefer the city, she said, because people are more broadminded there. The village is old fashioned and backward. Boys and girls can go out together in groups in the city, not just as couples. In Žerovnica, she said, boys just get drunk and do not know how to have a good time. They try to seduce the girls, but they do not respect those who succumb. Furthermore, Žerovnica girls are resented if they go out with a boy from another village. For example, one girl from Žerovnica went dancing with some relatives in a village far away, and for several years after she was ostracized by boys from Žerovnica. Yet, said the student, boys from Žerovnica like girls from other villages. But they do not want their girls to have the same privileges they have, because they know what boys do with girls from other villages. Boys, she said, want to marry girls from Žerovnica and gossip about strange girls. But, she concluded, girls prefer to marry boys from other villages.

Some of the young people who remain in the village are able to commute to nearby centers for special training. A few girls who wish to become dental assistants take the bus to Cerknica once a week for several weeks to attend a two-hour class that prepares them to take the entrance examination for the two-year program of dental training in Ljubljana. The competition is severe, and few succeed. Other girls receive training in Cerknica as seamstresses. A boy may learn a skill by becoming an apprentice or may receive training at the furniture factory, Brest, for a job there. It is at this point that young people begin to wear sophisticated urban clothing and to attend dances at the inn in Lipsenj. Traditionally, and often still today, when a boy (*otrok*) is considered to have become a young man (*fant*), this change in status is celebrated by a ceremony at the inn, at which he pays for drinks for all his friends; after that he is allowed to frequent the inn.

The traditional arranged marriages between the young people of families within the village or of families of neighboring villages, which required bargaining and discussions of inheritance and dowry, are part of the past. Today, not only land and homestead, but other possessions as well, are generally left to one son (or if there is no son, to one daughter), and dowries for girls and gifts to other sons are no longer considered of great importance. While some young people continue to marry within the village or to find partners in nearby villages, those who work outside the village now meet people from far wider areas, and today parents play little part in marriage plans. Engagements are becoming rare. Weddings, which were once two- or three-day celebrations with music, singing, and ceremony, are now brief, and frequently there is only a civil ceremony. Those who wish a religious ceremony may resort to a private, city wedding, in order to avoid arousing public disapproval.

Villagers remember that the village musician used to sing at weddings. In one refrain he would beseech all those invited to contribute money for presents to the bride. One traditional wedding custom is often still followed. On the wedding day the groom is required to invite every unmarried young man in the village who is eighteen or over for a drink at the inn. The groom himself cannot join the bachelors in drinking, because he is no longer one of them. If he marries into a strange village, he must invite all the unmarried young men in that village for the same ceremony.

Girls now often marry at eighteen or nineteen, while formerly they waited until well into their twenties. The greatest problem the young couple faces, unless one of them inherits the homestead, is finding a place to live, which may cause a postponement of the marriage for several years.

## Old Age and Death

The older peasant occupies an insecure position, for he does not receive retirement insurance as other workers do; his children may desert the land for other occupations and leave him dependent on other people in the village when he becomes too old to work. Peasants work as long as they are physically able, and when an old man can no longer work in the fields, there is little left for him to do. He may help watch an infant or prepare green branches for thatching a roof. An old woman can more easily occupy her time, caring for the grandchildren or preparing food. As one *gospodar* commented about peasant men, "The young can go to the factory, but an old man cannot go anywhere until he dies."

Old people frequently speak about illness or death, and they often answered promises to return to the village the next year with, "If I am still alive." In referring to an illness, an older *gospodar* remarked, "For us there is no doctor, only the ditch [*samo jama*]."

Funerals follow the traditional Catholic customs of the village. The body is washed and dressed in good clothes and placed in an open coffin on a bed in the main room of the house. For forty-eight hours friends and relatives may pay a last call and sprinkle the body (*pokropiti telo*) with holy water or salt. (Photographs of the body in the coffin surrounded by flowers are afterward frequently displayed by the family, along with other family pictures.) After the coffin is closed, it is placed in the open door, and the priest invokes a benediction and leads the prayers. After this comes the funeral mass (*pogrebščina*) at the church, a graveside benediction, and the burial. The funeral feast follows at the churchyard. For eight days thereafter friends visit the family of the deceased and pray, eat, and drink together. Finally, there are additional requiem masses eighteen and thirty days later.

Such funeral traditions are still adhered to by the older generation. For example, the four neighbors returning with us from the Whitsunday mass at Križna Gora asked us to stop at the village of Gorenje Jezero, for a friend had just died there, and they wished to sprinkle holy water on the body. After performing this ritual, they asked us to join them at the village inn, where they drank, and dispelled the solemn mood with jokes and laughter.

# 11

## *The Question of Modernization*

MODERNIZATION and economic development are complex processes that cover a wide range of changes affecting many and diverse communities and nations throughout the world. Certain ideal or general patterns are common to these manifold changes. In a recent analysis of economic anthropology, Dalton has said that modernization in the local community is a process that starts with impingement from the outside and entails integration with external groupings and increased dependence upon these groups, "with whom new economic and cultural transactions take place. Sustained income growth for the local community requires enlarged production for sale to regional, national, or international markets, and a return flow of consumption goods, producer's goods, and social services (health and education) purchased with the ever-increasing cash income."[1] Smelser notes that modernization frequently involves four processes: change from a simple toward a scientific technology; change from subsistence farming toward commercial farming; change from unmechanized toward mechanized industry; and, in ecological arrangements, a move from the village toward urban centers. These processes give rise to three kinds of structural changes, which pervade the society: structural differentiation, or the establishment of more specialized autonomous units (for example, in the economic sphere, increasing occupational specialization and division of labor); new forms of integration required by the process of differentiation, which makes the old social order obsolete (for example, new political parties); and social disturbances reflecting "the uneven march of differentiation and integration."[2]

The changing culture and social structure of Žerovnica can be related, though only to a certain extent, to the constructs offered by Dalton and Smelser. In the modern period Žerovnica has experienced increased impingement from the outside and growing integration with, and dependence on, external groupings. Income has increased in Žerovnica, though not dramatically, partly as a result of improved technology and the beginning of commercialization in farming. Primarily, however, it is not enlarged production, but rather wage labor in the factory that has brought increased income. Social services have improved, and there has been a move toward urban centers. Furthermore, the culture of Žerovnica has exhibited some of the structural changes that Smelser has associated with the processes of modernization. For example, differentiation has proceeded in the various realms discussed by Smelser—the economy, the family, the value system, and the systems of stratification. Also, new, if unstable, forms of integration have appeared as new loyalties have challenged, or have altered, traditional family-based and village-based organizations and have begun to alter traditional norms and rules as well. Finally, social disturbances reflecting the uneven change have developed, including factional splits and other kinds of internal tension.

While such typical patterns, characterizing modernization and economic development at the local and national levels, are of great analytical value, equally important are the wide range of specific variations in the patterns at all levels and the specific factors that distinguish national from local development. Smelser has pointed to five main sources of variation in economic development: variations in the premodern conditions of the society, in the impetus to change, in the path taken toward modernization, in the advanced stages of modernization, and in the effects of such dramatic events as wars and natural catastrophes.[3] In distinguishing the national from the local level, Dalton has emphasized that socioeconomic changes and development at the level of the state do not necessarily bring successful economic development at the level of the village or tribe. At the local level, according to Dalton, changes may range from degenerative ones, to cash income growth without development, to true socioeconomic development—three categories that are not mutually exclusive and that frequently overlap.[4] A critical variable factor affecting the character of local economic change in underdeveloped areas, Dalton has noted, is the role of the central government, for primitive and peasant communities, being poor, cannot afford unsuccessful experiments. Dalton points out that if the government is unwilling to bear some of the risks of innovation, "the local community is likely to perceive any governmentally initiated project to expand community output as a device to increase taxes, and therefore to be resisted." The method of successful socioeconomic development is, in Dalton's view, "to work with those powerful levers of new achievement which the people themselves perceive as desirable and which induce other positive changes," and thus to avoid "the personal and community malaise that characterizes degenerative change and growth without development."[5]

The specifics of economic change and development in Žerovnica can be discussed in terms of Smelser's categories of variation. Premodern conditions have been important determinants of the patterns of change. They include a traditional, subsistence-based, agricultural economy with only limited production for the market; the exploitation of small holdings by a traditional technology; traditional family and kinship forms; traditional patterns of stratification, corporate institutions, and value systems; and a structure of relations between the village and the larger society that stems from the feudal period. Moreover, the internal impetus to change has been important for a long period. Early in their history the inhabitants of Žerovnica had to search for solutions to the problem of population pressure on the land. How to survive and how to increase their income to meet the ever-growing impositions of taxes have been constant problems. Individual initiative, perseverance, and originality have characterized many of the solutions devised. In the traditional village, peasants smuggled, hauled wood over long distances, and traded widely; more recently they have turned to specialization in hog raising and to the semilegal sale of wood. Finally, the particular path toward modernization taken by this community has been marked by an uneven and contradictory sequence of technological changes. Villagers have found ways to obtain mechanized mowers, but only limited amounts of artificial fertilizer can be bought at prices villagers can afford; commercialization has centered around uneconomical hog raising; and all innovations have been imposed upon an essentially unchanged pattern of medieval land tenure based on dispersed small holdings. A unique and unpredictable influence on the recent pattern of change in Žerovnica was the storm of 1965 that provided the peasants with a new source of cash income through lumbering, which in turn accelerated technological advancement in the village. Other large events affecting the specific path of modernization included, of course, the depression of the thirties, the two last wars, and the Communist revolution.

Then also, in the terms of Dalton's observations concerning economic development at the local level, it can be shown that the changes that have occurred in the economic life of Žerovnica have ranged from the degenerative to the positive. Negatively, some millers, former leaders of village industry, have been forced into inactivity; and manpower shortages have caused hardship for cultivators of the land and have even, in spite of strong opposing traditions, led to the abandonment to grass or the sale of some land. Increasing specialization in hog breeding is perhaps best viewed as cash income growth without development. Positive changes, on the other hand, include an increase in education, more health measures, improvements in agricultural technology, the introduction of some mechanization, and an increase in cash income from outside occupations. Perhaps no other factor has been so critical in determining the character of economic changes within the village throughout the modern period as the role of the central government. While governmental policies have frequently been re-evaluated and changed, one principle appears to have been maintained fairly consistently—that is, rejection by the government of any significant portion of the financial risk of economic and technological innovation and development in the sector of private agriculture.

## Projected Agricultural Reforms: 1964–65

In our discussions with officials of the co-operative farm in 1964 some of them advanced the view that the peasant subsistence agriculture should be replaced by production for the market. Villages in the Cerknica area should specialize, they held, in dairy farming and cattle raising. The cultivation of potatoes and wheat should be abandoned as unprofitable, since the Slovenian peasant could not compete with the Banat wheat farmer, and potatoes were not in great demand in Croatia and Serbia. Furthermore, hog raising was too time-consuming. Officials recognized, however, that such an agricultural revolution required complicated land reforms and new technologies. Fields under cultivation would need to become pasture land in a rotating system. In order to consolidate peasant holdings, villagers would be obliged to exchange noncontiguous parcels of land. Adequate supplies of cheap chemical fertilizer would be required to replace the manure and insufficient modern products now used. Furthermore, it would be necessary to make available modern machinery for harvesting fodder crops. Many other changes would also be called for.

Whereas some officials advocated revisions in the traditional peasant economy, there was not much evidence of agreement on, or interest in, methods to effect land reforms; nor did officials concern themselves with new ways to introduce the technological changes they suggested. They have generally done little more than implement negative measures to force peasants to adopt new ways. Thus, in 1964 officials expressed the standard view that the government should render subsistence farming unprofitable by tightening forest regulation and increasing taxes on lumber, and even by threatening to confiscate forest land. If forestry as a source of income should diminish or disappear, the peasant would be forced, according to this logic, to look to more profitable forms of farming or to give up his land. Among other negative methods favored was a general increase in taxes. On the positive side, it was proposed that the peasant might be given some aid in carrying out land exchanges, although the general feeling was that such a reform probably could not be effected because it would be too expensive and because the peasant was too set in his ways. Furthermore, co-operative ventures between the peasant and the co-operative farm involving credit and the sale of machinery were being considered.

By 1965, as ill effects of the negative program became clearer (peasants in mountain areas of the *občina* began to abandon land and enter the factories, which in turn became overstaffed, while peasants still farming became increasingly shorthanded), new and more persuasive measures to encourage cattle breeding were considered. In 1965 the cattle-raising mountain lands in the Cerknica *občina* were placed in the tax-free fourth class, and the land of Žerovnica was reduced to class three, the change bringing with it certain tax advantages to those selling cattle to the co-operative. For a healthy, fat, and pregnant cow, the co-operative would award the villager a 25 per cent reduction in taxes, and for a bull calf, a 15 per cent reduction. Former partisans could claim further tax benefits. At the same time, officials expressed some doubt in 1965 that basic reforms, such as a shift to cattle specialization, could be effected in the Cerknica area in the near future. The general economic retrenchment and limitation of aid to the *občina* from the federal government and the republic was responsible for a more conservative approach toward any fundamental change.

A proposal to build dams around a part of the lake, making it permanent, and to drain the rest of the lake area was consistently presented as one positive measure that would raise the general economic level of the area. Drainage would provide more cultivable land; irrigation would compensate for droughts; water power available for electrification would encourage industrialization; and the peasant would profit from the tourists the enhanced lake would attract. The lake lands that would be reclaimed for cultivation are in the higher portion of the Cerknica basin, an area belived to be covered by a layer of topsoil thicker than that overlying the remainder of the Cerknica basin. One official stated that the soil may extend down three meters, with as many as thirty meters of rock beneath it. The realization of this project, however, depends upon the location and closing of drainage holes in the lake, and even its most enthusiastic supporters express uncertainties concerning the feasibility of this aspect of the plan. Since the largest part of the area to be reclaimed is still privately owned, and Žerovnica owns 225 hectares of lake land, the project directly affects the peasants. Officials implied that a part of the newly reclaimed land would be added to the area under Marof administration through *arondacija* and ten-year rentals.

# Attitudes of Landowners toward Reforms: 1965

In the light of numerous discussions concerning change, held with various officials at intervals over a year, in 1965 we asked a representative number of landowning *gospodars* a series of questions relating to the future economy of the village. The first question was a general one pertaining to economic relations with the co-operative. The more specific questions concerned attitudes toward the possibility of land exchanges, a change to production for the market, the plan to improve the lake lands, and the new taxation program.

To the question, "Do you feel the co-operative is increasing its aid to the peasant, and do you believe that there is any change in the attitude of the co-operative toward the peasant?" there were fifteen responses. Six were on the whole noncommittal, although they included a few mildly positive comments. One *gospodar* said that since the co-operative now recognized its mistakes, relations were improved, but that this change had come too late. Some referred to the tax reductions for cattle breeding and the higher prices the co-operative now pays for cattle. Of these six, five were members of the new elite and one was a former representative to the *občina*.

On the other hand, nine *gospodar*s flatly asserted that there was no improvement in relations between the co-operative and the peasant. One *gospodar* noted that before 1964 peasants were not allowed to buy tractors, but now it was possible to buy them from the co-operative. However, he added, a typical peasant could not afford one. The general theme was expressed by another *gospodar:* "Perhaps Marof may help some day, but if it had helped the private peasant during all these years, how much better it would be."

We asked villagers if they thought that they would benefit from a consolidation of their scattered landholdings. Of the twenty landowners who answered, six expressed qualified, but positive, attitudes toward land redistribution. Three of the six held a half *zemlja*, two of them representing the new elite; two of the six were quarter-*zemljak*s who were also members of the new elite; one was a quarter-*zemljak* who had been elected to political office in the *občina*. These *gospodar*s pointed out that consolidation would permit larger holders to employ tractors, that it would facilitate the rationalization of farming, and that a few peasants had already made partial exchanges privately. They noted, however, that such attempts in the prewar period had not succeeded. Several added that while young and progressive *gospodar*s wanted this reform, older people feared it, wished to keep things as they were, and felt that their land was the best. One *gospodar* believed that the government would help farmers in the exchange of land by waiving taxes on the documents required for such transactions. None of this group, however, expected any more government aid than this small measure.

Of the fourteen negative answers, three were from half-*zemljaks* and the remainder from quarter-*zemljaks*, none of whom were members of the new elite. These *gospodars* also recalled that voluntary exchanges had been attempted in the prewar period, but had failed because the land parcels were not of equal quality. Eleven *gospodars* believed that differences in the quality of the landholdings would continue to cause insurmountable difficulty in effecting exchanges. One asked, "Who will take the land with rocks?" Several remarked that each *gospodar* likes his own land best. The consensus, as expressed by one villager, was, "Today everyone has a little good land and a little bad land, and that is best." One *gospodar* added that the plan was pointless because people believed that regardless of changes in the village economy all land would eventually go to the co-operative.

To the question, "Do you think it would be better to shift toward one basic crop or to cattle specialization in order to produce for the market, thereby gaining more cash?" nineteen landowning *gospodars* responded, five positively and fourteen negatively. Three of the five who responded positively were quarter-*zemljaks* or smaller holders who belonged to, or identified with, the new elite, and two were half-*zemljaks*, one of whom belonged to the new elite.

Whereas the question concerning agricultural specialization was posed by us in the summer of 1965, one near-landless member of the new elite had spontaneously suggested such a solution in earlier discussions. His plan demanded a shift to one basic crop for the market, which would be supported by the co-operative through the provision of low-cost fertilizer, tractors, financial aid, and advice in effecting land redistribution. No other *gospodar* initiated discussions of agricultural reforms. The few *gospodars* who favored specialization believed that the most progressive younger farmers would support a change to specialization in cattle. One *gospodar* remarked that peasants have learned that those who have a little of everything have nothing.

The fourteen *gospodars* who opposed a shift toward specialization included five half-*zemljaks*, and the remainder held a quarter *zemlja* or less. Only one of these represented the new elite. The difficulty of changing old ways was stressed: "We have the habit of growing various crops and of not buying food." A frequent theme was the danger of gambling on the unknown: "Who knows? It hasn't been tested"; "What would happen if America stopped its wheat? How do we know that we will be able to buy wheat if we stop growing it?"; "Where would we get flour for bread? We might be hungry"; "What if prices go down? Once we planted too many potatoes and then the prices dropped."

Many believed that Žerovnica does not have enough land to support a cattle economy. One half-*zemljak* said that only if the holdings of Žerovnica were limited to four families would there be sufficient pasture land for a cattle economy. Others doubted that peasants could ever buy enough cattle or obtain adequate supplies of low-cost fertilizer. Should the cattle bring more income, some peasants feared, the government would increase taxes or appropriate more of the peasants' land.

When landowning *gospodars* were asked their attitude toward the plan to improve the lake land, it appeared that this project lacked reality for most of them, and consequently they were not greatly interested. However, nine *gospodars* expressed definite views. Three (a half-*zemljak*, and a new elite smallholder, as well as the quarter-*zemljak* who had held office in the *občina*) supported the project. They stressed the advantage to the peasant of the tourist trade that would be gained, although one *gospodar* noted that the peasants would apparently lose their lake land if the project was realized and so were afraid of the plan. Of the six *gospodars* who presented the other side, three held a half *zemlja*, three were quarter holders, and none represented the new elite. Several of them voiced skepticism concerning the realizability of the project: "It's just talk"; "It's nothing but planning"; and "Who knows if it will work, it will cost a lot of money." Furthermore, respondents feared negative effects of the project: "It is not good for the peasant, but no one asks them," said a young half-*zemljak*. "It will make the land around the permanent lake wet and muddy and consequently unplowable. It will bring mosquitos; it will ruin the parcels closest to the lake because the water level will rise." Most villagers feared that should the lake lands owned by peasants be drained, the peasants would lose the land and would therefore be forced to decrease their cattle holdings, and that more villagers would be obliged to go into industry. "No one knows if the peasant will be paid for the land he loses," said one *gospodar*.

In discussing tax reforms in 1965 many Žerovnicans spoke of nearby mountain villages that were fast becoming deserted as a result of heavy taxation. One peasant reported that in some of the mountain villages, where some families once had held twenty head of cattle each, peasants were forced to sell their cattle, abandon their land, which was too rocky and mountainous for the co-operative, and go to work in the factory. It was said that the government had been too late in realizing that the taxes were prohibitive and in reclassifying mountain land as tax free. Žerovnicans predicted that no one would return to these mountain villages, where fields must be worked entirely by hand. The deserted appearance of the villages reinforced such views, contrasting sharply with the activity and intensive cultivation of the plains in the Cerknica basin. In the mountain village of Topal, perhaps eight kilometers from Žerovnica, the mother of a *gospodar* in Žerovnica still owned six hectares that she had offered to rent to the co-operative; but the co-operative had refused to pay even the usual nominal rent for land of such poor quality. To give her land to the co-operative without compensation would be too great a humiliation, nor would she simply abandon the land where she and her forefathers were born; so she remained in her village. But most young people had left. Brest sends a bus to the villages in the area to transport young workers to the factory. It was said that in another hamlet, Sveta Troitsa, only one of seven families remained. The peasants had abandoned all but the forest land. As a *gospodar* in Žerovnica remarked, "Neither the co-operative nor the state wants their land, and they could not pay the taxes, so it goes to the deer." Villagers predicted a shortage of beef if such peasants continued to leave the land.

When we asked *gospodars* whether they considered the tax program in Žerovnica to have been changed in any way in 1965, the almost unanimous response was no, which was grudgingly qualified when we inquired further. Several villagers conceded that those who could document their partisan affiliation might benefit from tax reductions, the amount depending on how early a date they could establish for such affiliation. While many villagers were vague or ignorant concerning the possibility of tax benefits for those who sold cattle to the co-operative, several villagers discussed the new program. All seemed to feel that the regulations were complex, but that there might be ways to secure a 20 to 25 per cent reduction in taxation. But discussions were qualified by such remarks as: "They tighten, they soften, that's how they do it"; "They lower some taxes, but they will raise others"; "The wolf has to eat [Volk mora bit sit]"; "How long will this last? They change the laws every year"; and "The co-operative and state farms receive help in cattle raising, but the private farmers do not."

These reactions may be compared with conflicting views expressed to us in 1965 by government officials. In short, they stated that their aim was to relieve the peasant, eventually, of property taxes. They felt that peasant production must be stimulated but that tax reductions were not sufficient to do this. At the same time they stressed that the peasant must not be allowed to become too strong and exploit others as the kulak had—indeed, if lowering taxes and helping the peasant to effect technological and land reforms were to make him too powerful, the government might be "forced to crack down again."

# New Policies for Private Agriculture: 1969

In the summer of 1969 a new tone characterized our discussions with officials of the co-operative farm, reflecting the recent economic reforms. Indifference to the existence of private agriculture dominated the views expressed. The policy relating to the socialization of agriculture had shifted since 1965, we were told, because attempts to absorb peasants into the working co-operatives had not succeeded. The co-operative was no longer interested in expansion, an official said, "We do only what pays, and we have found that social and economic interests are one." And while the mechanization of private agriculture had been opposed, now it was looked upon as correct.

It is the central government, not the co-operative that should occupy itself with aid to the peasant, representatives of the co-operative asserted. The government should consider protective measures such as farm subsidies. Furthermore, the government should lift price controls from peasant products and let food prices find their own level, even if they should rise by 100 per cent.

In response to questions about specific reforms in peasant agriculture that we had discussed in 1965, the officials showed less enthusiasm and a different over-all perspective. The co-operative was now supporting the peasants' desire to cut and saw more wood and had secured some additional funds for loans for tractors. However, taxes had to remain disproportionately high, it was said, because the peasants had so little income. Still, if peasant income were increased, taxes would have to be raised again. The question of increasing social security and retirement insurance was being discussed by the government, but no decision was said to be in sight.

The gradual change to a specialized cattle economy was still advanced, in 1969, as the correct ecological and economic solution for the area. Yet this was now viewed as a long-term objective, not of immediate concern to the co-operative, which was occupied with finding its own way. In regard to the key question of the supply of artificial fertilizer to the private peasant, officials said that the time for a change to this feature of scientific farming had not yet come.

Only the lake improvement project seemed to be advancing. Our informants expected that there would be a permanent lake by the following year, but that the Žerovnica land, which is in the highest area, would be the least affected.

At the end of the discussion officials outlined the future they expected for private agriculture in the Cerknica area. There would be three categories of private farmers, the first consisting of the small remaining group of full-time peasants. The second and major category would consist of peasant-workers, who would devote half their time to the factory and half to the fields, and who would be expected to pay for the mechanization of their farms from income earned in the factory. (While mechanization of private agriculture had earlier been opposed, said the informants, now it was looked upon as correct; yet the peasant would not be allowed to expand his landholding beyond the limit of ten hectares of fields and meadows.) The third category would consist of old peasants who because of their sons' departure from the village would either sell their land to full-time farmers or peasant-workers, or perhaps give it to the *občina* in exchange for a promise of support. (When asked what kind of support was implied, the officials admitted that the *občina* would be prepared to guarantee very little.)

THESE ARE the programs of modernization advanced by a poor nation that must pay its own way. In these programs the peasant must finance his own improvements, with all the risks innovation entails. He does this by working double time with fewer helpers, while he also contributes to other forms of modernization within the larger society by paying ever higher taxes. Thus the peasant-worker bears a major part of the burden of the state's effort to achieve rural economic development. The conflicts within this program remain unresolved. Two are particularly apparent to the peasant. First, if he rationalizes production, his income goes up, but taxes will take almost all the new gains away from him. Second, mechanization is recommended, but it is expensive. Moreover, it has limited returns on small dispersed strips of land, yet the total holdings of land are strictly limited. The co-operative offers loans for tractors, but nobody can use tractors, and inexpensive fertilizer, which the peasant badly needs, is not made available.

For the peasant, hard work and innovation bring neither significant increase in real income nor other rewards, such as programs of technological aid and increased social security benefits from the state. He realizes that, essentially without aid from outside, he must try alone to maintain all the things in his environment that he desires and believes to be threatened: land, forests, and manpower, as well as honor, status, and respect. Motivation, then, for participation in the programs of the new society is primarily negative, since a peasant is penalized if he does not comply. Without factory wages he cannot hope to pay his taxes or keep up or improve his farm. He must work always harder, yet most of the rewards will not be reaped in the peasant world, but only outside of it by the young people who depart. What is the ultimate meaning of this labor, is a question peasants ask themselves. This remains the dilemma of the peasants in the village of Žerovnica.

# 12

## The Peasant World View

THE WAY participants in a given culture see their world and how
this view affects and integrates behavior are not new concerns in anthropological studies. Redfield, in the early fifties, defined the term
*world view* in a very broad sense that grew out of his earlier work on
peasant societies in Mexico. As he explained it,

> included in "world view" may be the conception of what ought
> to be as well as what is, and included may be the characteristic
> ways in which experiences are kept together or apart—the patterns
> of thought—and the affective as well as the cognitive aspect of
> these things also. "World view" may be used to include the forms
> of thought and the most comprehensive attitudes toward life . . .
> and the phrase is large enough and loose enough to include the
> emotional "set" of a people. . . . But if there is an emphasized
> meaning in the phrase "world view," I think it is in the suggestion
> it carries of the structure of things as man is aware of them.[1]

In a more systematic approach Kluckhohn attempted to define the
underlying and partially unconscious character of cultural behavior
and to clarify the relation between normative and existential aspects
of values.[2] He agreed with Northrop that concepts of nature and
postulates about nature underlie any value system and that conceptions of nature are " 'verified' by facts that are in some sense independent of culture." Yet, at the same time, "we live in a world where
the same sets of phenomena are being accounted for by different postulates and concepts. Different cultures are tied to different conceptu-
alizations."[3] Values "are manifested in ideas, expressional symbols, and
in the moral and aesthetic norms evident in behavioral regularities.
Whether the cognitive or the cathectic factors have primacy in the
manifestation of a value . . . both are always present."[4] Further, "*value*
implies a code or a standard which has some persistence through time,
or, more broadly put, which organizes a system of action." Thus, a

value is defined as "a conception, explicit or implicit, distinctive of an individual or characteristic of a group, of the desirable which influences the selection from available modes, means, and ends of action."[5] The phrase *or implicit* recognizes the unconscious determinants of behavior that make it necessary to look to more than verbal statements to understand values.[6] Lévi-Strauss has emphasized this point in his comment that norms, which he equates with conscious models, sometimes disguise the structure of behavior, since they "are not intended to explain the phenomena but to perpetuate them."[7] The term *desirable* in Kluckhohn's definition emphasizes the affective dimension. "Values are never immediaetly altered by a mere logical demonstration of their invalidity. The combination of *conception* with *desirable* establishes the union of reason and feeling inherent in the word *value*."[8]

In considering how values are organized into value systems, Kluckhohn wrote, "Value elements and existential premises are almost inextricably blended in the over-all picture of experience that characterizes an individual or a group." He called this over-all view a "value-orientation," a term he formally defines as "a generalized and organized conception, influencing behavior, of nature, of man's place in it, of man's relation to man, and of the desirable and nondesirable as they may relate to man-environment and interhuman relations." Like values, value-orientations "vary on the continuum from the explicit to the implicit."[9]

Kluckhohn concluded that "the distinctive quality of each culture and the selective trends that characterize it rest fundamentally upon its system of value-orientations."[10] In such a system there seems to be some kind of hierarchy of values and priority of values. Furthermore, values may have "symbolic and historic connections in addition to their internal logical relations." Finally, values may conflict, in which case the mode of resolving conflict is also an aspect of the organization of values.[11]

## Traditional and Changing Values

The traditional and changing world views of the inhabitants of Žerovnica may be conceptualized within the framework of Kluckhohn's definitions and system. It seems possible to isolate two groups of traditional values which, though not always verbalized, are still manifest in certain behavioral regularities and institutional patterns. Today, as in the past, these values seem to be complexly related to existential premises concerning nature, man's place in nature, and man's relation to man. There is also evidence of the growing importance to the younger generation of a third group of values relating to the new imperatives of, and opportunities in, the larger society. In a general way these values may be seen to be interrelated, suggesting a system of value-orientations in Kluckhohn's sense.

The first group of traditional values still in evidence include collective village solidarity, equalitarianism, kinship loyalties, and co-operative behavior. These values were once manifest in various institutions and norms that contributed to the corporate nature of the village—among them, traditional kinship forms based on patriarchal principles and loyalty of brothers; the norms of village endogamy and joint, or equal, inheritance; co-operative economic institutions such as the communal pasture and village markets; and the political institution of the village council. The partial survival of these values in the modern period is evidenced by the persistence of the village-wide crop rotation system, the social organization of the firemen's society, and the continued attachment to family and village of emigrant villagers. They are also implicit in normative statements still heard from villagers who assert that Žerovnica is a village composed of friendly peasants who all own equal shares of land, that Žerovnica is the best village, and that it is best to remain in the village.

A second group of traditional values, also partially maintained, and in apparent conflict with the first group, may have gained strength somewhat later. These are the values of individualism, self-reliance, competition, leadership, initiative, and hard work, which figured in such enterprises as competitive wood carting and horse smuggling, as well as the lonely fending for oneself required of the emigrant. These values, found also in the larger society in which the peasants participated, underlay the norms of single and impartible inheritance and primogeniture, which enjoined all sons but the eldest to leave the village and seek a living by their own efforts. Activities expressing these values contributed to the development of economic differences within the village, internal stratification, and the growth of elites.

These values are implicit in such statements as, "The peasants of Žerovnica are tough, hardworking, and clever"; "Villagers can find ways to survive without help"; and "Villagers do not go into debt but prefer to deprive themselves and suffer, if need be, to maintain their land." The continued, though diminished force of these values is indicated by attitudes of distrust of, and resistance to, proposed modernization measures that would be directed from the outside.

Underlying both the generalized values of social solidarity and collective pride, on the one hand, and those of individual pride and self-reliance, on the other, is a dominant value that continues to uphold the peasant way of life as characterized by ownership and cultivation of the land in a subsistence-oriented, family-based economy. The norms relating to primogeniture and marriage within the village, through a form of complementary opposition, contributed to the stable social structure necessary for maintaining this traditional way of life. Thus, single and impartible inheritance, preferably primogeniture, which replaced joint, or equal, inheritance, prevented the land from becoming unduly subdivided and ensured the continuity of family lines. But its requirement that all sons but the eldest leave the village was interpreted within the context of another norm, reflecting a different group of values—preference for marriage within the village and loyalty between brothers—which continued to help counteract dispersal of the population and loss of land to family lines from outside the village.

As Kluckhohn, Northrop, and others have observed, a world outlook is more than an ethic and a code of behavior for preserving or obtaining what is desired. For "the basic assumptions of any philosophy of culture make certain assertions about the character of nature and man," which, while they contribute to the definition of a cultural ideology, also can be empirically verified by an appeal to the facts of nature and man.[12] Thus, for the people of Žerovnica faith in the collective community as well as in individual efforts to maintain the peasant way of life was constrained by a less than optimistic view of their natural and cultural environment. Fatalism, stoicism, and even pessimism characterized the peasant's response to the threat, or the reality, of economic crisis, war and natural catastrophe, and limited resources, all of which seemed to emphasize the peasant's lack of power when confronted with the more powerful forces of nature and the state. At the same time this view reinforced the peasant's belief that he should look only to his own efforts, whether co-operative or individual, in his struggle to survive.

The traditional world view in Žerovnica and the related patterns of behavior do not suggest a simple determinism or a static view, for values are shaped by the perceptions of experience and therefore are subject to change. But they are also endowed with normative qualities and thus themselves contribute to shaping perceptions and related behavior. As Kluckhohn suggested, both existential and normative propositions "define the 'nature of things.' "[13]

It is from this perspective that one must assess the effect on the peasant outlook of the new values related to the many radically new experiences that have become a part of village life in the postwar period. It is evident that in spite of many drastic changes introducing new ways and new kinds of information, and supporting new norms that guide new trends of behavior, most landowning villagers have not abandoned traditional outlooks. Although traditional views may be questioned and altered, most villagers have continued to maintain much of the peasant way of life. Clearly this is partly because the peasant is unsure of the extent and final direction of the new trends. He is not convinced that in fact the state can dispense with the peasant economy, and this strengthens his desire to resist changes he perceives as threatening. Furthermore, his confidence in the promises of the state is limited, since he believes that hostility to peasantry underlies various policies directed toward peasant life. However, these assessments by the peasant of the facts and character of change are also related to the strength and persistence of traditional values. For example, to this day no family has willingly relinquished its land in spite of strong pressure at times to do so. A philosophy of the land is still a modal aspect of the total behavior of the older generation of peasants:

"They can't carry my land away on their backs," said a widow who wished to reclaim her land from the co-operative.

"I'm in love with the land," declared another widow. "If my son sold a field, I would cry. When I go to the fields and work, I forget all my tears and nothing hurts me. I don't even know what time it is or when I come home, I enjoy it so much."

"I can't buy more land, but what I have I'll hang on to," remarked a poor *gospodar.*

Another poor peasant said, "No one knows what the future will bring! In our village people are tough. They hang on to the land."

And according to an elder, rich *gospodar*, "Land is gold."

Nevertheless, retention of land is questioned, although rarely directly, by young people. While no young men have yet abandoned their heritage, even after the death of their parents, they sometimes assert their feelings of independence of this traditional "good." A few said that they would work the land as long as their parents were alive, but that they did not know what they would do after their parents died. Young people rarely assert, as do their elders, that life in the village is best. For the young the traditional norms of primogeniture and the preference for marriage and living within the village, related to the value of the land and the peasant way of life, are being replaced by other rules and norms, related to a new group of values implicitly depreciating the peasant way of life and stressing upward mobility in the larger society through education and the attainment of skills useful in an urban and industrial society.

This raises the question of the degree to which the new programs of the larger society, which seem to neglect private agriculture and to entice young people to leave the village, threaten and undermine the traditional values associated with the peasant way of life—social solidarity, collective and individual pride, self-reliance, and initiative. Today the peasant—as long as he remains a peasant—feels himself increasingly ineffective. Consequently the fatalism of the older generation sometimes turns to apathy. Declining confidence or resignation is revealed in many comments:

"People in Žerovnica are clever, but they cannot help themselves today."

"We could get along without the co-operative, if only we received help in the form of fertilizer and machinery; for nowhere else are there so many hard workers as in this village!"

"If young people can see that you can *live* as a peasant then they will come back. But they must see that the peasant is worth as much as a worker."

"Without machinery, farming cannot go forward. Farming is failing, and the young are going away."

"Private land will be taken by the state. I don't know whether this is good or bad, but we will all be dead then."

"It is too late to induce the young people to return to the land. No one wants to stay, but if there is no place to go, young people may have to remain."

I have pointed to two groups of traditional values in the culture of Žerovnica and have suggested the evolution of a third group, all of which, like Kluckhohn's value-orientations, include both cognitive and affective elements and appear to structure broad areas of peasant behavior. These three groups of values are frequently implicit and are never verbalized in an organized form. They may be viewed as a configuration in which the constituent elements have historic connections and are interrelated by varying principles, among them, harmony and balance, opposition and conflict, and hierarchical order and priority. While the values isolated in this discussion may not constitute the total picture, they do seem to be significant aspects of the world outlook and way of life of the village of Žerovnica.

# The Question of the Image of Limited Good

The preceding discussion has not suggested that one value orientation subsumes, or has subsumed, all or almost all of the behavior of the people of Žerovnica. Rather, it has stressed the differing priorities and conflicts between values in the past and in the present world outlook of this small group of peasants. Yet it may be useful to question how Foster's attempt to isolate a dominant theme that is applicable to peasant behavior in general relates to Žerovnica.[14] Foster states that what he calls the "image of limited good" is the model, or integrating principle, of the cognitive orientation of classic peasant societies. The term *cognitive orientation*, as used by Foster, both resembles and differs from Redfield's "world view" and Kluckhohn's system of "value-orientations." Foster writes: "A particular cognitive orientation cannot be thought of as world view in a Redfieldian sense, i.e., as something existing largely at a conscious level in the minds of the members of the group. The average man . . . cannot describe the underlying premises of which his behavior is a logical function."[15]

A common cognitive orientation is shared by the members of every society and is, Foster maintains, "an unverbalized, implicit expression of their understanding of the 'rules of the game' of living imposed upon them by their social, natural, and supernatural universes. A cognitive orientation provides the members of the society it characterizes with basic premises and sets of assumptions normally neither recognized nor questioned which structure and guide behavior in much the same way grammatical rules . . . structure and guide their linguistic forms."[16]

Although Foster suggests that his concept of a dominant model bears similarities to Kluckhohn's speculations on a "master configuration" in his writings of the 1940s, Foster's model departs from Kluckhohn's later configuration of value-orientations. For Kluckhohn does not suggest, as does Foster, that one model "subsumes the greatest [possible] amount of behavior in such a fashion that there are no mutually incompatible parts in the model, i.e., forms of behavior cast together in what is obviously a logically inconsistent relationship."[17] Furthermore, unlike Kluckhohn, Foster holds that "all normative behavior of the members of a group is a function of its particular cognitive orientation" and that "a peasant's cognitive view provides moral and other precepts that are guides to—in fact, may be said to produce —behavior."[18] In Kluckhohn's system the elements are more complexly organized, and the relation between normative and existential propositions is thought of as reciprocal, each affecting, and being affected by, the other.

Foster describes the "image of limited good," which he interchangeably terms the "dominant theme," "integrating principle," and "model":

> By "Image of Limited Good" I mean that broad areas of peasant behavior are patterned in such fashion as to suggest that peasants view their social, economic, and natural universes—their total environment—as one in which all of the desired things in life such as land, wealth, health, friendship and love, manliness and honor, respect and status, power and influence, security and safety, *exist in finite quantity* and *are always in short supply*, as far as the peasant is concerned. Not only do these and all other "good things" exist in finite and limited quantities, but in addition *there is no way directly within peasant power to increase the available quantities.*[19]

He says that he considers the peasant community a closed system, that "a peasant sees his existence as determined and limited by the natural and social resources of his village and his immediate area."

Consequently, there is a corollary to the image of limited good: "If 'Good' exists in limited amounts which cannot be expanded, and if the system is closed, it follows that *an individual or a family can improve a position only at the expense of others.*" Thus it follows that "an apparent relative improvement in someone's position with respect to any 'Good,' is viewed as a threat to the entire community."[20]

Foster believes that the image of limited good is the dominant theme in the cognitive orientation, not only of the Mexican peasants about whom he has written extensively,[21] but also of classic peasant societies in general (as defined by Kroeber), which Foster finds rimming the Mediterranean and existing in the Near East, India, and China, as well as in a large portion of Indian and mestizo villages in Latin America today.[22] This model is a part of the growing attempt to understand peasant behavior in a more organized way, and reflects changing conceptions of the nature of peasant society itself. Thus Redfield's early view of the folk society as traditional, integrated, homogeneous, sacred, familial, and co-operative[23] has been challenged as lacking realism. Oscar Lewis, in restudying Tepoztlán, found tension, fear, envy, lack of co-operation, distrust, and hostility in the village culture, which he believed Redfield had largely overlooked.[24] Foster goes farther than Lewis, to conclude that the behavior of peasants throughout the world is dominated by a negative view that sanctions extreme individualism and envy, and discourages all forms of co-operation.

In considering whether this model is applicable to Žerovnica, it should be noted that today Žerovnica must be considered a transitional peasant community, although until the postwar period it met the definition of a classic peasant society. Foster believes that his model is applicable, in some form, to transitional as well as to traditional peasant societies, for he says that the cognitive view of the modern peasant, living in a rapidly changing world, produces behavior "that may not be appropriate to the changing conditions of life he has not yet grasped."[25] Furthermore, while asserting that a peasant views his system as closed, Foster states that there is an important exception to this conclusion, since even a traditional peasant village has access to other systems. Moreover, economic success gained from outside sources has increased in importance in transitional peasant societies. He maintains, however, that today, as formerly, "such success, though envied, is not seen as a direct threat to community stability, for no one within the community has lost anything." Attitudes toward these new sources of wealth, according to Foster, are but modern variants of an older pattern in which luck and fate explain and sanction outside success in the peasant community.[26]

The basic economic resource, land, does appear to be viewed in Žerovnica as finite and in short supply (a reasonable view, since land has in fact been limited for a very long time). And while villagers have long recognized the existence of differences in size of landholdings in the village, they typically describe themselves as a group of peasants who own approximately a quarter *zemlja* each and who participate equally in the crop rotation system. Even when they concede the presence of landless families and larger-than-average landholders in the community, most villagers give unrealistically low estimates of the number of families that deviate from the ideal. It seems justifiable to assume that villagers uphold the norm of equal landholdings, although contrary to fact, because they traditionally perceived increased landholding in one family as a threat that could impoverish others in the group. It appears that this view has been strengthened by recent government policies and has encouraged an attitude of skepticism toward reforms purporting to increase productivity or the supply of economic resources. For example, many villagers believe that the project to improve the lake land cannot succeed, that an increase in peasant income resulting from conversion to a cattle economy would only enrich the government, and that land exchanges between families would probably only bring about a less equitable division of land resources. In short, today most landowning villagers fear risks and deny the effectiveness of economic reforms.

Although the image of limited good seems useful in analyzing the relation of Žerovnica villagers to the land, Foster's conclusions concerning the limitation of every economic good and his related assumption of a closed society have less utility. As to the first, although Žerovnica was always poor, not every economic good was viewed as absolutely limited. As to the second, Foster maintains his view of the closed society even though he accepts Kroeber's definition of peasant societies as constituting "part-societies with part-cultures," which assumes the partial openness of peasant society.[27] Specifically, Foster asserts that economic gains from outside sources are not seen as a threat to community stability, for no one within the community has lost anything. But in Žerovnica factory labor and other outside occupations do mean a loss to the community and are viewed as a threat as well as an opportunity; for although they enrich the village by providing additional income, which has always been necessary for survival, they also deprive the village by withdrawing manpower. Furthermore, the social and upward mobility of young people, which makes it possible for them to desert the village permanently, is an even more serious threat to community stability. Nor can one overlook the effect on the village of the impingement from the outside of institutions such as the co-operative farm, which has threatened village resources of land, and the *občina*, which appears to the peasant to restrict the riches of the forest and to withdraw increasing amounts of peasant income through taxation. Even in the traditional village, which was less affected by social mobility, the departure of young people, and the impingement of outside institutions, relations with the outside were far too significant to allow the assumption of a closed system. This does not mean that the traditional community did not have some characteristics of a closed society, among them a preference for endogamy, practices to prevent land dispersal, and integrating and corporate institutions. At the same time, however, markets and other forms of trade, wage labor, and emigration provided contact with systems of the larger society. Thus, while some aspects of economic behavior in Žerovnica seemed to reflect a perception of limited good, not all economic resources were viewed as finite, since there was always access to outside resources. And the consequences of this were so complex that the behavior of the inhabitants of Žerovnica cannot be explained without reference to the outside world as well as to the village framework.

To what extent in Žerovnica is the concept of limited good applied to other than economic good in society?[28] Although there is evidence of tension between brothers, generations, economic strata, political factions, and, in the modern young generation, between the sexes, friendship and love are not generally viewed as existing in finite and limited quantities. Family loyalty and strong feelings of obligation and affection are still an important part of the Žerovnica ethos; relations between mother and children are affectionate and close, and the conception that there is not enough love for all the children, which Foster has ascribed to peasants,[29] is alien to the village. Nor is there evidence that health is perceived as severely limited, as Foster implies, for today the benefits of modern medicine and the provisions of health insurance do affect peasant mentality. Again, manliness and honor, said by Foster to be viewed as limited, are not so conceptualized in Žerovnica.[30] Although the patriarchal tradition is still strong, and the *gospodar* does not wish to abandon his prerogatives, husband and wife have traditionally shared responsibility and decision making, and they do so increasingly today.

Finally, Foster's dichotomy between individualism and maximum co-operation does not apply. Foster says, "People who see themselves in 'threatened' circumstances, which the Image of Limited Good implies, react normally in one of two ways: maximum cooperation and sometimes communism, burying individual differences and placing sanctions against individualism; or extreme individualism." He believes that peasant societies always seem to choose the second alternative.[31] However, while the villagers of Žerovnica are individualistic, they are not extreme individualists. Traditionally, both group solidarity and individualism were a part of Žerovnica culture, and they were not viewed as contradictory. Foster's depiction of the ideal peasant as "a man who works to feed and clothe his family, who fulfills his community and ceremonial obligations, who minds his own business, who does not seek to be outstanding, but who knows how to protect his rights"[32] does not fully describe the Žerovnica ideal type. While the ideal man fulfills his family and community obligations, protects his own rights and minds his own business, and avoids boasting and ostentatious behavior, he also shares feelings of responsibility for the general welfare of the community. Traditionally he was not reluctant to assume leadership roles in the village community. Today, because such roles are less meaningful, there is less interest in community participation, although the tradition has not yet entirely disappeared. It would be inaccurate to apply to Žerovnica Foster's statement that "each minimal social unit (often the nuclear family and, in many situations, a single individual) sees itself in perpetual, unrelenting struggle with its fellows for possession of or control over what it considers to be its share of scarce values."[33] Thus even today, when opportunities for co-operative behavior within the peasant village have lessened and factions have developed, the "mentality of mutual distrust"[34] cannot be ascribed to the Žerovnica personality.

Foster has asserted that in a traditional peasant society "hard work and thrift are moral qualities of only the slightest functional value," and that in the peasant view success and progress, insofar as they are realized, are due more to luck and fate than to an individual's own resources.[35] In Žerovnica while traditionally, dramatic success came only to those who settled in what was looked upon as the almost miraculous land of America, such personal resources as talent, wisdom, and cleverness were also recognized and valued. Furthermore, villagers have upheld the moral value of hard work and thrift, and they continue to do so even though today they doubt that work and savings can significantly improve their material position. While the fruits of hard work have been limited, industry and thrift have been necessary for survival and thus are functional. Moreover, the motivation today to help sons and daughters to achieve success outside the peasant village provides new sanctions for work. In this respect, one must not discount the influence of the values of the great traditions in which peasants participate,[36] for the moral worth of work has been a value in the society of which Žerovnica has been a part since the Austrian period.

Foster concludes that in the traditional peasant society what McClelland has called the need for achievement ("*N* Achievement")[37] cannot be a significant motivation: "*n* Achievement is rare in traditional peasant societies, not because of psychological factors, but because display of *n* Achievement is met by sanctions that a traditional villager does not wish to incur. The villager who feels the need for Achievement, and who does something about it, is violating the basic, unverbalized rules of the society of which he is a member."[38]

Only in an open system of expanding opportunity, Foster asserts, could the peasant feel safe in displaying initiative.[39] Yet, historically, in the traditional peasant village society—less open and less threatened than today's—opportunities for display of initiative, although limited, were not insignificant. Nor did village sanctions rule against such behavior as long as the villager met his social obligations and continued to co-operate in the traditional village economy. Today the larger society has declared illegal many traditional activities that once demanded achieving behavior, but insofar as there is access to systems outside the contemporary village, new ways to display initiative are available to the younger generation. As opportunities for problem solving and risk taking are withdrawn from peasant society, one of the few ways left for the peasant to achieve is to help his children leave the peasant world. Yet traditions are not forgotten, even if they exert less force today, and it appears that in spite of the pressure exerted on the traditional peasant by the outside world, the basic unverbalized rules of the peasant community do not rule out the manifestation of the need for achievement, nor did they in the past.

THERE ARE two general reasons why, in Žerovnica—where land, the most important economic resource, was restricted in the past and still is today—the image of limited good nevertheless cannot be generally extended to behavior in Foster's idiom.

First, it is difficult to apply an over-all cognitive orientation to peasant behavior in general, for peasantry is composed of subtypes different enough to require additional specification of the conditions under which Foster's model is relevant.[40] For example, traditional values and characteristics of the larger society, and the traditional functioning of integrating social, economic, and political institutions, are important circumstances pertaining to the peasants of Žerovnica. And today particular circumstances related to the Yugoslav brand of independent socialism have also affected the peasant community. Thus, in relation to land the system has become more closed; yet in relation to the social mobility of young people it has become more open. In addition, the values of the new society are beginning to affect the traditional peasant outlook. Not only types of peasantry must be distinguished; even within a traditional peasant community, internal strata and groups need not share identical values, as has become evident in this study of the people of Žerovnica.

Second, Foster seems to suggest, as Piker has pointed out, that peasants proceed from the conclusion that material wealth, or good, is limited "to the general premises that 'Good' as a generic quantity is limited in all areas of life."[41] In Žerovnica the presence of limited economic resources does not lead to such a metaphysical view. As significant as economic conditions are in shaping world views, other factors are also at work. And these factors contribute to a restricted or more generous view of "generic good" in peasant society. Underlying Foster's reasoning seems to be an assumption that upholds the absolute priority of the cognitive aspect of the dominant theme of peasant behavior: "Show the peasant that initiative is profitable, and that it will not be met by negative sanctions, and he acquires it in short order. . . . Change the cognitive orientation through changing access to opportunities, and the peasant will do very well indeed."[42] Foster also asserts that if peasant behavior seems irrational within a changing world it is because the peasant has not grasped the changing conditions.[43] If Foster had given more emphasis to the dynamic inter-play between the normative and the cognitive aspects of peasant behavior, it seems likely that he would not have suggested the total priority of the cognitive conclusion that economic wealth is limited. In relation to change, he might have given more weight to the force of normative views, which, along with empirical observations, help to shape perceptions and also work for the persistence of cultural ways.

Therefore, while Foster's model does apply to some aspects of behavior in the village, it does not seem possible to apply the concept of limited good to behavior in general in Žerovnica. Even in considering the traditional village alone, the role of value conflict, the importance of normative elements within value systems, and the influence of the values of the great traditions in which peasants participate cannot be neglected. Today traditional values, though less functional than in the past, still affect behavior; but a strong influence on change is a new value that is related to the traditional one of individual initiative but is primarily a part of the new socialist morality. Thus upward mobility in the expanding economy of the larger society has become a new "good" valued by the young. This view is beginning to affect the mentality of traditional peasants and to change the internal structure of the peasant community. The conflict between the old and the new outlook explains some of the complexities of behavior in Žerovnica, where the peasant style of life is both preserved and questioned by the traditional villagers; where work is both useless in significantly improving the traditional economy and useful in supporting the young; where the successes of young people both threaten and enrich the older generation; and where the young both question land ownership and resist surrendering it. Except for those who compose, or identify with, the new elite group, it appears that most villagers of the adult generation share a world outlook that is characterized by apathy and pessimism toward their own fate, tempered, however, by the more positive values of the past and by identification with the young in their struggle to achieve success outside the village.

# NOTES
# BIBLIOGRAPHY
# INDEX

5. Kos, *Zgodovina Slovencev*, p. 25.

6. Ibid., p. 46.

7. Ibid., p. 77.

8. Tomasevich, *Peasants, Politics, and Economic Change in Yugoslavia*, pp. 130–31.

9. Grafenauer, *Zgodovina slovenskega naroda*, 2:105–6.

10. Ibid., p. 136.

11. *Jugoslavia*, Geographical Handbook Series, 2:8.

12. Grafenauer, *Zgodovina slovenskega naroda*, 4:57.

13. Ibid., 3:66.

14. Tomasevich, *Peasants, Politics, and Economic Change*, p. 131.

15. Grafenauer, *Zgodovina slovenskega naroda*, 5:23.

16. Ibid., p. 50.

17. Ibid., pp. 26–27.

18. Tomasevich, *Peasants, Politics, and Economic Change*, pp. 82–83.

19. Warriner, ed., *Contrasts in Emerging Societies*, pp. 3, 11.

20. Planina, ed., *Slovenija*, p. 27.

21. This folk tale and others quoted have been translated by Vladimir Rus.

22. *Nix*—colloquial German; *figl fajgl*—an onomatopoeic imitation of the noise of sharpening scythes; *durch mahaj*—Slovenized imperative of German verb *durchmachen*.

23. Auty, "Yugoslavia: Introduction," in *Emerging Societies*, ed. Warriner, p. 291.

24. Ibid.; and "Help for Home Industries," in ibid., pp. 358–61.

25. "Fragmentation," in ibid., p. 354.

26. "Causes of Agricultural Depression," in ibid., p. 363.

27. Tomasevich, *Peasants, Politics, and Economic Change*, p. 132.

28. Ibid., p. 4.

29. Ibid., p. 225.

30. The cadastral yoke (*catastral joch*) standardized in 1875, equals 0.57 hectares or 1.4 acres. Warriner, *Emerging Societies*, p. 112.

31. Tomasevich, *Peasants, Politics, and Economic Change*, pp. 347–49.

32. Ibid., p. 368; and Warriner, "Urban Thinkers and Peasant Policy in Yugoslavia, 1918–59," p. 65.

33. Warriner, "Urban Thinkers," p. 66.

34. Tomasevich, *Peasants, Politics, and Economic Change*, p. 479.

35. Ibid., p. 316.

36. Ibid., p. 324.

37. Ibid., pp. 672–73.

38. Melik, *Slovenija*, p. 384.

39. Grafenauer, *Zgodovina slovenskega naroda*, 5:27.

40. I cannot ascertain the accuracy of this statement since there was great reluctance to discuss this subject.

41. Since 1963 the official name of Yugoslavia has been the Socialist Federal Republic of Yugoslavia (SFRJ).

42. The entire peninsula was ceded to Yugoslavia by Italy.

43. Spulber, "Eastern Europe," p. 399.

44. *Informativni priručnik o Jugoslaviji, Opšti podaci o privrednom, kulturnom i prosvetnom živote u FNRJ* (Belgrade, 1948–51), 1:476, quoted in Markert, ed., *Jugoslawien*, p. 229.

45. Warriner, "Urban Thinkers," p. 67.

46. Ibid., p. 69.

# 3 The Early Society

1. According to Vilfan, *kmetija* and *zemlja* are general Slovene terms that traditionally referred to "a rounded-off economic unit in a one-family peasant operation that included a hut, farm buildings, a garden, fields, meadows, and various possibilities for participation in the exploitation of the forest and pasture land. This unit could be larger or smaller, in one piece or with fields distributed. . . . In short, *kmetija* is a broad term designating a peasant economic operation that could be of varied size, composition, and origin, and that nourished one peasant family." Vilfan, *Pravna zgodovina Slovencev*, p. 69.

The Slovenized German terms *huba* and *grunt* or Latin *mansus* also came to be used interchangeably with the Slovene *kmetija* or *zemlja* when the latter concepts acquired definite legal form and content under western feudalism as it developed in Slovene lands. Ibid., p. 75. The *huba* was calculated as the amount of land that the average peasant family could cultivate and from which the family could gain sufficient income for the landlord's rent. Ibid., p. 76.

2. Synonymous Slovene terms are: *kajžar, bajtar,* and *kočar,* all of which correspond to the English term *cottager* and the German *Hüttler.*

3. Mosely, "The Peasant Family," p. 95.

4. Tomasevich, *Peasants, Politics, and Economic Change in Yugoslavia,* p. 180.

5. Ibid., p. 181.

6. Dragutin Tončić, quoted in ibid., p. 180.

7. Tomasic, *Personality and Culture in Eastern European Politics;* idem, "The Family in the Balkans," pp. 301–7.

8. Mosely, "The Distribution of the Zadruga within Southeastern Europe," p. 222.

9. St. Erlich, *Family in Transition,* p. 32.

10. Gruden, *Zgodovina slovenskega naroda,* 1:28–29.

11. Grafenauer, *Zgodovina slovenskega naroda,* 1:139.

12. Ibid., p. 140.

13. Melik, *Slovenija*, p. 389.
14. Vilfan, *Pravna zgodovina Slovencev*, pp. 54–55.
15. Grafenauer, *Zgodovina slovenskega naroda*, 2:98.
16. Kos, *Zgodovina Slovencev od naselitve do petnajstega stoletja*, p. 128.
17. Grafenauer, *Zgodovina slovenskega naroda*, 2:137.
18. Melik, *Slovenija*, p. 389.
19. Vilfan, *Pravna zgodovina Slovencev*, pp. 54–55.
20. Kos, *Zgodovina Slovencev*, p. 332.
21. Ibid., p. 334.
22. Vilfan, *Pravna zgodovina Slovencev*, p. 260.

## 4 The Stem Family and Traditional Elites

1. LePlay, Frédéric, Focillon, and Delaire, *L'organisation de la famille* (Tours, 1884), cited in Arensberg and Kimball, *Culture and Community*, p. 235.
2. Ibid., p. 234.
3. Ibid., p. 235.
4. Ibid., p. 238.
5. Vilfan, *Pravna zgodovina Slovencev*, p. 261.
6. Mal, *Zgodovina slovenskega naroda*, p. 1062.
7. Arensberg and Kimball, *Culture and Community*, p. 235.
8. Wolf, "Cultural Dissonance in the Italian Alps," p. 9.

## 5 The Village Socioeconomic Structure and the Outside World

1. Wolf, *Peasants*, pp. 3–4.
2. Ibid., p. 9.
3. Ibid., p. 15.
4. "Fragmentation," in *Contrasts in Emerging Societies*, ed. Warriner, p. 354.
5. Ibid., p. 290.
6. Max Weber, "Class, Status, Party," *From Max Weber, Essays in Sociology*, pp. 181–95.
7. See Kennedy, " 'Peasant Society and the Image of Limited Good,' " p. 1216. Also, Goldkind, "Social Stratification in the Peasant Community," pp. 863–84; and Goldberg, "Elite Groups in Peasant Communities," pp. 718–31.
8. Goldberg, "Elite Groups."
9. Kennedy, "Peasant Society," p. 1217.

10. Stirling, *Turkish Village,* p. 221.

11. I have omitted a family in which mental deficiency has affected two generations. The church records of this family are incomplete, and few villagers are willing to discuss them.

12. *Statistički bilten: Savezni zavod za statistiku i evidenciju FNRJ,* no. 11 (July 1952), cited in Markert, ed., *Jugoslawien,* p. 231.

13. State farms are distinguished from working co-operatives. In the former, land is owned by the state and workers are employed as wage laborers. The assets of the working co-operative, in principle, are jointly owned by the members.

14. Warriner, "Urban Thinkers and Peasant Policy in Yugoslavia, 1918–59," p. 70.

15. Ibid., p. 71.

16. Ibid.

17. Ibid., p. 72.

18. Hočevar, *The Structure of the Slovenian Economy 1848–1963,* p. 229.

19. Mihailo Vučković, "The Transformation of the Peasant Cooperative," p. 28.

20. Ibid., p. 21.

21. *Minutes of the People's Assembly of the People's Republic of Slovenia,* quoted in Hočevar, *Slovenian Economy,* p. 230.

22. Vukčević, "The Legal Status of Private Agricultural Land," pp. 20–21.

23. Ibid., p. 13.

24. Fisher, *Yugoslavia,* p. 186.

25. Peasants, who are also classed as private producers, composed the largest group deprived of these privileges.

26. The dinar:dollar ratio in 1965 was 750:1, so the fee amounted to a little over $5.00 a month. Effective 1 January 1966, the dinar was revalued, one new dinar equaling one hundred of the previous dinars. Since that time peasants refer to "old" and "new" dinars. When I quote figures simply as dinars I am referring to old dinars.

27. David Binder in the *New York Times,* 20 October 1965, p. 17.

28. Two houses had been abandoned some time before World War II. A third was owned by an absent son whose parents were dead. As the only son, he surrendered his land to Marof and became a truck driver for the *občina,* but he hoped to regain his land when he married. A fourth house had been bought by a man who had not established residence in the village.

29. Two landless houses are occupied by young unmarried *gospodars,* and two other houses are each occupied by an elderly couple whose children have left the village.

30. In tables 9–15, if the *gospodar* is in nonagricultural employment, it is his occupation (in addition to his landholding) that is used as a criterion

of classification regardless of whether another member pursues another type of occupation. In such cases, and there are only three, the occupation of the second member is indicated. If the *gospodar* is a peasant and one family member is employed outside the village, the occupation of the second member is the one used in classifying the family. In one case two other members of the family are in nonagricultural employment, and the occupation of the eldest employed male is used. For an individual retired on social security, his last occupation is used, if it is known. Children are so classified until they graduate from the eight-grade school. In a household that includes three generations the eldest generation consists of one person unless otherwise indicated.

31. There were two others who had worked in the factory over a long period, but their circumstances differed. One (family 5) was the young *gospodar* who had recently bought his house and was unmarried. Another (family 8) was an elderly *gospodar* in ill health who had to retire without full benefits.

32. While these two *gospodars* were former specialists and held land as well, each secured his inheritance only after a dispute with a contending brother. As has been shown, most specialists were drawn from the landless class.

# 6 The Village Economy

1. Grafenauer, *Zgodovina slovenskega naroda*, 5:27.

2. The ditch results, a *gospodar* explained, when one is forced to plow in one direction and then plow in the other direction in the next furrow, because the plow on one side turns the land one way, and on the other side it turns the land the opposite way.

3. The strip is too narrow to allow mowing on the return. Should the *gospodar* attempt this, the oxen would trample on the next field, which is owned by another.

4. There were six widows in the village in 1965; three of them were aided by grown sons (only one of these sons was married), and three had no male helper.

5. True coffee, which is called Turkish coffee (*turška kava*), is an expensive delicacy that is ground and prepared in Turkish style and served in demitasses on special occasions and for guests. The wife does not include herself when she serves Turkish coffee to the *gospodar* and his visitors. The substitute coffee, called *kava* or *kava Frank*, after an Austrian and German brand, is a brew of roast ground grain.

6. Wolf, *Peasants*, p. 58.

7. According to a 1968 report, the rationale for the system of taxation of individual farmers is the following: "Under the Income Tax Decree of 1953 tax levied on income from agriculture was to be collected on the

basis of cadastral revenue, i.e. of average revenue that could accrue from the land of a definite category. This alteration made it possible to determine the tax base on the grounds of objective measurements and criteria for several years in advance. This tax system was intended to stimulate the farmers to use their land as rationally as possible, thus improving their economic position while indirectly reducing their tax charges." Vukčević, "The Legal Status of Private Agricultural Land," p. 15.

## 7 Local Government and the State

1. Hoffman and Neal, *Yugoslavia and the New Communism*, p. 224.
2. Ibid., p. 230.
3. Ibid., p. 211.
4. Ibid., pp. 224–25.
5. Wolf, *The Balkans in Our Times*, p. 434.
6. Djordjević and Pašić, "The Communal Self-Government System in Yugoslavia," p. 390.
7. Fisher, *Yugoslavia*, p. 149.
8. Ibid., p. 150.
9. Ibid., pp. 154, 155.
10. Djordjević and Pašić, "Communal Self-Government," p. 404.
11. Hoffman and Neal, *Yugoslavia*, p. 230.
12. Djordjević and Pašić, "Communal Self-Government," p. 405.
13. Hoffman and Neal, *Yugoslavia*, p. 216.
14. Ibid., p. 218.
15. Fisher, *Yugoslavia*, p. 153.
16. Hoffman and Neal, *Yugoslavia*, p. 216.
17. Ibid., p. 218.
18. Fisher, *Yugoslavia*, p. 153.
19. Zaninovich, *The Development of Socialist Yugoslavia*, p. 117.
20. "The Constitution of the Socialist Federal Republic of Yugoslavia," *Socialist Thought and Practice*, no. 10 (June 1963), p. 47.
21. Hoffman and Neal, *Yugoslavia*, pp. 225, 226.
22. Fisher, *Yugoslavia*, p. 185.
23. Ibid., p. 172.
24. Ibid., p. 152.
25. Ibid., p. 173.
26. Ibid., p. 181.
27. Ibid., p. 186.
28. Ibid., pp. 175, 181.
29. Hoffman and Neal, *Yugoslavia*, p. 296.
30. Auty, *Yugoslavia*, p. 169.
31. Fisher, *Yugoslavia*, p. 73.
32. Ibid.

33. *Krajevni Leksikon Dravske Banovine* (Ljubljana, 1937); *Krajevni Leksikon L. R. Slovenije* (Ljubljana, 1954); *Krajevni Leksikon Slovenije* (Ljubljana, 1968).

# 8 Social Aspects of Village Life

1. Two of the four families in the village that were reduced to one generation were composed of the generation whose children had left for other occupations. The case of the elderly miller who refused to abandon his land although he was ill and had to rely on relatives' help was described earlier. His only son, a partisan, was killed during the war, and his three daughters married outside the village. An elderly couple who held one-sixth of a *zemlja* also had to depend on the help of others. In lieu of close relatives, they had to ask neighbors to assist them. Their one child, a daughter, had left the village, and consequently the wife had to work in the factory and try to keep up her land while supporting her invalid husband. In 1969 we learned that her husband had died and she had been forced to sell her land.

2. Following is a list of the most important kinship terms and the appropriate forms of address, including recent variations:

| *Kinship Term* | *Forms of Address* |
|---|---|
| father: *oče* | *ata* or *oče;* usually *vi,* but sometimes *ti* |
| mother: *mati* | *mama;* usually *vi,* but sometimes *ti* |
| brother: *brat* | first name; *ti* |
| sister: *sestra* | first name; *ti* |
| grandfather: *stari oče* | *stari oče* or *stari ata; vi* |
| grandmother: *stara mati* | *stara mama; vi* |
| father-in-law: *tast* | *ata* or *oče;* usually *vi,* but sometimes *ti* |
| mother-in-law: *tašče* | *mama;* usually *vi,* but sometimes *ti* |
| son-in-law: *zet* | first name; *ti* |
| daughter-in-law: *snaha* | first name; *ti* |
| uncle: *stric* (maternal and paternal) | first name or *stric; vi,* but sometimes *ti* |
| aunt: *teta* (maternal and paternal) | first name or *teta; vi,* but sometimes *ti* |
| brother-in-law: *svak* | *svak* or first name; *ti* or *vi,* depending on his age |
| sister-in-law: *svakinje* | *svakinje* or first name; *ti* or *vi,* depending on her age |
| cousin (male): *bratranec* | first name; *ti* |
| cousin (female): *sestrična* | first name; *ti* |

3. See Wolf, *Peasants*, pp. 84–91; idem, "Closed Corporate Peasant Communities in Mesoamerica and Central Java," pp. 7–18; idem, "Types of Latin American Peasantry," pp. 452–66.
4. Wolf, *Peasants*, p. 86.
5. Ibid., p. 81.

# 9 Religion

1. "Margins of Existence," in *Contrasts in Emerging Societies,* ed. Warriner, p. 350.

# 10 The Life Cycle

1. Prišlo je jutro / Ko moram iti od tebe / draga mati, oče in sestrice; / Ne bom pozabil tudi vas, dragi bratje / Tudi vi se me kdaj spomnite / Ne grem jaz daleč / Dragi sošolce, sošolke, / V domovini svoji še bom ostal. / Draga šola in profesorji moji / Vse vas prosim, da bi vam roko podal / Še bom kratek spomin na vas ohranil / Še vam pošljem belo pismo / Drobno. Vendar ne bomo nikoli več / Tako srečni, kot smo bili v šoli ali domu.

# 11 The Question of Modernization

1. Dalton, "Theoretical Issues in Economic Anthropology," p. 78.
2. Smelser, "Toward a Theory of Modernization," pp. 30–31.
3. Ibid., pp. 31–32.
4. Dalton, "Theoretical Issues," p. 76.
5. Ibid., pp. 78–79.

# 12 The Peasant World View

1. Redfield, *The Primitive World and Its Transformations*, p. 86.
2. Kluckhohn and others, "Values and Value-Orientations in the Theory of Action," pp. 388–433.
3. Ibid., p. 392.
4. Ibid., p. 394.
5. Ibid., p. 395.
6. Ibid., p. 400.
7. Lévi-Strauss, *Structural Anthropology*, p. 281.

8. Kluckhohn, "Values and Value-Orientations," p. 400.

9. Ibid., p. 411.

10. Ibid., p. 412.

11. Ibid., pp. 419–21.

12. Northrop, *The Logic of the Sciences and the Humanities,* pp. 335–61.

13. Kluckhohn, "Values and Value-Orientations," p. 410.

14. Foster, "Peasant Society and the Image of Limited Good," pp. 293–315.

15. Ibid., p. 294.

16. Ibid., p. 293.

17. Ibid., p. 294.

18. Ibid., p. 295.

19. Ibid., p. 296.

20. Ibid., pp. 296–97.

21. Foster, *Tzintzuntzan,* and other works (see Bibliography).

22. Foster, "Image of Limited Good," pp. 296, 311, n. 3.

23. See Redfield, "The Folk Society," and other works (see Bibliography).

24. Lewis, *Life in a Mexican Village.*

25. Foster, "Image of Limited Good," p. 295.

26. Ibid., p. 306.

27. Ibid., p. 311, n. 3.

28. "It is as if the obvious fact of land shortage in a densely populated area applied to all other desired things: not enough to go around. 'Good,' like land, is seen as inherent in nature, there to be divided and redivided, if necessary, but not to be augmented." Ibid., p. 296.

29. Ibid., p. 298.

30. Ibid., p. 300.

31. Ibid., p. 301.

32. Ibid., p. 304.

33. Ibid., p. 302.

34. Ibid. (Foster refers to Friedmann, "The World of 'La Miseria.' ")

35. Ibid., p. 307.

36. See Kennedy, " 'Peasant Society and The Image of Limited Good,' " p. 1213.

37. McClelland, "The Achievement Motive in Economic Growth," pp. 74–96.

38. Foster, "Image of Limited Good," p. 309.

39. Ibid., p. 310.

40. See Kennedy, "Peasant Society," p. 1222.

41. Piker, " 'The Image of Limited Good,' " p. 1203.

42. Foster, "Image of Limited Good," p. 310.

43. Ibid., p. 295.

# Bibliography

ANDERSON, ROBERT T., and ANDERSON, GALLATIN. "The Indirect Social
    Structure of European Village Communities." *American Anthro-
    pologist* 64 (Oct. 1962):1016–27.
ARENSBERG, CONRAD M., and KIMBALL, SOLON T. *Culture and Community.*
    New York: Harcourt, Brace & World, 1965.
ARNEZ, JOHN A. *Slovenia in European Affairs: Reflections on Slovenian
    Political History.* New York: Studia Slovenica, 1958.
AUTY, PHYLLIS. *Yugoslavia.* New York: Walker & Co., 1965.
————. "Yugoslavia: Introduction." In *Contrasts in Emerging Societies:
    Readings in the Social and Economic History of South-Eastern
    Europe in the Nineteenth Century,* edited by Doreen Warriner, pp.
    283–93. Bloomington: Indiana University Press, 1965.
BADJURA, RUDOLF. *Bloško starosvetsko smučanje in besedje* [Traditional
    Skiing and Sayings in Bloke]. Ljubljana: Državna založba Slovenije,
    1956.
BANFIELD, EDWARD C. *The Moral Basis of a Backward Society.* Glencoe, Ill.:
    The Free Press, 1958.
BRITOVŠEK, MARIJAN. *Razkroj feodalne agrarne strukture* [The Develop-
    ment of the Feudal Agrarian Structure]. Ljubljana, 1964.
DALTON, GEORGE. "Theoretical Issues in Economic Anthropology." *Current
    Anthropology* 10 (Feb. 1969):63–102.
DJORDJEVIĆ, JOVAN, and PAŠIĆ, NAJDAN. "The Communal Self-Government
    System in Yugoslavia." *International Social Science Journal* 13
    (1961):389–407.
ERLICH-STEIN, VERA. "The Southern Slav Patriarchal Family." *Sociological
    Review* 32 (July–Oct. 1940):224–41.
FISHER, JACK C. *Yugoslavia: A Multinational State.* San Francisco: Chandler
    Publishing Co., 1966.
FOSTER, GEORGE M. "What is Folk Culture?" *American Anthropologist* 55
    (Apr.–June 1953):159–73.
————. "Interpersonal Relations in Peasant Society." *Human Organization*
    19 (1960–61):174–78.
————. "The Dyadic Contract: A Model for the Social Structure of a
    Mexican Peasant Village." *American Anthropologist* 63 (Dec.
    1961):1173–92.

———. "The Dyadic Contract in Tzintzuntzan, II: Patron-Client Relationship." *American Anthropologist* 65 (Dec. 1963):1280–94.

———. "Peasant Society and the Image of Limited Good." *American Anthropologist* 67 (Apr. 1965):293–315.

———. "Foster's Reply to Kaplan, Saler, and Bennet." *American Anthropologist* 68 (Feb. 1966):211–14.

———. *Tzintzuntzan: Mexican Peasants in a Changing World*. Boston: Little, Brown & Co., 1967.

FRIEDMANN, F. G. "The World of 'La Miseria.' " *Partisan Review* 20 (Mar.–Apr. 1953):218–31.

GILLIN, JOHN. "Ethos and Cultural Aspects of Personality." In *Heritage of Conquest: The Ethnology of Middle America*, edited by Sol Tax, pp. 193–212. Glencoe, Ill.: The Free Press, 1952.

GOLDBERG, HARVEY. "Elite Groups in Peasant Communities: A Comparison of Three Middle Eastern Villages." *American Anthropologist* 70 (Aug. 1968):718–31.

GOLDKIND, VICTOR. "Social Stratification in the Peasant Community: Redfield's Chan Kom Reinterpreted." *American Anthropologist* 67 (Aug. 1965):863–84.

GRAFENAUER, BOGO. *Zgodovina slovenskega naroda* [History of the Slovenian People]. 5 vols. Ljubljana: Kmečka knjiga, 1954–62.

GRUDEN, J. *Zgodovina slovenskega naroda* [History of the Slovenian People]. Vol. 1. Celovec [Klagenfurt]: Družba Sv. Mohorja, 1910.

HALPERN, JOEL. *A Serbian Village*. New York: Columbia University Press, 1956.

———. "Farming as a Way of Life: Yugoslav Peasant Attitudes." Paper presented at Conference on Soviet and East European Agriculture, 27 Aug. 1965. Mimeographed.

HOČEVAR, TOUSSAINT. *The Structure of the Slovenian Economy, 1848–1963*. New York: Studia Slovenica, 1965.

HOFFMAN, GEORGE W., and NEAL, FRED W. *Yugoslavia and the New Communism*. New York: Twentieth Century Fund, 1962.

HONIGMANN, JOHN J. "A Case Study of Community Development in Pakistan." *Economic Development and Cultural Change* 3 (Apr. 1960):288–303.

ILEŠIČ, SVETOZAR. *Sistemi poljske razdelitve na Slovenskem* [Systems of Field Division in Slovenia]. Ljubljana: Slovenian Academy of Sciences and Arts, 1950.

*Jugoslavia*. 3 vols. Geographical Handbook Series. London: Naval Intelligence Division, 1944–45.

KAPLAN, DAVID, and SALER, BENSON. "Foster's Image of Limited Good: An Example of Anthropological Explanation." *American Anthropologist* 68 (Feb. 1966):202–5.

KARDELJ, EDVARD. *Razvoj slovenskega narodnega vprašanja* [The Development of the Slovenian National Question]. Ljubljana: Državna založba, 1939.

KENNEDY, JOHN G. " 'Peasant Society and the Image of Limited Good': A Critique." *American Anthropologist* 68 (Oct. 1966):1212–25.

KERNER, ROBERT, ed. *Yugoslavia*. Berkeley and Los Angeles: University of California Press, 1949.

KLEMENŠIČ, VLADIMIR. *Pokrajina med Snežnikom in Slavnikom: Gospodarska geografija* [The Region between the Snežnik and the Slavnik: Economic Geography]. Ljubljana: Slovenian Academy of Sciences and Arts, 1959.

KLUCKHOHN, CLYDE, and others. "Values and Value-Orientations in the Theory of Action: An Exploration in Definition and Classification." In *Toward a General Theory of Action*, edited by Talcott Parsons and Edward A. Shils. Cambridge: Harvard University Press, 1951. (Harper Torchbooks, 1962.)

KOS, MILKO. *Zgodovina Slovencev od naselitve do petnajstega stoletja* [History of the Slovenes from the Settling to the Fifteenth Century]. Ljubljana: Slovenska Matica, 1955.

KRANJEC, SILVO, and LEBAN, VLADIMIR. *Zemljepis Jugoslavije za gimnazije* [Geography of Yugoslavia for High Schools]. Ljubljana: Državna založba slovenije, 1958.

KROEBER, A. L. *Anthropology*. New ed. New York: Harcourt, Brace & World, 1948.

KUHAR, ALOYSIUS L. *Slovene Medieval History: Selected Studies*. New York: Studia Slovenica, 1962.

KUNAVER, PAUL. *Kraški svet in njegovi pojavi* [The Karstic Area and Its Appearances]. Ljubljana, 1922.

———. *Cerkniško jezero* [The Cerknica Lake]. Ljubljana: Mladinska knjiga, 1961.

LÉVI-STRAUSS, CLAUDE. *Structural Anthropology*. Translated by Claire Jacobson and Brooke Grundfest Schoepf. New York: Basic Books, 1963.

LEWIS, OSCAR. *Life in a Mexican Village: Tepoztlán Restudied*. Urbana: University of Illinois Press, 1963.

MAL, JOSIP. *Zgodovina slovenskega naroda: Najnovejša doba* [History of the Slovene Nation: The Modern Period]. Celje: Družba Sv. Mohorja, 1928.

MARKERT, WERNER, ed. *Osteuropa-Handbuch: Jugoslawien*. Cologne and Graz: Böhlau-Verlag, 1954.

MC CLELLAND, DAVID C. *The Achieving Society*. Princeton, N.J.: D. Van Nostrand, 1961.

———. "The Achievement Motive in Economic Growth." In *Industrialization and Society*, edited by Bert F. Hoselitz and Wilbert E. Moore, pp. 74–95. New York: Humanities Press, 1963.

MC COWN, BEATRICE. "Agriculture." In *Yugoslavia,* edited by Robert Kerner, pp. 151–68. Berkeley and Los Angeles: University of California Press, 1949.

MELIK, ANTON. *Slovenija: Geografski opis* [Slovenia: A Geographic Description]. Vol. 1. Ljubljana: Slovenska Matica, 1963.

MODERNDORFER, VINKO. *Slovenska vas na Dolenjskom* [A Slovenian Village in Dolenjsko]. Ljubljana: Merkur, 1938.

MOSELY, PHILIP E. "The Peasant Family: The Zadruga or Communal Joint-Family in the Balkans, and Its Recent Evolution." In *The Cultural Approach to History,* edited by Caroline F. Ware, pp. 95–108. New York: Columbia University Press, 1940.

———. "The Distribution of the Zadruga within Southeastern Europe." In *The Joshua Starr Memorial Volume: Studies in History and Philology.* Jewish Social Studies Publications, no. 5. New York: Conference on Jewish Relations, 1953.

NEAL, EDWARD. "Reforms in Yugoslavia." *American Slavic and East European Review* 13 (Apr. 1954):227–44.

NORTHROP, F. S. C. *The Logic of the Sciences and the Humanities.* New York: Macmillan, 1947.

PIKER, STEVEN. " 'The Image of Limited Good': Comments on an Exercise in Description and Interpretation." *American Anthropologist* 68 (Oct. 1966):1202–11.

PLANINA, FRANCE, ed. *Slovenija: Turistični vodnik* [Slovenia: A Tourist Guide]. Ljubljana: Presernova družba, 1964.

RAMOVŠ, FRANC. *Dialektološka karta slovenskega jezika* [Dialectological Map of the Slovenian Language]. Ljubljana: Universitetna Tiskarna, 1931.

———. *Kratka zgodovina slovenskega jezika* [A Brief History of the Slovenian Language]. Ljubljana: Akademska založba, 1936.

REDFIELD, ROBERT. "The Folk Society." *American Journal of Sociology* 52 (Jan. 1947):293–308.

———. *The Primitive World and Its Transformations.* Ithaca, N.Y.: Cornell University Press, 1953.

———. *The Little Community: Viewpoints for the Study of a Human Whole.* Chicago: University of Chicago Press, 1955. (Phoenix Paperback, 1960.)

———. *Peasant Society and Culture: An Anthropological Approach to Civilization.* Chicago: University of Chicago Press, 1956. (Phoenix Paperback, 1960.)

SIEGEL, BERNARD J., and BEALS, ALAN R. "Pervasive Factionalism." *American Anthropologist* 62 (June 1960):394–417.

SMELSER, NEIL J. "Toward a Theory of Modernization." In *Tribal and Peasant Economies,* edited by George Dalton, pp. 29–48. Garden City, N.Y.: Natural History Press, 1967.

SPULBER, NICOLAS. "Eastern Europe: The Changes in Agriculture from Land Reforms to Collectivization." *American Slavic and East European Review* 13 (Oct. 1954):389–401.

*Statistički bilten: Savezni zavod za statistiku i evidenciju FNRJ* [Statistical Bulletin. Federal Office for Statistics and Records]. No. 11, Belgrade, 1952.

ST. ERLICH, VERA. *Family in Transition: A Study of 300 Yugoslav Villages.* Princeton, N.J.: Princeton University Press, 1966.

STIRLING, PAUL. *Turkish Village.* New York: John Wiley, 1965.

TOMASEVICH, JOZO. *Peasants, Politics, and Economic Change in Yugoslavia.* Stanford: Stanford University Press, 1955.

TOMASIC, DINKO A. *Personality and Culture in Eastern European Politics.* New York: George W. Stewart, 1948.

———. "The Family in the Balkans." *Marriage and Family Living* 16 (Nov. 1954):301–7.

VALOCH, KAREL. "Evolution of the Paleolithic in Central and Eastern Europe." *Current Anthropology* 9 (Dec. 1968):351–68.

VALVASOR, JOHANN W. *Die Ehre des Erzherzogthums Crain.* Laibach [Ljubljana], 1686–89.

VILFAN, SERGIJ. *Pravna zgodovina Slovencev: Ot naselitve do zloma stare Jugoslavije* [Legal History of the Slovenes: From the First Settlement to the Destruction of Old Yugoslavia]. Ljubljana: Slovenska Matica, 1961.

VUČKOVIĆ, MIHAILO. "The Transformation of the Peasant Cooperative." In *Yugoslav Economists on Problems of a Socialist Economy,* edited by Radmila Stojanović, pp. 17–29. New York: International Arts and Sciences Press, 1964.

VUKČEVIĆ, DRAGOLJUB. "The Legal Status of Private Agricultural Land." *Yugoslav Survey* 9 (Feb. 1968):13–22.

WARRINER, DOREEN. "Urban Thinkers and Peasant Policy in Yugoslavia, 1918–59." *Slavonic and East European Review* 38 (Dec. 1959): 59–81.

———, ed. *Contrasts in Emerging Societies: Readings in the Social and Economic History of South-Eastern Europe in the Nineteenth Century.* Bloomington: Indiana University Press, 1965.

WEBER, MAX. *From Max Weber, Essays in Sociology.* Edited and translated by Hans H. Gerth and C. Wright Mills. New York: Oxford University Press, 1946.

WOLF, ERIC R. "Types of Latin American Peasantry: A Preliminary Discussion." *American Anthropologist* 57 (June 1955):452–71.

———. "Closed Corporate Peasant Communities in Mesoamerica and Central Java." *Southwestern Journal of Anthropology* 13 (Spring 1957):1–18.

——. "Cultural Dissonance in the Italian Alps." *Comparative Studies in Society and History* 5 (Oct. 1962): 1–14.

——. *Peasants.* Foundations of Modern Anthropology Series. Englewood Cliffs, N.J.: Prentice-Hall, 1966.

WOLF, ROBERT LEE. *The Balkans in Our Times.* Cambridge: Harvard University Press, 1956.

ZANIVOVICH, M. GEORGE. *The Development of Socialist Yugoslavia.* Baltimore: Johns Hopkins Press, 1968.

ŽIROVNIK, JOZEF. *Cerkniško jezero* [The Cerknica Lake]. Ljubljana: Slovenska Matica, 1898.

# Index